The Hidden Gulag

Second Edition

The Lives and Voices of
"Those Who are Sent to the Mountains"

Exposing North Korea's Vast System of Lawless Imprisonment

David Hawk

A Report by the Committee for Human Rights in North Korea

ISBN: 0615623670

Library of Congress Control Number: 2012939299

The Hidden Gulag
Second Edition
The Lives and Voices of
"Those Who are Sent to the Mountains"

Committee for Human Rights in North Korea
1001 Connecticut Avenue, NW
Suite 435
Washington, DC 20036

ABOUT THE COMMITTEE FOR HUMAN RIGHTS IN NORTH KOREA

In October of 2001, a distinguished group of foreign policy and human rights specialists launched the Committee for Human Rights in North Korea (HRNK) to promote human rights in that country. HRNK seeks to raise awareness and to publish well-documented research that focuses international attention on North Korean human rights conditions, which have been so closed off from the rest of the world.

The Committee's studies have established its reputation and leading role in the growing international network of organizations committed to opening up and promoting reform and transition in North Korea. The Committee's reports have addressed many of the fundamental human rights issues in North Korea. Its 2003 report, "The Hidden Gulag: Exposing North Korea's Prison Camps" (by David Hawk), was the first comprehensive study of the camps. Other reports published by the Committee have included:

• "Hunger and Human Rights: The Politics of Famine in North Korea" (by Stephan Haggard and Marcus Noland, 2005)
• "The North Korean Refugee Crisis: Human Rights and International Response" (by Stephan Haggard and Marcus Noland, 2006)
• "Failure to Protect: A Call for the UN Security Council to Act in North Korea" (published with DLA Piper LLP, 2006)
• "Legal Strategies for Protecting Human Rights in North Korea" (published with Skadden, Arps, Slate, Meagher & Florn LLP, 2007)
• "Failure to Protect: The Ongoing Challenge of North Korea (published with DLA Piper LLP, 2008)
• "Lives for Sale: Personal Accounts of Women Fleeing North Korea to China" (by Lee Hae-young, 2009)
• "After Kim Jong-il: Can We Hope for Better Human Rights Protection?" (by Kim Kwang-jin, 2009)
• "Taken! North Korea's Criminal Abduction of Citizens of Other Countries" (by Yoshi Yama-moto, 2011)
• "North Korea after Kim Jong-il: Can We Hope for Better Human Rights Protection?" (by Kim Kwang-jin, 2011)

The Committee is currently finalizing reports on: "Songbun," North Korea's social classification system, which is at the root of human rights violations in North Korea; the structure and operation of North Korea's public security agencies, which shows the system of political repression employed by North Korea; and the restrictions on information circulation inside North Korea.

II

TABLE OF CONTENTS

EXECUTIVE SUMMARY

The second edition of *Hidden Gulag* utilizes the testimony of sixty former North Koreans who were severely and arbitrarily deprived of their liberty in a vast network of penal and forced labor institutions in the Democratic People's Republic of Korea (DPRK or North Korea) for reasons not permitted by international law. This contradicts the formal December 2009 proclamation by North Korea to the United Nations Human Rights Council that the term 'political prisoners' is not in the DPRK's vocabulary, and that the so-called political prisoner camps do not exist.

At the time of the research for the first edition of *Hidden Gulag* in 2003, there were some 3,000 former North Koreans who recently had found asylum in the Republic of Korea (ROK or South Korea) among whom were several scores of former political prisoners in the DPRK. By the time of the research for the second edition in 2010 and 2011, there were some 23,000 former North Koreans who recently arrived in South Korea. Included in this number are hundreds of persons formerly detained in the variety of North Korea's slave labor camps, penitentiaries, and detention facilities. Included in this number are several former prisoners who were arbitrarily imprisoned for twenty to thirty years before their escape or release from the labor camps, and their subsequent flight through China to South Korea. This newly available testimony dramatically increases our knowledge of the operation of North Korea's political prison and labor camp system.

This second edition of *Hidden Gulag* also utilizes a recent international legal framework for the analysis of North Korea's human rights violations: the norms and standards established in the Rome Statute of the International Criminal Court for defining and determining crimes against humanity, which became operative in July 2002. This international legal framework enables a much more accurate and penetrating analysis of the various phenomena of repression associated with North Korea's system of arbitrary detention, political imprisonment, and forced labor. This more recent framework for analysis facilitates a series of detailed recommendations that would, if implemented, effectively disable and dismantle the prison labor camp system. This legal framework also facilitates a series of recommendations to other member states within the international community on how to better respond and take action against the massive and severe human rights violations in North Korea.

In addition to the testimony and accounts from the former political prisoners in this report, this second edition of *Hidden Gulag* also includes satellite photographs of the prison camps. The dramatically improved, higher resolution satellite imagery now available through Google Earth allows the former prisoners to identify their former barracks and houses, their former work sites, execution grounds, and other landmarks in the camps. The report provides the precise locations—exact degrees of latitude and longitude—of the political prison camps that North Korea proclaims do not exist.

Part One introduces the research methodology, sources, and information base used in the report and contains a glossary of terms associated with repression in North Korea.

Part Two describes the phenomena of repression associated with the North Korean *kwan-li-so* political penal labor colonies where scores of thousands of political prisoners—along with up to three generations of members of their families—are banished, deported, imprisoned without any judicial process, and subjected to slave labor for mostly lifetime sentences in mining, logging or various agricultural enterprises operating within a half-dozen sprawling encampments, enclosed in barbed wires and electrified fences, mostly in the north and north central mountains of North Korea. The report describes who the political prisoners are: real, suspected or imagined wrong-doers and wrong-thinkers, or persons with wrong-knowledge and/or wrong-associations who have been deemed to be irremediably counter-revolutionary and pre-emptively purged from North Korean society.

This part also provides an overview of the prison-labor camp system: the guilt-by-association collective punishment, forced disappearances and incommunicado detention without trial, systemic and severe mistreatment, induced malnutrition, slave labor and exorbitant rates of deaths in detention, informants and intra-prisoner hostilities, executions and other extreme punishments, sexual relations, "marriage" and prison camp "schools," the sexual exploitation of women prisoners, prisoner releases, the economic role of the forced labor camps, and the complete removal from any protection of law, along with the arbitrary and extra-judicial nature of the system.

It outlines the successive waves of political imprisonment over the fifty-odd years the prison camps have been in operation, and provides a brief recounting of how, over several decades, information about the secret and officially denied prison camps has become knowable and known to the world outside North Korea.

Part Two then presents the heart-rending stories and testimonies of fifteen former *kwan-li-so* prisoners—the lives and voices of "those who are sent to the mountains"—and several former guards at a half-dozen prison-labor camps who were interviewed for this report.

The total number of those currently incarcerated in prison labor camps is estimated between 150,000 and 200,000, as reported by North Korean state security agency officials who defected to South

Korea. From virtually all former prisoners' testimonies, it is evident that there has been an extraordinarily high rate of deaths in detention (measured by the deaths of family members or those in work or residence units). Whether the rate of new imprisonment is as high as the rate of deaths in detention is not known. The International Committee of the Red Cross would have to gain entry to the camps in order for a precise number of prisoners to be established.

Part Three describes North Korea's *kyo-hwa-so* long-term, felony level penitentiaries and prison camps. These facilities hold persons convicted of criminal acts, as defined in the DPRK criminal codes, as well as large numbers of persons suspected of political malfeasance—actions which would not, by international norms and standards, be regarded as criminal offenses. Some of the *kyo-hwa-so* resemble the sprawling *kwan-li-so* encampments and prisoners also engage in mining, lumber cutting and agricultural labor. Other *kyo-hwa-so* resemble penitentiaries: a small campus of several buildings surrounded by high turreted walls, where prisoners labor in terrible conditions in industrial factories or agricultural plots within the prison.

Some of these prisoners were tried in North Korean courts, but many were not. Some of the women's prisons have very large numbers of women who were forcibly repatriated from China. The brutal conditions of imprisonment are a far cry from international standards, which are for ease of comparison appended to the present report. The *kyo-hwa-so* prisons and penitentiaries are also characterized by very high rates of deaths in detention. *Kyo-hwa-so* prisoners are released back into society upon completion of their sentences. In fact, many prisoners are given sickness-related early releases to lower the number of deaths in detention and spare the prison officials from the need to return the bodies to their families.

Part Three presents the stories and testimonies of twelve former *kyo-hwa-so* prisoners from ten different prisons.

Part Four focuses on three additional North Korean institutions of arbitrary detention, brutal interrogation, severe punishment and forced labor that are primarily directed at North Korean citizens who have been *refouled*—forcibly repatriated—from China: *ku-ryu-jang* police interrogation and detention facilities; *jip-kyul-so* misdemeanor level prisons; and mobile labor brigades termed *ro-dong-dan-ryeon-dae* "labor training centers." These facilities are characterized by shorter periods of detention. But they are no less brutal than the longer term *kwan-li-so* and *kyo-hwa-so* prisons and camps detailed in Parts Two and Three. Beatings and more systematic torture are commonplace, if not routine, in the initial *ku-ryu-jang* police detention-interrogation facilities located along the China-North Korea border. And it is at these detention-interrogation facilities, or the "collection places" known as *jip-*

kyul-so, where the horrific practices of racially-motivated forced abortions, infanticides and other forms of humiliation and violence against women take place.

Part Four begins with an examination of the conditions that lead to the flow of North Koreans into China, the situation of North Koreans in China, including the unavoidable contact with South Koreans and South Korean culture, contact with Korean-Chinese Christian churches, and the situation that leads to the trafficking of North Korean women inside China.

It then examines four of the main forced repatriation corridors through which North Koreans are *refouled* by Chinese police to the awaiting North Korean police agencies. Testimony is presented from six North Koreans forcibly repatriated at Sinuiju, one person repatriated at Hyesan, five persons forcibly repatriated at Musan, one person forcibly repatriated at Hoeryong, and eleven persons repatriated at Onsong. Their stories trace the former prisoners' punishing travails through one, and often more than one, police interrogation facilities before being dispatched, often without any judicial processes to one of the prison labor camps or penitentiaries described in Parts Two and Three or to one or more of the misdemeanor level prisons or mobile work brigades described in Part Four.

Part Five summarizes the torture and racially-motivated-infanticide and forced abortion experienced or directly witnessed by former North Korean prisoners and detainees interviewed for this report.

Part Six concludes that the prison labor camp system as it has operated in the DPRK for some fifty years, and continues to so operate today, constitutes a clear and massive crime against humanity. This section utilizes the best available contemporary norms of international human rights law and international criminal law—the International Covenant on Civil and Political Rights, and Article 7 of the Rome Statute of the International Criminal Court—to analyze the human rights violations detailed in Parts Two, Three, Four and Five. This analysis concludes that 10 of the 11 actions proscribed in Article 7 of the Rome Statute as crimes against humanity are being committed in North Korea against civilian populations imprisoned in the *kwan-li-so* political labor camps: enforced disappearance, deportation, massive and prolonged extra-judicial and incommunicado imprisonment in violation of the fundamental rules of international law, enslavement, torture, murder, extermination, rape, persecution against identifiable groups on political grounds, and other inhumane acts committed knowingly in a systematic and widespread manner by state police agents operating on behalf of the state authority.

In addition, Part Six finds the serial atrocities committed by DPRK police agents against North Korean citizens forcibly repatriated from China, as detailed in Parts Four and Five (held in the *kyo-hwa-so*, *ku-ryu-jang*, *jip-kyul-so*, and *ro-dong-dan-ryeon-dae* prisons and other facilities), to constitute crimes against humanity. Such crimes include imprisonment in violation of the fundamental rules of international law, enslavement, torture, sexual violence of comparable gravity to rape, murder, persecution on political grounds, and other inhumane acts of similar character causing great suffering and serious injury to mental and physical health.

The report posits that international recognition that the consistent pattern of gross violations of human rights, documented in this report, constitutes crimes against humanity, would, in the long run, be conducive to halting such violations. Such recognition could encourage the North Korean authorities, who presently deny that the camps even exist, and who presently refuse to cooperate with key United Nations human rights procedures, to admit that the political prison forced labor camp system is a matter that they cannot fail to address and resolve.

Part Seven. Based on the facts of the operation of the North Korean gulag system, as detailed in the report, and utilizing the international legal framework for analysis outlined in Part Six, this section makes a series of detailed recommendations to the DPRK, to the People's Republic of China, and to other member states of the international community. Recommendation highlights include:

<u>To the DPRK</u>: With respect to the *kwan-li-so* prison labor camp system, the report recommends a schedule for prisoner releases and sets forth the measures that would fully restore to those detained the liberties of which they have been so severely deprived. In effect, it provides a blueprint for disabling and dismantling the prison labor camp system.

With respect to the other prison and forced labor facilities described, the report recommends the release of all persons who have not been charged, tried and convicted of violations of the DPRK Criminal Code in a DPRK court of law operating under international standards for due process and fair trial. It also recommends that all detention and re-education through labor facilities be brought into line with international standards.

Further, it is recommended that all persecutions and prosecutions cease against North Koreans who have exercised their right to leave their country of origin; and that the practices of torture, forced abortions and infanticide be halted immediately and absolutely. More generally, it is recommended that the DPRK allow the International Committee of the Red Cross to have access to detention facilities, and cooperate with United Nations human rights personnel and programs.

<u>To China</u>: The report recommends that the office of the UN High Commissioner for Refugees be granted immediate access to North Koreans seeking protection and first asylum in China, and that all forced repatriation of pregnant Korean women be halted immediately and unconditionally.

<u>To UN Member States</u>: As a step toward international recognition that the human rights violations detailed in this report constitute crimes against humanity, it is recommended that a commission of inquiry or group of experts be created to examine DPRK breaches of international human rights law and international criminal law.

<u>To the United States, South Korea and Japan</u>: It is recommended that the human rights concerns raised in this report be factored into any future normalization of political and economic relations with the DPRK.

An *Appendix* provides the texts of the UN Standard Minimum Rules for the Treatment of Prisoners, and the UN Body of Principles for the Protection of All Persons Under any Form of Detention or Imprisonment.

Satellite Photographs. The report contains 41 satellite photographs of numerous North Korean prison labor camps and penitentiaries holding North Koreans for essentially political offenses. The locations have been confirmed by former prisoners in these facilities.

ABOUT THE AUTHOR:
DAVID HAWK

A prominent human rights researcher and advocate, David Hawk is a former Executive Director of Amnesty International USA, and a former United Nations human rights official. His career began with involvement in voter registration and desegregation campaigns in Mississippi and Georgia in the early-and-mid-1960s. After post-graduate studies, Hawk began directing AIUSA in 1974, overseeing a rapid expansion and extension of influence at a time of surging international interest in human rights. Hawk later served on the Board of Directors of AIUSA and became a founding member of the Board of Directors of Human Rights Watch/Asia.

In 1981, while based in Thailand to monitor the situation of Cambodian refugees and famine relief, Hawk kicked-off groundbreaking investigation, documentation and analysis of the Khmer Rouge genocide—a project that he would continue through the decade—traveling regularly to Cambodia and obtaining and publishing original Khmer Rouge prison documents, prisoner/execution and mass grave photographs, and supplying first-person eye-witness testimony from Cambodians inside the country and in refugee camps, along with a framework to understand the system of repression within the terms of international human rights law.

In August 1995 Hawk traveled to Rwanda to document genocidal massacres for the US Committee for Refugees, and in 1996 he returned to Kigali on mission for Amnesty International. In the mid-to-late 1990s, he directed the Cambodia Office of the UN High Commissioner for Human Rights, helping to train and sustain fledgling Cambodian human rights civil society organizations, monitor current violations, and stand up for accountability. Returning to the USA in 1999, Hawk consulted for the Washington DC-based Landmine Survivors Network, advocating the landmine ban and disability rights conventions, and assisting in humanitarian aid for landmine victims in Cambodia and Vietnam.

Since 2002, Hawk has focused on the grievous situation of human rights in North Korea. His publications on the DPRK include: *Hidden Gulag: Exposing North Korea's Prison Camps—Prisoner Testimonies and Satellite Photographs*, The Committee for Human Rights in North Korea, 2003; *Thank You Father Kim Il Sung: Eyewitness Accounts of Violations of Freedom of Thought Conscience and Belief in North Korea*, U.S. Commission on International Religious Freedom, 2005; "Human Rights and the Crisis in

1

North Korea," North Korea: 2005 and Beyond, APARC/Stanford University, Brookings Institution Press, 2006; *Concentrations of Inhumanity: An Analysis of the Phenomena of Repression Associated with North Korea's Kwan-li-so Political Penal Labor Camps*, Freedom House, 2007; "Factoring Human Rights into the Resolution of Cold War Conflict on the Korean Peninsula" in *Human Rights in North Korea: Toward a Comprehensive Understanding*, eds. Park and Han, The Sejong Institute, Seoul, 2007; and *Pursuing Peace While Advancing Rights: The Untried Approach to North Korea*, The U.S.-Korea Institute at the John's Hopkins School of Advanced International Studies, 2010.

Currently he is a Visiting Scholar at the Columbia University Institute for the Study of Human Rights, and teaches at Hunter College, City University of New York.

ACKNOWLEDGEMENTS

This report benefited from the help of many people in the United States, South Korea and elsewhere—the author is extremely grateful to each and everyone.

But some assisted in ways that can only be described as over and above the call of duty. Ms. Sarah Kim, my research assistant is at the top of that category. A graduate student in international affairs at George Washington University, Sarah assisted in translating, conducting and transcribing interviews, organizing files, assisted in Korean and Japanese word usage, and copy-editing. She made the computerized illustrations from the former prisoners' hand-drawn sketches of detention facilities, and her enthusiasm for the project—regardless of the assignment—never flagged.

Special thanks also to Committee Chair, Roberta Cohen, for taking so much care and time for substantive comments and detailed copy-editing of successive draft manuscripts, which imparted more clarity and a smoother read. Thanks also to former HRNK Executive Director, Chuck Downs, for his patience and guidance during the research and writing of this report, and for obtaining the important testimony of Mrs. Kim Hye-sook. And to current HRNK director Greg Scarlatoiu, for his work to complete the publication.

Locating former North Korean prisoners and detainees to participate in my interviews was helped so much by "Free the North Korean Gulag" (NKGULAG), a Seoul-based NGO of former North Korean political prisoners, and by Mr. Chung Tae-ung, who previously assisted the Stephen Haggard and Marcus Noland refugee survey, *Witness to Transformation: Refugee Insights into North Korea*. Thanks to Ms. Lee Hae-young for assistance in translating during interviews with former prisoners and for briefing me on Korean language memoirs by former prisoners. Lee Hae-young also reviewed the sections of the text on North Koreans in China and their repatriation to the DPRK.

Thanks to Prof. Haruhisa Ogawa and his colleagues at the Japanese NGO, NO FENCE, for arranging my interviews with former North Koreans in Tokyo and Osaka.

There are others who gave their time and expertise. Among these are Mr. Joshua Stanton, a Washington attorney and blog manager (OneFreeKorea); Mr. Curtis Melvin, Editor of North Korea Economy Watch (NKEconWatch); HRNK interns, Jason Keller, Chung Hae-gun, James Do, and Lee Hyung-chang, who helped with Google Earth satellite photo images; Mintaro Oba for help with copy editing; Geena An, Suzanne Lee Riopel and Grace Oh for help with translating background documents; and Rosa Park for graphic design, and help with copy editing and text arrangement. Thanks also to Mr. Kim Sang-hun, Chairman of the Board of Directors of NK Data Base (NKDB) for finding the former residents of Chongjin who confirmed the location of Prison Camp No. 25.

Thanks to those who generously reviewed the report's legal analysis and recommendations, who include Jared Genser, an international human-rights lawyer and Managing Director of Perseus Strategies; Sir Nigel Rodley, Professor of Law and Chair of the Human Rights Centre at Essex University; and Prof. George Andreopoulos, Director of the Center for International Human Rights at the John Jay College of Criminal Justice, City University of New York. Needless to say, remaining errors of fact or interpretation are the responsibility of the author.

Special thanks to Joan Libby Hawk, for her unflagging patience, valued advice and editing assistance during the research and writing of this report.

David Hawk

PREFACE

Upon receipt of the Nobel Prize for Literature in 1980, Czeslaw Milosz, a defector from communist Poland and author of *The Captive Mind,* observed that "those who are alive receive a mandate from those who are silent forever." In publishing the first and second editions of *Hidden Gulag,* the Committee for Human Rights in North Korea has assumed that mandate. By means of these reports, it gives voice to those silenced in the remote labor camps and prisons of North Korea.

There may be as many as 200,000 North Koreans locked away on political grounds behind barbed wire and subject to extreme cruelty and brutality. Many are "not expected to survive," according to the State Department's 2010 human rights report, in particular those incarcerated in the *kwan-li-so* (political penal labor colonies). Others are held in long-term prison-labor penitentiaries or camps, shorter-term detention facilities, mobile labor brigades and interrogation detention facilities. The vast majority are arbitrarily arrested with no reference to any judicial procedure and for "offenses" that are not punishable in most countries, namely listening to a foreign radio broadcast, holding a Protestant religious service, watching a South Korean DVD, leaving dust on Kim Il-sung's picture, exiting the country without permission, expressing critical remarks about government policies, or having a father or grandfather who was a landowner or defected to South Korea or worked for the Japanese, thereby placing the family in a "hostile" category under North Korea's social classification or *songbun* system.

Starvation food rations, forced labor, routine beatings, systematic torture and executions put the North Korean camps in the ranks of history's worst prisons for political offenders. Originally modeled on the Soviet gulag, the North Korean camps have developed distinctive features of their own for which no terminology has yet been devised. Particularly horrifying is the incarceration of entire families, including children and grandparents, in order to isolate them from society and punish them because of their relationship to family members accused of political crimes. Rooting out "class enemies for three generations" was specifically ordered by Kim Il-sung, which at times has led to comparisons with Nazi death camps. An equally horrifying practice distinctive to North Korea is forced abortion regularly carried out and in the most brutal manner on women prisoners who illegally crossed the border into China, became pregnant by Chinese men and were forcibly repatriated to North Korea. In cases where the pregnancy is too advanced, guards beat the infants to death or bury them alive after they are born. Still another point of departure in North Korea is that all the residents of the *kwan-li-so* are denied any correspondence, visits or life saving parcels from family and friends. They are totally *incommunicado.*

Estimates of the numbers who have died in the camps over the past 40 years have run well over one hundred thousand. The existence of the political prison camps, however, is soundly denied by North Korean officials. "We must envelop our environment in a dense fog to prevent our enemies from learning anything about us," Kim Jong-il reportedly said. Human rights specialist David Hawk in his first edition of *Hidden Gulag* (2003) and now in its second edition (2012) challenges North Korea's deliberate effort to hide the truth. With painstaking care he has unearthed and compiled evidence from the period 1970 to 2008 to demonstrate an extensive prison camp system hidden away in North Korea's isolated mountains. Amassing satellite photographs and hand drawings of the different camps, testimonies from former prisoners and interviews with former guards, he has documented beyond a doubt the existence of penal labor camps and other political prisons. He has met with almost all of the former *kwan-li-so* prisoners who were either released or escaped to South Korea. Of the more than 23,000 defectors who have made the treacherous journey to the South over the past decade, hundreds are former prisoners. In telling their stories, they are making the world aware of the crimes and atrocities upon which Kim family rule has long been based.

It is worth recalling that some forty-five years ago, political prisoners in China were an undifferentiated mass of people unknown to the rest of the world. In fact Andrei Sakharov, the renowned Soviet scientist and dissident, together with other Soviet dissidents in the 1970s publicly called on their Chinese counterparts to establish lines of communication with the outside world in order to prevent the authorities "from crushing them without a trace in the remote labor camps and prisons." They pointed out that international exposure of human rights violations was an important way to deter governments and bring about change. Today, North Korean prisoners are the ones coming to the fore. Their country, now led by Kim Jong-un, continues to be closed to the world, but the conspiracy of silence surrounding the camps is nonetheless being breached.

More than 120 states at the UN General Assembly in 2011 expressed "serious concern" about the "the existence of a large number of prison camps and the extensive use of forced labour" in North Korea. This must be followed by bilateral and multilateral efforts to gain access to the camps so that international organizations can bring in food and medicines, help reduce the high death rates and end the horrifying isolation of these prisoners. For too long, it has been considered too difficult, too controversial, and too confrontational to point to the camps in discussions with North Korean officials. That is precisely why the report's recommendations are so important in calling for access to the starving, abused and broken men, women and children held captive. It is not just nuclear weapons that have to be dismantled in North Korea but an entire system of political repression.

Roberta Cohen

Co-Chair

Committee for Human Rights in North Korea

MAP OF NORTH KOREA

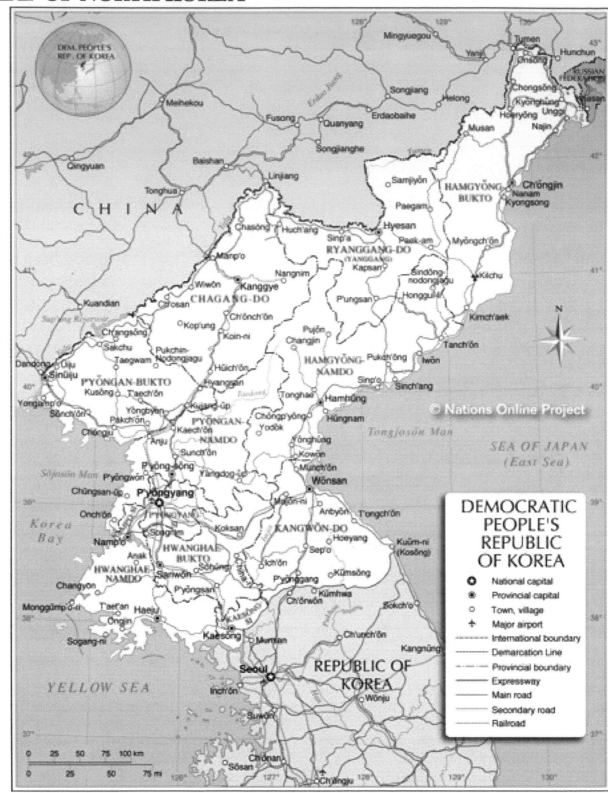

PART ONE

INTRODUCTION

"The term 'political prisoner' does not exist in the DPRK's vocabulary … the so-called political prisoner's camps do not exist."

Or so asserted the representative of the Democratic People's Republic of Korea (DPRK or North Korea) to the United Nations Human Rights Council on December 7, 2009.[1]

The second edition of Hidden Gulag is based on information provided by former North Koreans who were incarcerated in the DPRK prisons and prison-labor camps. It challenges the denial of political prisoner camps and outlines the operations of a large scale and far reaching system of arbitrary and extra-judicial detention coupled with a regime of forced labor that abuses scores of thousands of North Koreans at any one time, and brutalized hundreds of thousands of North Koreans from the period 1970 to 2008.

The first-person testimony on which this report is based, along with brief biographies of the former prisoners interviewed, is now available to the international public because these individuals took long and dangerous journeys outside the DPRK and agreed to give accounts of what happened to them. After their release, or, in a very few cases, escape from imprisonment, they

fled to the area of Northeast China, formerly known as Manchuria. From Northeast China, a few crossed the Gobi desert to Mongolia and travelled from Mongolia to South Korea. Many more undertook an arduous "underground railroad," a 4,000 to 5,000 mile trek of several months duration (without travel documents and permits) from Northeast China down through Beijing, Shanghai, Guangzhou, Kunming, and further down into Southeast Asia through Vietnam, Laos, Cambodia or Thailand. This was before reaching Bangkok, where they found asylum and protection via the South Korean consulate, which transported them to Seoul. In the last decade, some 23,000 former North Koreans have found refuge and citizenship in the Republic of Korea.[2]

Included among them are hundreds of North Koreans previously detained in the network of prison camps, penitentiaries, police detention facilities and mobile forced labor brigades described in this report. This network of arbitary, often extra-judicial, detention and forced labor facilities constitutes the North Korean "gulag," appropriating the common name for the Stalinist prison-labor camps of the former Soviet Union.[3] Some 60 former North Koreans, previously detained in these facilities, were interviewed for this report. Their testimony and personal stories detail egregious suffering.

---

1 "Report of the Working Group on the Universal Periodic Review: DPRK," UN Doc. A/HRC/13/13, 4 January 2010, para. 45.

2 There are also several hundred former North Koreans who have found asylum in Europe or North America.

3 Literally, *gulag* is the Russian language acronym for "Chief Administration of Corrective Labor Camps." The term has come to signify not only the labor camps established by Stalin after 1929, but the whole system of slave labor, and the repressive system itself: the arrests, interrogations, transport, destruction of families, the years in exile, and the early and unnecessary deaths. Michael Scammell, "Circles of Hell" *New York Review of Books*, April 28, 2011 citing Anne Applebaum, *Gulag, A History*, Random House, 2003.

The official denial cited above is, in part, semantic legerdemain.[4] It is also a corollary of the stock, Orwellian assertion used by North Korean representatives and diplomats from the late Kim Jong-il on down, "There can be no human rights problem in our people-centered socialism.[5]

In actuality, the only real way for North Korea to refute, contradict or invalidate the claims and testimonies of the North Korean refugees interviewed in South Korea for this report would be to permit officials of the United Nations, the International Committee of the Red Cross (ICRC), the International Labour Organization (ILO), or experienced international human rights organizations such as Amnesty International or Human Rights Watch, or a delegation of Pyongyang-based Ambassadors to verify or invalidate on-site the allegations of the former prisoners.[6] In the absence of reliable on-site refutation, the refugee testimonies stand.

This report also provides extensive testimony about the severely inhumane punishments meted out to North Koreans who are *refouled*, that is forcibly repatriated, from China for having exercised their internationally recognized "right to leave their country of origin" in search of food, employment, or refuge and asylum. At the December 7, 2009 session of the UN Human Rights Council cited above, DPRK representatives made the astonishing admission:

"Border crossers linked to outside forces who perpetrate anti-state acts will be strongly guarded against and punished."[7]

Testimony from scores of "border crossers"—North Koreans forcibly repatriated from China and severely punished upon return to the DPRK—who eventually fled again to China and made their way to South Korea amply demonstrates that virtually any encounter with South Koreans or South Korean culture (which in the ethnic-Korean region in Northeast China is virtually impossible to avoid) is regarded as "an anti-state act." There is, however, no basis in contemporary international norms and standards for imprisonment on the grounds of meeting foreign nationals or listening to foreign TV programs, videos or music, or attending church in a third country.

The testimony reveals that forced repatriation from China is a pathway to pain, suffering, and violence. Arbitrary detention, torture and forced labor are inflicted upon many repatriated North Koreans, and sexual humiliations, forced abor-

---

4 The term used by DPRK officials and guards for those confined in the labor camps is "migrant" (*e-ju-min*). And, it is possible to define "prisoner" (as opposed to a "detainee") as someone convicted in a court for violating what is defined in law as a crime, whereas, the North Korean political penal labor camp system, as described in this report, is virtually extra-judicial – outside the DPRK court and legal system. Thus, the inmates in the North Korean gulag, with a few exceptions noted below, have not been tried or convicted. However, contrary to North Korean semantics, the standard international legal definition is "imprisonment or other severe deprivation of physical liberty in violation of the fundamental rules of international law." As can be seen in the testimonies in this report the deprivation of physical liberty in the prison camps, penitentiaries, detention-interrogation facilities and mobile forced labor brigades is severe in the extreme. And severely contrary to the norms and standards of modern international human rights and criminal law.

5 Recently reiterated in the offical Korea Central News Agency (KCNA) Bulletin, 26 October 2011: "There are no 'human rights issues' for us. There can be no such things in the light of the intrinsic nature of the socialist system which serves the people, placing them in the center of everything."

6 This report provides the precise locations (degrees, minutes and seconds of latitude and longitude) of the prison camps.

7 Author's notes from the UN-provided oral translation at the Human Rights Council meeting, Geneva, 7 December 2009.

tions and infanticides are inflicted upon repatriated North Korean women, many of whom are pregnant after having been trafficked and tricked or coerced and sold into "marriage" to men in China. The testimonies from former women prisoners and detainees also reveal the racial prejudices that North Korean prison officials and guards hold toward half-Chinese fetuses and newborn babies, which are aborted or killed immediately upon birth, a practice documented at multiple detention facilities along the North Korea-China border.

In recounting the stories of victims and survivors, *Hidden Gulag* provides testimony and analysis of arbitrary and largely extra-judicial detention in a variety of penal and forced labor facilities:

> *Kwan-li-so* political penal labor colonies, where North Koreans suspected of wrong-doing and wrong-thinking, along with up to three generations of family members are summarily deported without trial to disappear into fenced-in and heavily guarded mountainous areas where they are subjected to forced labor in mines, logging, state farming and factory work, for mostly life–time duration.

> *Kyo-hwa-so* penitentiaries or camps, where persons deemed to have committed felony level criminal and political offenses are sent for fixed-term forced labor often under very strict regime and brutal conditions.

> *Jip-kyul-so* shorter-term detention facilities for misdemeanor-level offenses, both criminal and political.

> *Ro-dong-dan-ryon-dae* mobile labor brigades,

localized "labor training" facilities largely for repatriated North Koreans, set up originally because the numbers of repatriated Koreans overwhelmed the *jip-kyul-so* detention facilities.

Ku-ryu-jang interrogation-detention facilities run by either the *Bo-wi-bu* political police or the *An-jeon-bu* criminal police agencies.

The above facilities are listed in the descending order of length of detention. But the length of detention should not be equated with the harshness or brutality of mistreatment. Brutality and abuse reign, regardless of the length of detention. While the phenomena of repression varies according to the type of detention facility, the stories and testimonies of the victims and survivors of these facilities contained in this report show extreme brutality—across the board—characterizing the arbitrary detention to which hundreds of thousands of North Koreans are subjected. Deliberately below-subsistence level food rations, coupled with routine beatings and systematic torture, and onerous forced labor lead to very high rates of deaths in detention. The entire system, with all of its components, is rife with human rights violations so brutal and severe as to shock the conscience of mankind. In the words of one scholar, the term "gulag" has "come to stand with the word 'Holocaust' as the name of one of the two great aberrations of twentieth century civilization."[8] The gulags of Kim Il-sung, Kim Jong-il, and Kim Jong-un continue into the twenty-first century with, at present, no end in sight.

---

8 Scammell, *op cit.*, p.46.

Not in a Vacuum

The prison and labor camp atrocities detailed in this report do not take place in a socio-political vacuum. To the contrary, these severe human rights violations occur in an environment of large-scale denial of human rights and fundamental freedoms. The systematic and widespread human rights violations in North Korea are comprehensively surveyed in the annual White Paper on Human Rights in North Korea published by the Seoul-based Korea Institute for National Unification (KINU).[9] The White Paper follows the categories and provisions of the International Covenants on Human Rights, and references or incorporates up-to-date information and accounts from international and national human rights NGOs, and the findings in the US Department of State's annual "country reports."[10]

In the words of noted Korea specialists:

"The DPRK is the single most controlling state in history, bar none... [the Chosun dynasty feudal] system, already transformed by decades of guerilla war against Japanese colonialism and occupation, was supplemented after 1948 by the political-surveillance techniques grafted onto the traditional control system by Soviet and Chinese 'best practice,' thereby achieving a truly totalitarian level of individual monitoring, reporting, and control without precedence in human history. This control system is designed to sustain a social system that is based on political loyalty..."[11]

The broad array of human rights violations involved with the population "control system" in North Korea has been set forth in a series of reports by the UN Special Rapporteur on the situation of human rights in the DPRK.[12] In his 2010 report to the UN Human Rights Council, the Special Rapporteur characterized the human rights violations in North Korea as "harrowing," "horrific" and "sui-generis," putting North Korea "in its own category."[13] Based largely on these reports, the United Nations Human Rights Council and General Assembly have passed a series of resolutions recognizing and condemning the "systematic, widespread, and grave violations of civil, political, economic, social and cultural rights in the D.P.R.K."[14]

---

9 Korea Institute for National Unification, Insu-dong, Gangbuk-gu, Seoul, Korea, pp.142-728, http://www.kinu.or.kr.

10 See also the reports and web sites of Amnesty International and Human Rights Watch, the Committee for Human Rights in North Korea (hrnk.org) and the Seoul-based Citizen's Alliance for North Korean Human Rights (nkhumanrights.or.kr), the Network for North Korean Democracy and Human Rights (nknet.org), and Database Center for North Korean Human Rights (NKDB.org). In 2008 the (South) Korean Bar Association also published a 700 page *White Paper on Human Rights in North Korea* in both Korean and English containing chapters on important aspects of the human rights situation (koreanbar.or.kr). For readers interested in general accounts of life in North Korea which reference the overall human rights situation, see Barbara Demick, *Nothing to Envy: Ordinary Lives in North Korea*, Spiegel and Grau, New York, 2009; Ralph Hassig and Kongdan Oh, *The Hidden People of North Korea: Everyday Life in the Hermit Kingdom*, Rowman and Littlefield, Lanham, Maryland, 2009; and Stephan Haggard and Marcus Noland, *Witness to Transformation: Refugee Insights into North Korea*, Peterson Institute for International Economics, Washington DC, 2011.

---

11 Peter Hayes, Scott Bruce and Dyana Mardon, "North Korea's Digital Transformation: Implications for North Korea Policy," Nautilus Institute, November 8, 2011, p. 2.

12 The first Special Rapporteur was Vitit Muntarbhorn, a professor of international and constitutional law at Chulalongkorn University, Bangkok Thailand. The second, and current, Special Rapporteur is Marzuki Darusman, the former Attorney General of Indonesia.

13 UN Doc. A/HRC/13/47, 17 February 2010.

14 In 2011, the UN General Assembly resolution condemning the human rights violations in the DPRK passed by a vote of 123 in favor and only 16 against (with 51 abstentions and three absences). For the text of this resolution see UN Doc. A/C.3/66/L.54, 28

But, just as they deny the existence of the political prison forced labor camps, the North Korean authorities have long denied that there are any human rights problems or issues in the DPRK. In 1988, the North Korean Ambassador to the United Nations wrote to the Minnesota Lawyers International Human Rights Committee that violations of human rights do not take place and are "unthinkable" in North Korea.[15] In 1994, an official publication, *The People's Korea* proclaimed, "... there is no 'human rights problem' in our Republic either from the institutional or from the legal point of view."[16] North Korean diplomats at the United Nations in Geneva routinely deny that there are any violations of human rights. The General Assembly resolutions are regularly and officially denounced by the Korean Central News Agency (KCNA) as a smear campaign by the United States and its "sycophants."

The Second Edition of Hidden Gulag

There are three major differences between the 2003 first edition of *Hidden Gulag*[17] and the present, second edition: first, a substantial increase in the amount of available testimony from former prisoners; second, many more and clearer resolution satellite photographs; and third, the availability of an important new international legal framework for the evaluation of severe human rights violations. This new legal framework for analyzing the North Korean violations enables a fresh and more penetrating series of recommendations to the DPRK on how to dismantle the camp system, and a more focused set of recommendations to the international community on appropriate and efficacious responses to the DPRK violations.

More Sources, New Dimensions

In 2002 and 2003, during the research for the first edition of *Hidden Gulag*, there were roughly 3,000 former North Koreans who had re-settled in South Korea. In-depth interviews were conducted with thirty former prisoners. By 2009 and 2010, during the research for the second edition, the number of recently arrived

---

October 2011.

15 *Human Rights in the Democratic People's Republic of Korea* (North Korea), Minnesota Lawyers International Human Rights Committee and Human Rights Watch/Asia, December 1988.

16 The People's Korea, No. 1661 (August 13, 1994), p. 8, as cited in *North Korea Through the Looking Glass*, Kongdan Oh and Ralph C. Hassig, The Brookings Institution Press, Washington DC, 2000, p. 134. (What are described herein and elsewhere as political prisoner camps are proclaimed by The People's Korea to be instead "... industrial establishments and cooperative farms animated with creative labor and rows of modern apartment houses and rural houses overflowing with the happiness of the people.")

17 The first edition, entitled *Hidden Gulag: Exposing North Korea's Prison Camps*, published in 2003, was the first systematic and comprehensive account of political prisons, prison camps, and the subsidiary sub-systems of of arbitrary detention in the DPRK.

Prior to the report's publication, the different types of DPRK detention facilities had been translated from Korean to English as "political prisons" and those detained therein as "political prisoners." This was accurate, but not descriptive of the considerable variations in the systems of arbitrary detention in North Korea. Some prisoners had judicial proceedings. Many others did not. Some were imprisoned for life, others for a few months. North Koreans use different names for the different kinds of detention facilities, and these differences are similarly understood by South Koreans. The report therefore sorted testimonies according to their Korean language designations, providing more descriptive translations in English, and then detailed the various phenomena of repression associated with the varieties of political imprisonment. Further, Hidden Gulag was the first time that satellite photographs were used by an NGO report to document the sites of human rights violations. The satellite images allowed former prisoners to locate and identify their former houses, barracks, worksites, execution grounds, and other facilities within the camps, thereby enabling them to confirm the precise location of the camps.

North Koreans residing in South Korea had grown to over 20,000. Included in this number are hundreds of former North Koreans who were subjected to arbitrary detention and other mistreatments documented in this report. For the present edition, an additional thirty in-depth interviews were conducted in 2009 and 2010.

These additional interviews corroborate and re-confirm the testimonies, findings and analysis of the first edition. They also extend, by nearly two decades, the time frame of political imprisonment testimony. The first edition covered political imprisonment between the years 1977 to 1999. The testimony available for the second edition covers 1970 to 2008. Two of the newly interviewed former political prisoners were held in the prison camps for two-and-a-half and nearly three-decades, respectively. Their decades-long incarceration provides significant new details and perspectives on how the prison labor camp system works, and how it can be ended.

Higher Resolution Satellite Photographs

The satellite photography of the camps used in the first edition was provided by two private companies that specialize in commercial satellite photos, Digital Globe and the Space Imaging Corporation. Obtaining the photographs and inputting the citations and designations by the former prisoners into the satellite photographs was a laborious and time consuming process. The Committee for Human Rights in North Korea (HRNK) obtained very detailed maps of North Korea that included degrees of latitude and longitude. The maps were airmailed to our local NGO partners in Seoul, who called the former prisoners into their offices and showed them the maps. If and when the former prisoners could locate the camps at which they were held, the degrees of latitude and longitude were plotted. We then contacted the two satellite photo firms to see if they had any imagery for those coordinates in their database. If so, we would order detailed satellite images for those coordinates. Those photographs would then be airmailed to our NGO colleagues in Seoul who would again call the former prisoners to return to their offices and identify any recognized landmarks in the photographic images. The translated identifications were then entered by computer onto the photographic images published in the first edition. This process required several months of consultation and analysis.

By the time of the research for the second edition, Google Earth made satellite images, often of much higher resolution, of the entire Korean peninsula available to anyone with a computer and Internet connection. Using the coordinates from the first edition of *Hidden Gulag*, Korea specialists pored over the higher resolution images of the camps, identifying the fences and guard towers that demarcate the prison camp boundaries. Google Earth enables pinpointing landmarks with efficiency.

During interviews with former North Koreans for the second edition, the author and a Korean translator would sit with former prisoners using the Korean language version of Google Earth, which is better apt at finding North Korean locations, including *ri* and *kun* designations for counties and townships, entered into "search boxes" in Hangul. We would pinpoint landmarks that the former prisoners could identify with confidence.

Additional Normative and Legal Framework for Analyzing Human Rights Violations

The first edition used, as its framework for analysis, the standard, internationally accepted terminology of a "consistent pattern of gross violations of internationally recognized human rights," based on violation of the human rights norms contained in the International Covenants on Civil and Political and Economic, Social and Cultural Rights, and the UN Standard Minimum Rules for the Treatment of Prisoners. Just as the research for *Hidden Gulag* was underway, an important new framework for analyzing and evaluating severe violations of human rights became available when the Rome Statute of the International Criminal Court (ICC) entered into force in mid-2002. The Rome Statute contains an updated and refined definition of crimes against humanity. The second edition of *Hidden Gulag* utilizes this important additional normative framework for analyzing severe human rights violations in the DPRK.

Breaking down the phenomena of repression in North Korea into the separate criminal acts defined in the Rome Statute reveals a detailed guide to dismantling the prison camp system. Article 7 of the Rome Statute enumerates twelve discrete actions, which, under the requisite circumstances, constitute crimes against humanity. Eleven of those acts, clearly and massively carried out under the requisite circumstances, are detailed in this report. Ending the violations of international human rights and criminal law would effectively dismantle the prison camps.

Notes On Research, Limits of Information, Sources, Translations, and Transliterations

Research

This report is based on more than sixty in-depth personal interviews with former prisoners in North Korea's detention facilities who subsequently escaped to South Korea. This is in addition to interviews with several former guards at the camps who later defected to South Korea.[18]

There is a noteworthy difference between the interview data obtained from the former prisoners in the *kwan-li-so* prison-labor camps and the interview data obtained from former prisoners and detainees in the other North Korean detention facilities described and analyzed in this report. I have interviewed almost all of the former *kwan-li-so* prisoners who were released or escaped from detention, fled North Korea, and made their way to South Korea. While each of their accounts—and many interviewees for this report have extraordinary personal histories—could be amplified in much greater detail, as could their descriptions of the section of the sprawling labor camps where they were held (for periods varying from three to thirty years), this report outlines in summary what is known and presently knowable about the DPRK's *kwan-li-so* political-penal labor camp system.

---

18 As is described in this report, most of the prisoners have been deported to the camps for hard labor for the rest of their lives without the possibility of release or parole. Only a small number of prisoners in the labor camps are even eligible for release. While there are a fair number of escape attempts—every former *kwan-li-so* prisoner interviewed for this report witnessed multiple public executions of persons caught trying to escape—there are only two known successful escape attempts. Their stories are recounted herein.

In contradiction to the first person eye-witness interview base for the former prisoners from the *kwan-li-so* camps, there are among the 23,000 former North Koreans who have fled to South Korea in the last decade, hundreds more former North Koreans who were detained in the *kyo-hwa-so, jip-kyul-so, ro-dong-dan-ryeon-dae* and *ku-ryu-jang* detention facilities. This is in addition to the score of former prisoners and detainees at these facilities interviewed for the present report. In this situation, I sought out enough interviews to ascertain what in human rights terminology is called a "consistent pattern of gross violations of internationally recognized human rights." Thus, it should be noted at the outset that there are, literally, scores of additional witnesses to the phenomena of repression detailed in Parts Three, Four and Five of this report who could, potentially, be sought out and interviewed.

Most of the interviews were conducted in English in downtown or suburban Seoul using South Korean or Korean-American translators of the highest expertise, virtually all of whom had prior experience speaking with North Koreans. A few interviews were conducted in Tokyo and Osaka with former Korean-Japanese who had previously migrated from Japan to North Korea before escaping to China and returning to Japan.

More and more recent information can be obtained from North Koreans currently hiding without entrance visas or legal papers in China. However, upon the recommendations of South Korean colleagues, such interviews are best left to non-Western investigators.[19]

There is, thus, an unavoidable delay between the time the former prisoner is released or escapes from detention, and the time the former prisoner becomes accessible to researchers in South Korea. The former prisoner may spend several months or years before deciding to leave the land of his or her birth, and making the necessary connections to flee to China. The former prisoner may spend several months or years in China to make preparations and connections for the onward journey to South Korea, usually via Southeast Asia or Mongolia. Upon arrival in South Korea, asylum seekers undergo several months of debriefing by South Korean intelligence officials, who try to ferret out North Korean spies or operatives who may have been put into the North Korean refugee flow to South Korea. Then, the new arrivals, now in effective receipt of South Korean citizenship, are provided with several weeks or months of orientation sessions by the South Korean Ministry of Unification. Only after these arrangements are the former prisoners and detainees accessible to journalists, scholars or human rights investigators.

Limits of Information

While there is easily more than enough data to outline and detail with confidence "consistent patterns" of gross human rights violations, the unavoidable delay described above means that

---

19 There are large numbers of South Korean tourists, students and business people in the areas along the China-North Korea border

where the undocumented North Koreans are working or seeking asylum. There are also Japanese business people as well. There are very few Western tourists or business people in the areas of Northeast China along the DPRK border. Thus, it is feared that a Western researcher conducting multiple in-depth interviews with North Koreans hiding in China, might bring unwanted and dangerous police attention to the undocumented North Koreans who risk forced repatriation and severe punishment if sent back to the DPRK.

gaps remain, only some of which can be bridged by additional research interviews. For example, much of the recent information about one of the most well known *kwan-li-so* labor camps comes from relatively short-term prisoners from a recently constructed section for single men and single women in the "revolutionizing process zone" at Camp 15 (Yodok) for prisoners who are eligible for release. Even though the former North Korean prisoners now residing in South Korea try to track information very closely through their extensive information networks back in North Korea, there have been no known releases from Yodok since 2009. Thus, as of the publication of this report in 2012, we do not know if releases from the "revolutionizing process zones" continue or if the policy and practice has changed.

Similarly, a number of prisoners in the *kwan-li-so* labor camps interviewed for this report were sent to the family sections of the camps under the "three generation collective guilt and responsibility system" for the real, perceived or imagined political stances, actions or associations of their parent or grandparent. Yet, as much as our recent information comes from former prisoners from "singles" sections of the camps, we cannot know with certainty the extent to which the familywide "guilt-by-association system" operates currently for new prisoners deported to the camps. All we can know with certainty is that there are persons remaining incarcerated who were imprisoned for the perceived political associations or perceived misdeeds of their parents or grandparents.

Lastly, new construction can be seen in more recent satellite photographs of the camps. But without first person or eye-witness testimony, we do not know if the new construction means the prisoner population is expanding or if the new construction is for the prison guards and officials, who are also housed within the sprawling encampments.

Sources

Many of the former North Koreans interviewed for this report, believing their relatives to be either dead or now living in South Korea, agreed to have their names and, in some cases, their photographs published. Many others, fearing that the North Korean government practices collective punishment, would agree to be interviewed and provide testimony only under condition of anonymity, lest relatives remaining in North Korea be punished for the interviewees' crime of escaping to the Republic of Korea. Such individuals are identified in this report with a number rather than a pseudonym.

For some prison camps and detention facilities described in this report, more than one source of information was available, allowing a comparison of accounts. In other cases, the description of a particular camp or facility rested on the testimony of a single former prisoner. In those instances, the coherence and internal consistency of the testimony and my professional experience[20] had to be relied upon. In more than sixty interviews, only three struck me as too inconsistent to be reliable—one, from a very recent arrival

---

20 In the course of several decades of human rights work, I have interviewed large numbers of victims of repression from a variety of political systems and country situations: perhaps, most notably, hundreds of survivors of the Khmer Rouge genocide in Cambodia between 1975 and 1979 and scores of survivors of the genocide in Rwanda in 1994.

who wanted to make a declaration against Kim Jong-il but whose story and assertions dissolved under close questioning, and two interviewees who may have suffered greatly, but whose testimonies were too confused to be usable.

Because violations of human rights happen to individual human beings, the personal stories of the prisoners are as important to our understanding of repression in North Korea as the first-hand eyewitness information they provide. Most former North Korean prisoners, like the Cambodian and Rwandan survivors I interviewed in the 1980s and 1990s, have extraordinary stories of suffering and survival. Thus, brief sketches of their personal histories are provided along with their descriptions of the prison camps they survived. To a large extent, this report uses the practice of briefly profiling a witness (under the heading "Witness") before providing his or her testimony about the particular camp or facility in which he or she was incarcerated and the phenomena of repression endured and observed there (under the heading "Testimony").

This is not to say that the interviewees' memories are always entirely accurate or that some details have not been lost in translation. Nonetheless, I am convinced that the overwhelming bulk of testimony is reliable. The stories in this report create a fuller picture of the phenomena of repression in North Korea than what has previously existed in English-language sources.

Translation and Transliteration

In reviewing the North Korea prison literature available in English and after initially conduct-

ing interviews through multiple translators, it became apparent that there is no standard or consistent translation of Korean prison or police terminology into English. Further, North Koreans sometimes use the same word inconsistently. For example, the term *ku-ryu-jang* is used generically by some to mean "detention facility" and more narrowly by others to mean "interrogation facility." In most cases, the usage employed by the interviewee was retained for this report. The term for "jail" (*ka-mok*) is sometimes used interchangeably with *ku-ryu-jang*.

There are also different ways that Korean terms are romanized or transliterated into alphabetically rendered versions of the Korean Hangul characters. Recently, the South Korean government formally introduced a newer transliteration system. But many older books or articles use the earlier version, which is the same transliteration system used in North Korea. For example, the new official South Korean transliteration for the prison camps is *gwalliso* whereas the former transliteration, and the one still used by North Koreans is *kwan-li-so*. Generally, this report uses the older transliteration system, as this transliteration reads more like the way the words sound phonetically when used by former North Koreans.

More problematically, some Korean prison terms are frequently translated in ways that are literally accurate but are either meaningless or misleading in what the words convey in English. For example, the term *kwan-li-so* is sometimes literally translated as "management center," which sounds rather like a business-consulting firm, and is a meaningless translation for a political prison and slave-labor camp. The term *kwan-li-so* is also variously translated as "political-detention camp," "prison camp," or "concentration camp," which are better translations. In this report, the term *kwan-li-so* is translated as "political penal-labor colony," a more descriptive English rendering.

If the term *kwan-li-so* has been meaninglessly translated as "management center," even more misleading is translating the term *kyo-hwa-so* (alternatively transliterated as *gyohwaso*) as "re-education center," or even as "enlighten-ment center," or "edification center." Judged by the testimonies of the former prisoners, there is nothing remotely educational, enlightening, edifying or rehabilitative about these penitentia-ries and long-term prison-labor facilities, as they are more accurately called in this report. Many are characterized by staggeringly high rates of deaths in detention resulting from forced labor under brutal conditions combined with starva-tion-level food rations.

For ease of reference, this report includes a "Glossary of North Korean Repression"—a chart of common North Korean prison and police terms, which lists the Hangul charac-ters, the Chinese characters from which the Korean language expression is based, the formal and common Romanized renderings of the Korean characters, and a literal and a descrip-tive translation into English. For clarity, so that Korean readers will know precisely what is being described, the running text of this report includes the Korean terms used by the inter-viewees as adjectives in front of the descriptive English translation.

To improve accuracy of usage, the second edition of Hidden Gulag introduces changes in the translations of North Korean detention facilities into English. In the first edition, the term "camps" was used for three different kinds of detention facilities: the *kwan-li-so* political labor colonies, the *kyo-hwa-so* long-term, felony-level prison labor facilities, and the *ro-dong-dan-ryeon-dae* mobile labor brigades. In the present, second edition, the term "camp" is used only for the sprawling *kwan-li-so* encampments. The *kyo-hwa-so*, and the related *kyo-yang-so*, which in satellite photographs look like penitentiaries—a small cluster of multiple buildings surrounded by clearly visible high walls with gates and often identifiable guard towers—are termed "felony-level detention or prison-labor facilities." And the *ro-dong-dan-ryeon-dae* are referred to as "labor training centers" or more descriptively, "mobile labor brigades."

Korean names usually appear with the family name followed by the given name, except for a few individuals who have, for English usage, adopted the Anglicized form of their given names and followed these with their family names. In this report, Korean family names appear first followed by the given name, which is often indicated with a hyphen between two syllables of the given name.

Organization of the Report

Part One, following this introduction, contains a chart detailing the "Scope of Information," which lists the times and places of detention experienced by the former North Koreans interviewed for this report and a "Glossary of Repression" which provides literal and explana-tory translations of the terminology associated with North Korea's policy and practice of arbi-trary and extra-judicial imprisonment.

Part Two describes the general characteristics of the *kwan-li-so* political penal labor colonies, and provides the testimony of 14 former inmates detained therein, along with the observations of three former prison guards, and workers at the camps.

Part Three describes the characteristics and provides testimony from 12 former prisoners in the *kyo-hwa-so* long-term penitentiaries that utilize forced labor with both criminal and political prisoners.

Part Four describes the brutal punishments and mistreatments meted out to North Koreans forcibly repatriated from China, all of whom were detained and interrogated in police *kyu-ru-jang* detention-interrogation facilities before being sent to *jip-kyul-so* short-term detention facilities or *ro-dong-dan-ryeon-dae* "labor training centers" which are, in effect, mobile labor brigades, or else the previously described *kwan-li-so* forced labor camps or *kyo-hwa-so* penitentiaries.

Part Five summarizes two particularly abhorrent atrocities—torture and racially motivated infanticide/forced abortion—that occur in the various detention facilities described in this report.

Part Six analyzes the phenomena of repression according to the terms and provisions of contemporary international human rights law and international criminal law.

Part Seven provides a series of recommendations to the DPRK and to other UN Member States of the international community.

Scope of Information: Documenting the Hidden Gulag

Former North Korean prison detainees and prison guards interviewed for this report were detained, imprisoned or employed at the following places and times[21]:

Kwan-li-so Political Penal-Labor Colonies

Kwan-li-so No.14
Kaechon, S. Pyongan Province
- August 1993 – Oct.1995
- 1982–2005

Kwan-li-so No. 15
Yodok, S. Hamgyong Province
- 1970–1978
- 1977–1987
- Nov. 1987–Feb. 1989
- March 1988–1992
- April 1995–Jan.1999
- 1999–2000
- March 2000–April 2003
- 2003–2006
- 1999–2006

Kwan-li-so No. 18
Bukchang, S. Pyongan Province
- 1977–1983
- 1967–1987
- Oct. 1995–Sept.1998

Kwan-li-so No. 22
Hoeryong, N. Hamgyong Province
- 1990–1994
<Closed *Kwan-li-so*>
Kwan-li-so No. 105 (closed) Danchun, S.

---

21 Some of the interviewees who requested anonymity also asked that the precise dates of their imprisonment be withheld from publication.

Hamgyong Province
    mid-1980s

Kwan-li-so No. 11 (closed in 1989) Kyongsong, N. Hamgyong Province
    Feb 1985–June 1986
    May–August 1987

Kwan-li-so No. 13 (closed in 1990) Jongsong, N. Hamgyong Province
    1987–1989

Kwan-li-so No. 26
Sungho-ri (closed in 1991) Pyongyang
(1964–1984)
1986–1989

Kyo-hwa-so Long-Term (Felony level) Prison-Labor Facilities

Kyo-hwa-so No.1
Kaechon, S. Pyongan Province
- Nov. 1987–Dec.1992
- Early 1993–late 1995

Kyo-hwa-so No.3
Sinuiju, N. Pyongan Province
- Late 1980s–early 1990s

Kyo-hwa-so No. 4
Samdung-ri, Kangdong, S. Pyongan Province
- April–Nov. 1997

Kyo-hwa-so No. 8 "Yongdam"
Wonsan, Kangwon Province
- Early to mid–1980s

Kyo-hwa-so No. 12
Chongo-ri, N. Hamgyong Province
- Dec. 1998–July 1999

- April 2003–March 2006

Kyo-hwa-so No. 22 "Two-Two"
Oro, S. Hamgyong Province
- Sept. 1996–Sept. 1997

Kyo-hwa-so No. 77
Danchun, S. Hamgyong Province
- Sept. 1985–July 1987

Kyo-hwa-so
Hamhung, S. Hamgyong Provice
- 1.5 year, June 2000–Dec. 2001

Kyo-hwa-so
Hoeryong, N. Hamgyong Province
- 1991–1995

Oro *Kyo-yang-so*,
Hamhung, S.Hamgyong Province
-June 2004–July 2005

Jip-kyul-so Provincial (Misdemeanor level) Detention Centers

Chongjin City, N. Hamgyoung Province
- March 2004
- 4 days, mid–2006
- Late March 2007
Nongpo, Chongjin City
N. Hamgyong Province
- Oct. 1986–May 1987
- December 1997
- December 1999
- May 2000
- Mid 2000
- July – Sept. 2000

Onsong, N. Hamgyong Provincce
- Sept. 2000

Ro-dong-dan-ryon-dae
**Labor Training Centers/
Mobile Labor Brigades**

Onsong, N. Hamgyong Province
- Jan.–Sept.1996
- June 2000
- 2 months, 2002
- 1 month, Nov. 2003
- 1 year, 2005
- 17 days, mid 2006
- Mid–late March 2007

Musan, N. Hamgyong Province
- October 1998
- Nov.–Dec. 1999
- 20 days, April 30th 2007

Sinuiju, N. Pyoung-an Province
- 3 months, 2002
- 3 months, end of 2003

Youngkwang district, S. Hamgyong Province
- Oct. 2000

Ka-mok and *Ku-ryu-jang*
Police Detention/Interrogation Facilities[22]

Chung-san, S. Pyongan Province
-2004–2005

Chongjin *An-jeon-bu*, N. Hamgyong Province
- May–Nov. 1987
- Dec. 2001–Feb. 2002

Chongjin *Bo-wi-bu*, N. Hamgyong Province
- Dec. 1987–March 1988
- 8 months, 1998
- 3 months, 2000

Hamju district *An-jeon-bu*, S. Hamgyong Province
- Jan. 1993

Hoeryong *An-jeon-bu*, N. Hamgyong Province
- Couple of days, 2004
- 40 days, July 2008

Hoeryong *Bo-wi-bu*, N. Hamgyong Province
- July 2001
- 2.5 months, late 2004
- June 2008

Hyesan *An-jeon-bu*, Yang-gang Province
- Early 1991

---

22 Identified by the shorthand colloquial names used by former detainees for the two distinct and separate police forces that operate the detention-interrogation facilities.

Kyongsong *An-jeon-bu*
3 months, early 2004

Kyongsong *Bo-wi-bu*
- 2 months, early 2004

Maram *Bo-wi-bu*, Pyongyang
- Early–mid 1993
- Nov. 1994–April 1995
- March–Sept. 1997
- Jan. 1996–Nov. 1997

Moonsu *Bo-wi-bu*, Pyongyang
- Early–mid 2003

Musan *An-jeon-bu*, N. Hamgyong Province
- Jan.–June 2000
- 50 days, early 2004
- April 7th, 2007
Musan, *Bo-wi-bu*, N. Hamgyong Province
- 3 days, Oct. 1999
- 6 months, 2000
- 40 days, Jan. 2004

Myungchun district *An-jeon-bu*, N. Hamgyong Province
- Jan.–July 1993

Namindang *Bo-wi-bu*, Sinuiju, N. Pyongan Province
- Dec. 1999

Onsong *An-jeon-bu*, N. Hamgyong Province
- 5 months, Oct. 2002–March 2003
- 1 day, mid March 2007

Onsong *Bo-wi-bu*, N. Hamgyong Province
- 15 days, 2001
- September 2002
- 5 months, around December 2002
- 6 months, early 2003
- 3 months, 2003
- 15 days, Dec. 2003
- 25 days, 2004
- 15 days, early/mid 2006
- 21 days, late February 2007

Sambong, Musan, *Bo-wi-bu*, N. Hamgyong Province
- July 2001

Sinuiju *An-jeon-bu*, N. Pyongan Province
- 3 months, late 2002

Sinuiju *Bo-wi-bu*, N. Pyongan Province
- Nov.–Dec. 1999
- 3 months, mid 2002
- 5 months, Jan. 2003
- 25 days, March 2003

Glossary of Repression

Korean	관리소	교화소	집결소	노동단련대	감옥	구류장
Chinese	管理所	敎化所	集結所	勞動鍛鍊隊	監獄	句留場
Colloquial Korean Phonetic Romanization	kwan-li-so	kyo-hwa-so	jip-kyul-so	ro-dong-dan-ryeon-dae	ka-mok	ku-ryu-jang
Formal Korean Romanization	gwal-liso	gyohwaso	jipkyulso	nodong-danryeon-dae	gamok	guryujang
Literal English	control and managing place	a place to make a good person through reeduca-tion	gathering place	labor-training corps	jail	detention facility
Descriptive English	political penal-labor colony	long-term prison labor facil-ity	shorter-term labor/detention facility	mobile labor brigades	jail (often pre-sentence deten-tion)	interroga-tion and detention facility

Korean	교양소	수용소	완전통제구역	혁명화구역
Chinese	教養所	收容所	完全統制區域	革命化區域
Colloquial Korean Phonetic Romanization	kyo-yang-so	soo-yong-so	wan-jeon-tong-je-koo-yeok	hyeok-myong-hwa-koo-yeok
Formal Korean Romanization	gyoyangso	sooyongso	wanjeontongje-gooyeok	Hyeogmyongh-wagooyeok
Literal English	a place to make a refined person through teaching and nurturing	a place where many people are put in together.	total control zone	revolutionizing zone
Descriptive English	labor detention facility, often for women border crossers	a generic South Korean term for a place of incarceration; occasionally used by North Korean defectors	isolated lifetime political labor colony	non-lifetime prisoner area of the camp

Korean	국가보위부	사회안전부	인민보안성
Chinese	國家保衛部	社會安全部	人民保安省
Colloquial Korean Phonetic Romanization	Kuk-ga-bo-wi-bu* "Bo-wi-bu"	Sa-hoe-an-jeon-bu** "An-jeon-bu"	In-min-bo-an-seong
Formal Korean Romanization	Gukgabowibu	Sahoeanjeonbu	Inminboanseong
Literal English	State Security Agency	Social Safety Agency (pre-1998)	People's Safety Agency (post-1998)
Descriptive English	political police	regular police	regular police

* Former North Koreans interviewed for this report frequently used the shorthand *Bo-wi-bu*, meaning political police, rather than its full name (it is also sometimes translated into English as the National Security Agency or State Security Department).

** Former North Koreans interviewed for this report continued to use the shorthand *An-jeon-bu* to refer to regular police rather than the newer formal name *In-min-bo-an-seong*.

Korean	고문	공개형	영아살해	강제낙태	연좌제
Chinese	拷問	公開死刑	嬰兒殺害	强制落胎	緣坐制
Colloquial Korean Phonetic Romanization	ko-mun	kong-gae-sa-hyeong	yeong-a-sal-hae	kang-je-nak-tae	yeon-jwa-je
Formal Korean Romanization	gomun	gonggae-sahyeong	yeongasal-hae	gangjaenak-tae	yeonjwaje
Literal English	torture	public execution	killing babies	forced abortion	association system
Descriptive English	torture	public execution	infanticide	involuntary abortion	guilt by association

Korean	도강자	비법월경자
Chinese	渡江者	非法越境者
Colloquial Korean Phonetic Romanization	to-kang-ja	pi-bup-wol-kyoung-ja
Formal Korean Romanization	dogangja	bibupwolgyoungja
Literal English	river crosser	illegal border crosser
Descriptive English	person who left the country through crossing a river at the border	person who left the country by border crossing

PART TWO

THE *KWAN-LI-SO* POLITICAL PENAL-LABOR COLONIES

Arbitrary Detention and Forced Labor: Generations Imprisoned Without Trial and Enslaved

The Prisoners: Who They Are

The *kwan-li-so* labor camps are the incommunicado repositories for those North Korean citizens who have been cleansed or purged and deported to areas of North Korea "outside the protection of the law" because of their perceived counter-revolutionary attitudes or associations. They are deemed to be social, political, economic or ideological deviants who do not fit into or who pose a risk to what the North Koreans themselves term the "Kim Il-sung nation."

The presumed political, ideological, and sociological deviants deported to and imprisoned in the labor camps include persons suspected of *wrong-doing, wrong-thinking, wrong-knowledge, wrong-association*, or *wrong-class-background*. This report provides the stories and testimonies of real persons subjected to severe punishment for this catalogue of perceived wrongs—"crimes that are not really crimes" in the words of one former prisoner.

• Imagined or perceived *wrong-doing* can include being on the "wrong" or losing side of a bureaucratic, factional, or political dispute within the Korean Workers' Party, skipping too many of the compulsory ideological education classes all North Koreans are required to attend, defacing or failing to take adequate care of photographic images of Kim Il-sung, complaining about conditions, expressing criticism of regime policies, or leaving the country without permission, and in particular, meeting South Koreans while outside North Korea.

• Imagined or perceived *wrong-thinking* includes expressing or supporting ideas at variance with the official ideology. At times this could have been belief or evidence of belief in Protestant Christianity. At other times wrong-thinkers were orthodox Marxists who thought that "juche ideology" or dynastic succession within Kim Il-sung's family was contrary to the spirit and tenets of Marxism-Leninism.

• An example of *wrong-knowledge* includes the situation of North Korean students or diplomats who had been studying or posted in Eastern Europe in the late 1980s during the collapse of socialism, and who were recalled to the DPRK only to be immediately dispatched to labor camps to prevent their knowledge of the collapse of state socialism in North Korea's allies from spreading to the North Korean population. An earlier example of wrong-knowledge was the exposure to and knowledge about capitalist prosperity, democracy and civil liberties in Japan by ethnic Koreans who "repatriated" to the DPRK in the 1960s to build socialism in the Korean fatherland, but found Kim Il-sung's version of totalitarian socialism not what they had imagined.[23]

• *Wrong-association* is being part of a family whose husband, father or grandfather had collaborated with the Japanese occupation of Korea, or who was a Presbyterian elder or deacon, or

---

23 Substantial numbers of the ethnic Koreans who emigrated to the DPRK from Japan ended up in their own sub-sections of the labor camps.

part of a family whose patriarch was part of a purged faction of the Korean Workers' Party, or who was suspected of supporting South Korea during the Korean War or having subsequently defected to South Korea.[24]

• *Wrong-class* background includes those who had been aristocratic land-owners or otherwise privileged bourgeoisie during the Japanese colonial regime in Korea.

Thus, the purged elements of the population deported to the camps mirror North Korean society. There are "high level" individuals and families as well as members of the lowest socio-political orders in North Korea's rigidly hierarchical *songbun* social classification system.[25] Prisoners include Christian religious believers and orthodox Marxist-Leninist Workers' Party members, as well as large numbers of apolitical citizens who ran afoul of the many rules and regulations put in place to achieve and enforce the unity of heart and mind between the populace and the "Great Leader" Kim Il-sung, and his dynastic successors.

As noted, those deemed irremediably counter-revolutionary were, and are, deported to the camps designated exclusively as "zones under special dictatorship," or to the "total control zones" of mixed-zone camps. Those elements of the population deemed capable of rehabilitation were, and are, sent to the "re-revolutionizing areas" of the labor camps.[26]

Perhaps inevitably, a large ongoing, secretive, extra-judicial camp system such as has long existed in the DPRK becomes a convenient dumping-ground for other individuals or groups that do not fit in. Thus, it is thought that some of the South Korean POWs from the Korean War not repatriated to South Korea ended up in labor camps. Likewise, it is suspected that South Korean soldiers who fought for the Americans in Vietnam and were captured by the North Vietnamese and then turned over to North Korea also ended up in the North Korean labor camps.

Notwithstanding North Korean claims that there are no human rights violations in the DPRK, both Kim Il-Sung and Kim Jong-il have defended and justified the forced labor prison camp system. According to Kim Il-Sung, the imprisonments were:

> "... a legitimate measure to protect the country's democracy from its hostile and impure elements who have abused democratic order and attempted to destroy our socialist system...The type of democracy which can guarantee freedoms and rights to the People, including workers, peasants and the working intelligentsia, and which at the same time can punish a small number of class enemies, is the type of socialist democracy we have in our country."[27]

---

24 Even decades after the Korean War, wives and children in North Korea whose father was believed to have aided or fled to the South, were being tracked down and sent to the camps.

25 See HRNK report, *Marked for Life: Songbun, North Korea's Social Classification System*, (forthcoming in the summer of 2012).

26 See Heo Man-ho, "North Korea's Continued Detention of

South Korean POWs since the Korean and Vietnam Wars," The Korean Journal of Defense Analysis, Vol. XIV, No.2, Fall 2002.

27 Kim Il-sung, "Let us strengthen the Peoples Regime," Works of Kim Il-Sung 32, January-December 1977, Korean Workers Party Press, Pyongyang, cited in Jiyong Song's *Human Rights Discourse in North Korea*, Routledge, London and New York, p. 104 . (N.B. In reality North Korea never guaranteed civil and political rights to its people, including its workers, peasants and intellectuals. It no longer guarantees economic freedoms such as freedom from hunger or the right to adequate health either. And the number of "punished enemies" is not small.)

Kim Jong-il, in turn, entirely inverted human rights protection and human rights violations:

> "The fact that the People's regime uses dictatorship against the forces violating the interests of the People is indeed the protection of human rights, not the violation of human rights...The original meaning of People's Democratic Dictatorship is a powerful function of the People's regime in an aim to guarantee democratic rights and freedoms for the People as the master of state and society."[28]

Following a descriptive overview of the North Korean system to "punish" the "enemies" of the self-described "People's Democratic Dictatorship," there is a brief account tracing the pattern and evolution of the regime's perceptions of the "hostile and impure elements" that sent successive waves of persons deemed to be among the "forces violating the interests of the People" to the forced labor camps.

Overview of the Prison Labor Camp System

The *kwan-li-so* political penal forced-labor facilities consist of a series of sprawling encampments measuring many miles long and many wide. They are located in the mountains and valleys, mostly, in the northern provinces of North Korea. There are between 5,000 and 50,000 prisoners per *kwan-li-so*, totaling some 150,000 to 200,000 prisoners throughout North

Korea.[29] The perceived or suspected wrong-doers and wrong-thinkers and up to three generations of their extended families are apprehended by police authorities and forcibly deported to the *kwan-li-so*, without any judicial process or legal recourse whatsoever, usually for lifetime isolation and punishment comprised of hard labor in mining, timber-cutting, farming and related enterprises. The prisoners live under brutal and severe conditions in permanent situations of intentional, deliberate semi-starvation.

The *kwan-li-so* are usually surrounded at their outer perimeters by barbed-wire (often electrified) fences, punctuated with guard towers and patrolled by armed guards. The encampments include self-contained, closed compounds (sometimes called "villages") for single persons, usually the alleged wrong-doers, and other closed, fenced-in compounds for the wrong-doers' extended families. Two of the camps, 15 and 18, are divided into sections called *wan-jeon-tong-je-kyoo-yeok* (total-control zones) where the incarceration is for life; and sections called *hyuk-myung-hwa-koo yeok* (best translated as "re-revolutionizing zones"), from which prisoners may be released.[30] North Koreans deemed by DPRK authorities to be implacably or irre-

---

28 Kim Jong-il, "For the promotion of the superiority of the People's regime" Selected Works of Kim Jong-il 13, February 1992-December 1994, Korean Workers Party Press, Pyongyang, cited in Siyoung Song, ibid, p.156.

29 The 200,000 figure comes from a former guard, Ahn Myong-chol, who previously worked at four different prison camps. Yoon Dae-il, a former official of the *Bo-wi-bu* State Security Agency, the police organization that administers the prison camps, says the 200,000 figure is "the minimum." It is obvious from the testimony of former prisoners that the rate of deaths in detention is very high. It is also clear from prisoner testimony that new prisoners continue to be sent to the camps.

30 Much of our information about the *kwan-li-so* camps comes from former prisoners released from the "re-revolutionizing zones" who subsequently fled to China and made their way to South Korea. Other information comes from the few prisoners who managed to escape prison camps Nos. 14 and 18, and from former guards at a number of the camps who also fled to China and made their way to South Korea.

mediably counter-revolutionary are deposited in the total control camps or zones. Those deemed capable of rehabilitation through intense labor and political indoctrination and "re-education" and hence eligible for eventual release back into North Korean society are placed in the "re-revolutionizing" zones.

Resident and family policy varies. There are sections and dormitories for single men and single women, sometimes in rather close proximity. There are other areas for families (without the primary wrongdoer who is often the family patriarch). Only a very few privileged or model young prisoners are allowed to conjugate and have children. Otherwise, sex between men and women prisoners is prohibited. Except for a number of persons at Camp 18, prisoners have no correspondence or contact with the world outside the political penal-labor colony. The *kwan-li-so* are also sometimes referred to as *teuk-byeol-dok-je-dae-sang-gu-yeok*, which translates as "zones under special dictatorship." The *kwan-li-so* political penal labor colonies are also variously translated into English as "control centers," "management centers," "concentration camps," or "political prison camps."

Over the past decades, there has been a gradual consolidation of the *kwan-li-so*, according to former guards and police officials. Originally there were a dozen, but several have been closed, for a variety of reasons. Camp 11, at Kyong-song, North Hamgyong province was closed to convert the location into a villa for Kim Il-sung at the foot of scenic Mount Gwanmo. Some closed camps were deemed too close to the Chinese border. In these cases, the prisoners were transferred to other camps. Accord-

ing to former police officials, there are now six *kwan-li-so* in operation. Four of these six prison camps, numbered by the North Koreans as 14, 15, 18 and 22 were confirmed by persons interviewed for this report. The location of a fifth camp, 25, has been confirmed by former North Koreans who resided near the prison camp and went to it for various reasons. Former prisoners from Camp 15 relate that there is at least one former prisoner from Camp No. 16, located at Hwasong, North Hamgyong province, who has fled North Korea and presently resides in South Korea, but who declines to be interviewed by journalists or researchers.[31]

Originally, the prison-labor camps were run by the *In-min-bo-an-seong* (People's Safety Agency), regular police forces that are part of the Ministry of Interior (before 1998 called the *Sa-hoe-an-jeon-bu*, meaning Social Safety Agency). Former North Koreans continue to use the older abbreviation, "*An-jeon-bu*," for North Korea's regular police force. Except for *Kwan-li-so* No. 18 in South Pyongan province where the *An-jeon-bu* police agency retains an administrative role, the administration of the *kwan-li-so* prison-labor camps was taken over by *Kuk-ga-bo-wi-bu* (commonly abbreviated as "*Bo-wi-bu*") police force. This is variously translated as the State Security Agency, National Security Agency, National Security Police, State Political Protection Agency, or State Safety and Protection Agency. Reportedly, this political security force was created in 1973 and reported not to the

---

31 The annual *White Paper on Human Rights in North Korea*, ROK Korea Institute for National Unification (KINU) also notes a camp No. 17 at Hoeryong in North Hamgyong Province. (The KINU *White Paper* does not identify Camp No. 18. at Bukchang, South Pyongan Province as a *kwan-li-so* camp because it is largely administered by the regular *An-jeon-bu* police force rather than the *Bo-wi-bu* political police authorities.)

Ministry of Interior or Defense, but according to former *Bo-wi-bu* officials, directly to Kim Jong-il through Chang Song-taek, Kim Jong-il's brother-in- law.[32] The outer perimeters of the *kwan-li-so* are patrolled by privileged members of North Korea's army.

Guilt by Association

A striking feature of the *kwan-li-so* system is the penal philosophy of "collective responsibility," or "guilt by association" (*yeon-jwa-je*) whereby the mother, children and sometimes grand-children of the offending political prisoner are imprisoned in a "three-generations" practice.[33] Former prisoners and guards align this prac-tice with the 1972 statement by "Great Leader" Kim Il-sung: "Factionalists or enemies of class, whoever they are, their seed must be eliminated through three generations."According to the testimony of a former guard at *Kwan-li-so* No. 11 at Kyongsong, North Hamgyong province, this slogan was carved in wood above the prison guards' headquarters building.

The three-generation guilt-by-association is a revival of feudal penal practices associated with the five-hundred-year-old Chosun dynasty (1392–1897). The practice was discontinued in the early twentieth century following the collapse of the dynasty, but, as is described

"Great Leader" Kim Il-sung: "Factionalists or enemies of class, whoever they are, their seed must be eliminated through three generations."

below, was revived by Kim Il-sung after the Korean War along with other feudal Korean practices such as dynastic succession and extreme ideological orthodoxy. According to the testimony of a former police official, the number of family members abducted and sent to the lifetime labor camps depends on the severity of the presumed political offense.

Forced Disappearances and *Incommunicado* Detention without Trial

Another striking characteristic of the *kwan-li-so* system is that those citizens who are to be deprived of their liberty are not arrested, charged (that is, informed of their offense of, or against, a particular criminal act delineated in the DPRK Criminal Code), or tried in any sort of judicial procedure. There is no chance to appear before a judge, confront their accusers, offer a defense or have benefit of legal counsel. The presumed offender is simply picked up, taken to an inter-rogation facility and frequently tortured to "confess" before being deported to the political penal-labor colony. The family members are also picked up and deported to the *kwan-li-so*. None of the interviewees reported having been told of the whereabouts or alleged misconduct of the presumed wrong-doing or wrong-thinking head of family.

---

32 Kim Jong-un succeeded Kim Jong-il in December 2011. Chang Song-taek has recently been promoted. The lines of authority and command for the State Security Agency during and following North Korea's leadership succession process is not known by the present author.

33 Sometimes, the wife of a purged high ranking official is allowed or required to divorce her deported husband rather than accom-pany him to the labor camps.

Friends, neighbors, co-workers, or more distant family members not sent to the camps are not given any information as to the whereabouts of those who have "disappeared" into the mountains. "Forced disappearance" leading to arbitrary detention or execution is a modern day phenomena of repression.[34] But nowhere else does it take place on the massive and prolonged scale—hundreds of thousands of persons over half a century—as is the case in North Korea.

Systemic and Severe Mistreatment

United Nations Member States have developed a series of penal guidelines that "set out what is generally accepted as being good principle and practice in the treatment of prisoners and the management of institutions."[35] Among the most important of these guidelines are *The Standard Minimum Rules for the Treatment of Prisoners*, commonly called the "Standard Minimum Rules," adopted by the Economic and Social Council of the United Nations General Assembly,[36] and the *UN Standard Minimum Rules for the Administration of Juvenile Justice*, commonly

termed the "Beijing Rules" after the city where these standards were drafted.[37]

The prison camp system in North Korea described by the former prisoners interviewed for this report is at marked variance with these norms and standards. For example, Rule 13 of the Standard Minimum Rules says that adequate bathing and shower installations shall be provided... as necessary for general hygiene. Rule 20 says that every prisoner shall be provided with food of nutritional value adequate for health and strength. Rule 31 says that corporal punishment and all cruel, inhumane or degrading punishments shall be completely prohibited as punishments for disciplinary offences. Rule 37 says that prisoners shall be allowed, under necessary supervision, to communicate with their family and reputable friends at regular intervals. Rule 75 (2) says that the hours fixed for prison labor shall leave one rest day per week. Rule 89 says that an untried prisoner shall be offered the opportunity to work, but shall not be required to work and if he chooses to work, he shall be paid for it.

Three former inmates interviewed for this report were imprisoned as youths, two were brought in with their mothers for political offenses committed by their grandfathers, and one was born in the camps as a result of the assigned mating of two model prisoners.[38] The former juvenile prisoners report frequent beatings in their schools

---

34 For example, during the military dictatorships in Chile and Argentina during the "dirty wars" of the 1970s, although in these situations "disappearance" frequently resulted in execution not long-term detention without trial. "Enforced disappearance" is "the arrest, detention, abduction or any other form of deprivation of liberty by agents of the State...followed by a refusal to acknowledge the deprivation of liberty or by concealment of the fate or whereabouts of the disappeared person, which places such a person outside the protection of the law." (Article 2, International Convention for the Protection of all Persons from Enforced Disappearance.)

35 The Standard Minimum Rules for the Treatment of Prisoners, para. 1.

36 ECOSOC Res. 2076, 13 May 1977.

37 In May 1984. Submitted to General Assembly, 29 November 1985 Res. A/RES/40/33. Additional norms and standards for the penal practice and administration of justice were similarly discussed and defined at conferences in Japan and Venezuela and are known as "The Tokyo Rules" and "The Caracas Declaration Rules," adopted by the UN General Assembly in Res. 45/110, 14 December 1990 and Res. 35/171, 15 December 1980 respectively

38 See p. 49, 59 and 71 below.

by the *Bo-wi-bu* guards assigned to be teachers. Apart from the question of why these children were incarcerated in a labor camp to begin with, Rule 17.3 of the Beijing Rules for the Administration of Juvenile Justice provides that juveniles should not be subject to corporal punishment.

As noted above,[39] DPRK officials deny that they have political prisoners and instead refer to the *kwan-li-so* inmates as "moved people" or "migrants" (*e-ju-min*).[40] However, international human rights norms, including the Standard Minimum Rules, explicitly refer to persons who have been deprived, or severely deprived, of their personal liberty. No matter what they are called, the residents in the political penal labor colonies are severely deprived of their liberty.

The Standard Minimum Rules "cover the general management of institutions, and [are] applicable to all categories of prisoners, criminal or civil, untried or convicted, including prisoners subject to 'security measures.'"[41] These rules, as can be seen in the examples above, offer minimal standards. Yet, in the stories and testimonies that follow in this report, these minimum standards are grossly ignored or abused.

Induced Malnutrition, Slave Labor and High Rates of Deaths in Detention

The most salient feature of day-to-day prison labor camp life is the combination of below-

subsistence food rations and extreme hard labor. In a system of intentional, administratively inflicted hunger, the regimen of chronic semi-starvation provides only enough food to be kept perpetually on the verge of starvation. Prisoners are driven by hunger to eat, if they can get it (and avoid being caught) anything remotely edible: plants, grass, bark, rats, snakes, the food-stuffs of the labor camp farm animals. According to the testimony of former prisoners, deliberate below-subsistence-level food rations in the camps preceded by decades the severe nationwide food shortages experienced by North Korea during the famine of the 1990s.

When entire families are deported to the camps, much of their household and personal belongings—clothing, blankets and bedding, pots, pans, cooking utensils, etc.—are trucked along with them. However, these material possessions are soon bartered away for food. The former prisoners interviewed for this report recall their shock upon initial arrival at the camps at the sight of the malnourished inmates: stick figures dressed in tattered, patched and threadbare clothing; and literally, rags. The prisoners are occasionally issued shoes, but not socks, so that rags are frequently wrapped around ankles for warmth. The prisoners are covered in dirt from the infrequency of bathing privileges, and marked by physical deformities: hunched backs, from years of bent-over agricultural work in the absense of sufficient protein and calcium in the diet; and missing toes and fingers, from frostbite; and missing hands, or arms or legs, from work accidents.

Many of the *kwan-li-so* labor camps feature multiple production areas. These include: mining coal, iron, gold, and other ores; logging on the mountainsides within the boundaries of

---

39 See p. 7-8.

40 Former prisoners, however, relate that prison officials and guards also address them as "traitors" or "animals without tails."

41 *The Standard Minimum Rules for the Treatment of Prisoners*, para. 4 (1).

the encampments, agricultural production in the valleys between the mountains; and artisan work such as furniture-making and woodworking from the logs felled by other prisoners; animal husbandry, chicken or rabbit-raising, or bee-keeping in the agricultural sections of the camps. Camp 14 includes a large textile factory.

Backbreaking agricultural, mining or manufacturing labor is usually performed twelve or more hours per day, seven days per week, with only one day of rest per month and on the three national holidays such as New Year's Day, and Kim Il-sung's and Kim Jong-il's birthdays. Prisoners receive small food rations, mostly corn-meal. No former prisoner interviewed for this report received payments in money or redeemable or transferable coupons. The small amount of money provided to the prisoners was, in their words, cigarette money, about one pack a month. Most prisoners are assigned daily production quotas, accompanied by threats of reduced food rations, and/or beatings. Labor is performed in work groups; the whole group can be punished for failure to meet production quotas. These work units are required to participate in evening "mutual work criticism" sessions.

The combinations of forced labor in very inhumane conditions and below-subsistence-level food rations lead to very high rates of deaths in detention. Clearly, North Korea does not publish statistics on the population levels of the prison camps that they deny exist. However, the former prisoners interviewed for this report describe extraordinary death rates in their work groups and the sections of the camp in which they resided.

A comparison to the labor camps of the Soviet Union demonstrates the extreme inhumanity of the North Korean prison camp system. In the USSR, the gulag camps were divided into four "regimes" or regimens: ordinary, re-enforced, strict, and special. The "special regime" camps were essentially punishment facilities in which the prisoners were confined to cells (rather than subjected to forced labor), and were not eligible for visits or parcels. The other "regimes" were denominated in terms of the amount of correspondence, brief or prolonged visits (measured by hours and/or days), and the number of food parcels the prisoners could receive after completing a part of their sentence of hard labor. Prisoners in the "ordinary regime" labor camps could receive four brief and two prolonged visits and up to three parcels per year. Those in the "re-enforced regime" camps could receive three brief and two prolonged visits and two parcels per year, while prisoners in the "strict regime" camps got only one short, one prolonged visit and one parcel per year.[42]

In the North Korean prison labor camps, all the residents, while subjected to arduous forced labor, are entirely *incommunicado*, unable to have any correspondence, visits, and most importantly, unable to receive life saving parcels of food, clothing, soap or medicines from family members, friends, neighbors or former colleagues outside the camps. According to the former prisoners interviewed for this report, the prisoners who are sent to the equivalent of "special regime" detention facilities within the DPRK camps most usually die there or shortly after release to the general prison camp population.

---

42 Information on the Soviet camps is taken from Joshua Rubenstein and Alexander Gribanov, *The KGB File of Andrei Sakharov*, Yale University Press, 2005; and *Prisoners of Conscience in the USSR: Their Treatment and Conditions*, Amnesty International, April 1980.

Prisoner Informants and Intra-Prisoner Surveillance and Hostility

Semi-starvation generates large numbers of informants among the prisoners, leading to a prison-camp culture of extreme distrust and hostility. Complaints from one prisoner to another about life in the prison camps are frequently reported to camp authorities. Conditions drive people to violence and aberrant behavior. Former prisoners report that inmates beat each other in retaliation for the non-achievement of production quotas for which the entire work unit will be punished. Prisoners fight each other over scraps of food, or over the clothing of deceased inmates.

Execution and Extreme Punishments

The camps contain disciplinary punishment facilities for inmates who violate camp regulations. Former prisoners describe these facilities as tiny underground or partially underground cells in which prisoners cannot fully stand up or lie down. Punishment cell detention within the prison camps is reportedly accompanied by severe beatings or systematic torture and even more drastically reduced food rations. Former prisoners report that fellow inmates came back from the punishment cells "in very bad shape" and frequently die shortly thereafter.

Such punishments are meted out for various infractions of camp rules: unauthorized food gathering or eating, stealing the food provided for animals or live-stock, repeated failure to meet production quotas, losing or damaging tools or equipment, suspected sabotage of camp facilities, reported complaints about camp life, or unauthorized sexual conduct between prisoners.

Escape attempts are punished by public execution, sometimes by hanging but more often by firing squad. The prisoners are compelled to assemble and witness the executions at close range. Virtually all former prisoners interviewed for this report witnessed numerous executions. Sometimes the prisoners were compelled to file by the corpse and throw stones at or strike the corpse. Former prisoners relate that they hated this gratuitous indignity, and held in contempt those prisoners who stoned the executed corpse with obvious force.[43] And former prison guards reported that they also hated the public executions because the prisoners wailed and cried out in distress. The guards recounted that they feared the distraught prisoners might revolt and thus attended the public executions in force and heavily armed.

Former prisoners also report that other prisoners were taken away, never to return, and are widely believed to have been executed in secret. Detentions in the labor camp punishment cells, disappearances, and public executions are all extra-judicial in nature. Neither the DPRK Criminal Code, Criminal Procedures Code nor court system, such as it is, has any reported reach, applicability, or presence inside the *kwan-li-so* encampments. The camps appear to be entirely outside North Korea's constitution, courts and laws.

---

43 Testimony on the compulsory defilement of the corpses of executed prisoners does not extend past 1985. It is possible that the use of this gratuitously dehumanizing practice has declined.

Sexual Relations, "Marriage" and Prison Camp Schools

The practice of imprisoning the family members of suspected wrong-doers and wrong-thinkers brings numbers of young people into the camps. Sexual relations between young men and women camp residents are prohibited. Young women who become pregnant are severely punished: they are often taken away by the guards and not seen again. The former prisoners assume they have been executed.

A very small number of "model" young prisoners are rewarded by being allowed to "couple," often with a mate selected by prison authorities to reward "model" prisoners of the opposite sex. However, the mated couples do not thereafter live together. Rather, they remain in the sexually segregated housing facilities. The "married" couples are allowed to meet periodically, with the resulting children living with the mother up to age twelve or thirteen, and rarely seeing their fathers.[44]

For the young children brought into the camps with their parents or grandparents, and for the small number of children born to model prisoners, primary schools offering limited instruction in basic literacy and very basic math (addition and subtraction, but not even multiplication or division, according to the former prisoners) exist. Uniformed police officers serve as teachers. There are also so-called "middle schools". But the former prisoners describe these as, in reality, bases for young people's mobile labor brigades, the students having already learned in primary schools the basic reading, writing and math

---

44 See the story and testimony of Shin Dong-hyuk, who was born and raised in Camp No. 14. pages 48-51.

necessary to perform prison camp labor. The children are indoctrinated to inform on other prisoners, even their parents.

The Sexual Exploitation of Women

Grossly inadequate food rations and forced labor under harsh conditions inevitably lead to sexual exploitation of young women vulnerable to offers of additional food or less arduous work such as record keeping or cleaning guards' offices or quarters in exchange for sexual favors. Such practice is, reportedly, not in accordance with camp policy, but former prisoners relate that it was widespread, and understood by other prisoners as a necessity for survival. Contemporary international human rights law regards sex between prisoners and prison guards to be so inherently coercive as to constitute rape.

Prisoner Releases

Reported releases from the labor camps that take place from the "re-revolutionizing" areas in Camps 15 and 18 took place on the birthdays of Kim Il-sung or Kim Jong-il. The prisoners from those areas are assembled, and speeches are made praising the hard work and rehabilitation of those soon to be released. They, in turn, are required to publically pledge their appreciation and loyalty to the regime. The prisoners are sworn to secrecy, promising not to disclose information about the camps to persons outside. On some occasions the prisoners are required to affix their fingerprints to their oaths of secrecy and silence. A return to the camps, or worse, would be the punishment for talking to North Koreans outside the camps about the camps.

The released prisoner is given a travel pass and a food rations coupon that identifies the released prisoner as a worker at specially designated Military Units that North Korean police will recognize as the political penal labor colonies.

Notwithstanding the regime's attempt to prevent information about political imprisonment from reaching the general population, recent surveys of larger numbers of former North Koreans now living in South Korea indicate that much of the population knows of the camp system,[45] even if it is safer within North Korea to use the euphemistic phrase "those who are sent to the mountains."

The Economic Role of the Forced Labor Camps

The "gulag archipelago" in the former Soviet Union, with its combination of political and criminal prisoners, had a clear economic function: to open up the vast areas of Siberia for the exploitation of the mineral wealth beneath the frozen earth. The production of the forced labor camps contributed measurably to the Soviet economy. The DPRK does not publish national macro-economic statistics, let alone production figures for the prison labor camps they claim do not exist. Thus, the economic role of the political penal labor colonies cannot be quantified.

However, what we do know is that much of the coal mined in the prison camps goes directly to

nearby power plants for the generation of electricity. Some of the lumber cut down from the mountainsides goes into factories to make furniture for government offices and schools. The fur of the rabbits raised by juvenile prisoners is used to line winter coats for army officers. Some of the textile factory output also reportedly goes into army uniforms. Prior to recent sanctions, rare mushrooms collected in the mountainsides were reportedly exported to Japan.[46]

The agricultural production by prisoners is used in part to feed the prison population, but was, at one point, also provided to the state-run Public Distribution System (PDS) for distribution to the general population. Probably, some of the food produced by the prisoners is sold by prison officials in the public markets that sprung up during and after the 1990 famine. Also, much of the honey produced by prison camp bee keeping or the whiskey and *soju* (a popular inexpensive Korean liquor) distilled in the prison camps most likely ends up in local markets. But whether profit from these sales finds its way into the pockets of the prison camp officials or goes to the national treasury is anybody's guess.

Nonetheless, what is clear from the testimonies of the former prisoners is that prison camp slave labor is notoriously inefficient. Sending malnourished men down into the earth to mine coal with picks and shovels, while malnourished women and children workers pick up the coal pieces and put them in carts and trolleys to pull and push to the surface, is very old-fashioned mining. Having malnourished loggers walk for an hour or two up into the mountains to cut down trees with saws and axes and then drag the

---

45 See Survey Report on Political Prisoners' Camps in North Korea, National Human Rights Commission of Korea, Seoul, 2009, p. 188. In a survey of over three hundred former North Koreans now residing in South Korea, one-third had experienced political imprisonment, another third knew about it, leaving only one third of the respondents unaware of political imprisonment.

46 Japanese imports from the DPRK have largely, if not entirely, stopped.

trimmed logs down the mountainside with ropes seems similarly inefficient compared to chain-saw logging practices in other developing countries. Even if the productivity of agricultural and industrial enterprises throughout North Korea is not high, productivity in the prison labor camps seems, likely, even lower, even if the prisoners are punished and beaten if they do not fulfill their production quotas.

In theory, slave or forced labor should be cheaper than work remunerated by wages or salaries. But almost all of the North Korean economy, prior to the economic breakdown of the 1990s, was substantially demonetized. Most work throughout North Korean society was rewarded by the provision of food and clothing, with the amount and quality of food and clothing linked to the person's employment and to the *songbun*, the social-political status of the male head of household. But when the PDS broke down in the 1990s, the rations provided to citizens across the board plummeted. Even before that, it seems difficult to calculate the economic significance of the marginal savings that accrued to the state from the lesser amounts of food provided to prison versus non-prison labor.

The Absence of Due Process: Arbitrary and Extra-Judicial Detention

Virtually all of the prisoners in the *kwan-li-so* are victims of "arbitrary detention," as this phenomena of repression is called by international human rights bodies, such as the UN Working Group on Arbitrary Detention.[47] The severe

---

47 The UN Working Group on Arbitrary Detention, which reports to the Geneva-based UN Human Rights Council and is

deprivations of physical liberty in North Korea's *kwan-li-so* political penal labor colonies are extra-judicial, that is, outside of, and without regard to, the provisions of the DPRK constitution, the DPRK Criminal Code and Criminal Procedures Code, and the North Korean court system, which, as noted above, has no existing jurisdiction or presence within the labor camps.

Former prisoners from the *kwan-li-so* camps now residing in South Korea and their South Korean translators sometimes apply legal and judicial language to imprisonment in the *kwan-li-so*. For example, the amount of "time served" in the prison camp is called a "sentence." More accurately, in legal usage of the English language, a "sentence" is the duration and/or place of punishment pronounced by a judge in a court of law following a legal process resulting in a conviction, which should not be conflated with the amount of "time served" in the prison camp.

Similarly, the former prisoners spend significant mental energy trying to figure out what it is they did wrong to bring such misery into their lives. And sometimes, it is quite possible to reconstruct from the endlessly repeated questions of the police interrogators, what it is that the regime was concerned about. Thus, some of the former prisoners refer to the presumed reasons for their imprisonment as "charges," a misleading appropriation of legal and court of law terminology.

---

supported by the Office of the High Commissioner for Human Rights, has defined three categories of arbitrary detention: (1) when there is no legal basis for the deprivation of liberty; (2) when a person is deprived of their liberty because they have exercised the rights and freedoms guaranteed in the Universal Declaraton of Human Rights (UDHR) and the International Covenant on Civil and Political Rights (ICCPR); and (3) when a person is deprived of liberty after a trial which did not comply with the standards for fair trial set out in the UDHR and ICCPR and other relevant international instruments.

Further, some accounts mention that within the *Bo-wi-bu* political police force, there are "prosecutors" and that "sentences"—the decision to send someone or a whole family to the camps—are made by a "judge" deciding on behalf or in the the the name of, and/or reporting to the North Korean Central Court. It is possible that one or more *Bo-wi-bu* police officials are termed "prosecutor" or that the person who makes the judgment to send a person or family to the camps is called a "judge." It is also possible that the DPRK court system is informed of the names of persons deported from society to life-long servitude in the labor camps.

However, fundamentally, the use of the language of law in such instances is misleading. International conventions, which the DPRK has officially adhered to, particularly Article 14 of the International Covenant on Civil and Political Rights, spell out the minimum requirements for fair trial and due process of law. This sets the standards of a judicial process that enables a government to lawfully deprive a citizen of his or her liberty. Clearly, the practice of abducting and deporting North Koreans, not to mention foreign nationals, to the *kwan-li-so* labor camps violates international norms. With one or two exceptions discussed below, nothing in the testimony of the former prisoners about their interrogation or deportations indicates any reference by North Korean political police authorities to the DPRK Criminal Code, the Criminal Procedures Code, or the DPRK court system. The system of severe deprivation of physical liberty described below, to which hundreds of thousands of North Koreans have been, and continue to be, subjected is essentially, and certainly by international standards, extra-judicial.

Such a massive and enduring system of arbitrary and extra-judicial detention would likely itself be deemed a crime against humanity under contempory international human rights law.

Successive Waves of Political Imprisonment: A Historical Overview

There is a sequence to political incarceration in North Korea—a dynamic that will be familiar to students of communist party rule: first, suppression of the opposition to the revolution; then, the elimination of enemies from within the revolution; and finally, the elimination of successive victims of, and scapegoats for, the failure of the revolution. The pattern of deporting purported opponents to the North Korean gulag follows Kim Il-sung's successful struggle to achieve power and gain complete control over the North Korean people, society, economy and state. More recent deportations include those who complained about or sought to escape from the economic, social and political failures of the regime.

After Japan's defeat in WWII and the end of Japanese colonial rule in Korea, Kim Il-sung, under Soviet tutelage, instituted what is usually termed a "national democratic revolution" in Korea north of the 38th parallel. This included genuinely popular reforms, such as the official establishment of an eight-hour workday, positing formal equality of the sexes and prohibiting prostitution, concubinage and female infanticide. It included a sweeping and popular land reform that expropriated the landholdings of absentee Japanese landlords and the native Korean land-owning aristocracy. It also included a purge of Koreans in the colonial bureaucracy, who thought that Korea should follow the Japanese path to economic, social and political modernization, and Korean police officers who had collaborated with the harshly repressive Japanese rule in Korea. Many purged police officials and dispossessed Korean landlords fled to the south. Many of their family members who remained in the north ended up in labor camps.[48]

Kim Il-sung's drive for political power and his earliest plans for Korea were initially challenged by political parties affiliated with two popular religions in Korea: Protestant Christianity (*Kiddokyo*) and an indigenous syncretic faith known initially as "Eastern Learning" (*Tonghak*) and subsequently as the "Followers of the Heavenly Way" (*Chondokyo*).[49] Protestant Christian and *Chondokyo* leaders had spearheaded the internal Korean opposition to the Japanese occupation, most famously the March 1919 "Korean Declaration of Independence" and subsequent mass demonstrations. After Japan's defeat, the Korean Christians and *Chondokyoists* established political parties and rejected the proposed Soviet-American plan for a five-to-ten-year Korean

trusteeship in favor of immediate independence with full Korean sovereignty.[50] Kim suppressed these rival, non-communist, nationalist political parties through the arrests and executions of Protestant and *Chondokyo* leaders.[51] Many of their followers fled to the south. Again, family members who remained in the north were under suspicion and many ended up in prison camps.

The Soviets had tasked Kim Il-sung, the former leader of a Manchuria-based band of partisan anti-Japanese guerrilla fighters, with forming the Korean Workers' Party out of various ethnic Korean members within the Chinese, Japanese or Russian communist parties. This was along with incorporating Korean leftists, many previously based in the southwest corner of Korea who fled north of the 38th parallel after 1945.

However, following the Korean War (1950–53), Kim instituted a series of intense purges within the communist Korean Workers' Party. First, he purged his leftist rivals who had fled north from the southern portion of Korea. He scapegoated them for their failure to launch a successful popular uprising to coincide with the military invasion from the North and thus liberate the South from American 'imperialist' occupation.

48 For a general description of this process see, Charles Armstrong, *The North Korean Revolution, 1945-1950*, Cornell University Press, 2002.

49 In the late 19th century, Pyongyang became the epicenter of Protestant Christianity in Asia. In other parts of Asia, Christianity was associated with European colonial powers. But Korea was colonized and occupied by Shintoist and Buddhist Japan. Protestant Christianity, introduced by medical and educational missionaries, was perceived as a modernizing and nationalistic force, opposed to Japanese colonization. (Kim Il-sung's family members were Protestant Christians and his mother and her family were particularly devout). *Tonghak/Chondokyo* was a synthesis of neo-Confucianism, Buddhism, and Catholic Christianity distilled by a disaffected Confucian scholar earlier in the 19th century. A millenarian and eschatological belief system, it attracted large numbers of dispossessed peasants to fight for heaven on earth against corrupt feudal officials and then against Japanese encroachments on Korean sovereignty during the terminal decline of the five-hundred year old Chosun dynasty.

50 During the time of the trusteeship, the USA, the USSR and China would "prepare" Korea for full independence. It was thought at the time that the Americans and Russians could restrain the rival Korean nationalists they had installed in the south and the north, and thus prevent civil war. But the Americans and Russians failed to work out the terms of a trusteeship, leading to the proclamation of competing and implacably hostile regimes in the north and south of the peninsula, followed shortly by the Korean War.

51 While Kim Il-sung was suppressing Christian and Chondokyo religious leaders north of the 38th parallel, Syngman Rhee, the US-installed leader in the south, was repressing Korean leftists with even more violence. Many southern leftists fled north, while others fled to Japan. Many of the southern leftists who fled north were later purged and sent to the camps. Many of the southern leftists who fled to Japan later migrated to North Korea, where, again, many ended up in the camps.

Next, Kim purged rival Korean communist leaders who had been affiliated with the Chinese communist party and army.[52] Subsequently, he purged the Koreans who had previously lived in and had been affiliated with the Soviet Union.[53] According to Korea scholar Charles Armstrong, "By the 1960s, the former Manchurian partisans [the Kim Il-sung-led anti-Japanese resistance fighters] were at the apex of the power system in the DPRK, and those who had been aligned with the Southern Workers' Party, the Soviets, and the Chinese in Yan'an had almost all been purged, executed, exiled or otherwise eliminated from positions of power."[54]

These purges usually involved executing the leaders, initially after Stalinist-type show trials, and sending their networks of supporters in the party, the army and the bureaucracy to the camps. According to Hwang Jang-yop, the highest level North Korean official to defect to South Korea, the "total control zones" were established after 1956 for the "purged factionalists."[55] Korea specialists have noted subsequent purges:

> "After Kim Il-Sung designated his son as his successor, the elder Kim purged military officers in 1976-77 who voice[d] displeasure with the move. Another purge of military officers occurred in 1987-88 … when the SSD [the *Bo-wi-bu* State Security Department, the police agency that runs the *kwan-li-so* political prison camps] exposed an alleged military coup attempt in 1992, six hundred officers were purged."[56]

Another development following the Korean War profoundly affected the nature of North Korean society, including the peopling and operation of the prison labor camps. Following the death of Stalin in 1953, the Soviet Union and most of Eastern Europe curbed some of the worst excesses of Stalinism[57] seeking a measure of return to "socialist legality," and in anticipation of what became known as "revisionism," the possibility of "peaceful co-existence" between capitalism and socialism. Ruling communist parties in East Asia took a dramatically different course that has been described as "national Stalinism." Most famously, in China, Mao Zedong set off on the radical and disastrous policies of the "Great Leap Forward" and "Cultural Revolution." Cambodia's Pol Pot set off on an even more disastrous "Super Great Leap Forward." In North Korea, in an attempt to Koreanize Stalin-

---

52 There have always been large populations of ethnic Koreans on the China side of the China-Korea border. Because of the Japanese occupation of Korea, many ethnic Koreans in China joined Mao's Red Army to fight the Japanese who were seizing larger and larger parts of China. Immediately after World War II, the ethnic Korean divisions of Mao's Red Army played a major role in China's civil war, defeating Chiang Kai-shek's US-backed Kuomintang army in Manchuria and handing northern China over to Mao. Mao returned the favor by handing over these battled-hardened ethnic Korean troops to Kim Il-sung for use in the 1950 invasion of South Korea. But following the Korean War, Kim Il-sung did not trust the loyalty of the "Yan'an faction" of the Korean Workers' Party (named after Mao's headquarters in China during WWII and the Chinese civil war) and had them purged, executed or imprisoned.

53 In the late 19th and early 20th centuries, thousands of ethnic Koreans from Korea or Manchuria moved into Siberia and the Russian Maritime Provinces. Many of these Korean residents in the USSR and their families returned to the north of the peninsula as administrators or members of the Communist Party of the USSR or simply as administrators and Russian-Korean translators.

54 Armstrong, *op cit*, p. 72-73. Quite a large number of the purges in the 1950s and 1960s are detailed in Robert Scalapino and Chong-Sik Lee's two volume *Communism in Korea*, University of California Press, Berkeley, 1972.

55 See *White Paper on Human Rights in North Korea*, KINU, Seoul, 2003, p. 177-180.

56 Patrick McEachern, *Inside the Red Box: North Korea's Post-Totalitarian Politics*, Columbia University Press, New York, p. 94.

57 For a discussion of the term and its unfolding in the DPRK, see Andrei Lankov, *Crisis in North Korea*, University of Hawaii Press, 2005.

ism, usually referred to as "socialism in our style" (*urisik sahoejuui*), Kim Il-sung turned to the only Korea he and his Manchurian partisans knew, or imagined—the Korea that had existed prior to the Japanese occupation where the feudalist Chosun dynasty had ruled for nearly five hundred years.

Chosun dynasty feudal practices were revived and incorporated into the Stalinist system bequeathed to North Korea by the Soviet Union including a return to "hermit kingdom" self-styled isolation, prohibiting travel abroad and rigorously excluding foreign influence in order to develop a distinctive and unique Korean political culture. With rare exceptions, North Koreans were, and still are, forbidden to leave North Korea. People who did were caught and sent to a variety of detention facilities including the prison camps. These numbers skyrocketed when tens of thousands of North Koreans fled to China during the famine of the 1990s.

The entire North Korean population was divided into three more-or-less hereditary classes (*songbun*): "loyal" or "core," "wavering," and "hostile" or "antagonistic." As characterized by Professor Armstrong:

> "Social stratification had been one of the most enduring characteristics of Korean society before the twentieth century...The hereditary three-tiered structure...that became explicit in North Korea from the 1960s onward was based on the actions of oneself or one's ancestors during the colonial period and the Korean War. Such stratification was made possible by the careful categorization of all North Korean citizens by social strata beginning in 1946

and resonated with the three-class structure of *yangban* [scholar/bureaucratic or land-owning aristocrat], commoner, and outcast/slave that dominated Choson society." [58]

The prisoners exiled to the political penal labor camps are the modern day "outcasts/slaves" of Kim Il-sung's re-feudalization of North Korean society.

An extreme version of collectivism was instituted as well. The North Korean Workers' Party determined residence, educational opportunities, occupations and work sites for the citizenry, largely based on calculations of loyalty toward the Kim regime. A Public Distribution System that dispensed food and clothing according to social class *songbun* ranking and occupation replaced salaries and wages. Agricultural production was collectivized. Private selling of goods and services was prohibited. The regime re-instituted the feudalistic *yeon-jwa-je* "guilt-by-association" three-generation collective punishment system for political opposition or deviance. This provided the rationale for populating the labor camps with the families of purged or offending deviants.

As in the Chosun dynasty, a rigid and extreme ideological orthodoxy was instituted.[59] Variously

---

58 Armstrong, *op. cit.*, p.72-73.

59 Prior to the Chosun dynasty (1392-1910) Buddhism, as the state religion, and Confucianism, as a theory of social and political relations, co-existed for a thousand years. Starting in the 15th century, for four hundred years, neo-Confucianist Chosun dynasty officials persecuted Buddhism almost to the point of extinction. When in the 18th century, Roman Catholic Christianity was introduced by Korean diplomats who had learned of it at the Emperor's court in Ming Dynasty Beijing, those bringing these new ideas about the "Lord of Heaven" back to Korea were executed, as were subsequent Korean and foreign Catholics in Korea for a hundred years. In the 19th century when itinerant scholars-visionaries constructed the syncretic Tonghak (Eastern learning) system of

termed "*ju-che* thought" or the "*ju-che* ideology" or simply "Kim Il-sungism," the regime vigorously promulgated *ju-che* as "the one-and-only ideology system" (*yuil sasang chegye*). North Koreans, and even foreign leftists working in the North Korean Foreign Ministry, who were overheard saying that "*ju-che* thought" was contrary to Marxism were sent to prison camps.[60]

An extreme cult of personality was organized around Kim Il-sung and his family, going back to his great grandfather, and extending to his son, Kim Jong-il, as dynastic succession was reintroduced. Kim Il-sung was venerated as the founder of a new dynasty, comparable to the founders of the previous Koryo and Chosun dynasties. Kim was even elevated to the status of a Korean messiah, destined to liberate the Korean people from the consecutive and seamless evils of Japanese colonialism and American imperialism. Portraits of the one or both Kims were required in every house. Everybody was required to affix a Kim button to his or her lapel. Hallowed, church-like "study halls for General Kim Il-sung revolutionary activity" (*Kim Il Sung Wonsu hyukmyeong hwaldong yeongusil*) were set up in every factory, farm, school and office. The entire population was required to attend weekly sessions to venerate Kim Il-sung and master his teachings. Failure to attend these classes or to show sufficient respect to the portraits of the "Great Leader" risked exile to the camps.

Further purges and arrests from within the Party, the army, and state bureaucracy coincided with the development of the "cult of personality" around Kim Il-sung and the feudal-dynastic succession of Kim Jong-il, the first son of Kim Il-sung's first wife.

The extreme ideological orthodoxy effectively criminalized the *wrong-thought* and some of the *wrong-doing* described previously. A heavy gloss of pseudo-religiosity[61] began to coat this extreme ultra-orthodoxy. As expressed by a former *kwan-li-so* prison guard interviewed for this report, North Korea is similar to a gigantic religious cult. Not thinking in accord with the thinking of the cult is simply not allowed. If noncompliance is suspected, it is punished severely.

How Do We Know: A Brief Historical Recounting

In his 1997 history, *Korea's Place in the Sun*, Bruce Cumings predicted, "… if and when the [North Korean] regime falls, we will probably learn of larger numbers [of people held in prisons and reform-through-labor camps] and various unimaginable atrocities…"[62] Historians will continue to anxiously await the regime archives and police files. But, as reflected in Professor Cuming's prediction, for fifty years, information about North Korea's prison

---

ideas, they too were hunted down and executed. Today, DPRK police officials hunt down and vigorously prosecute North Koreans who convert to Protestant Christianity while in China or who attempt to bring Christian literature, primarily Bible verses, back with them to North Korea.

60 See p. 25 above.

61 Miracles in the skies and forests, signifying the joy of both heaven and nature, were attached to the birth of Kim Jong-il on Mount Paektu, long regarded as the sacred birthplace of the Korean people. (Historians of Korea outside of the DPRK commonly record that Kim Jong-il was born in the USSR at a Soviet army base.) The portraits of Kim Il-sung in the ubiquitous "study halls for General Kim Il-sung revolutionary activity" are arranged in a sacred-like, altar setting.

62 Bruce Cumings, *Korea's Place in the Sun*, Norton, NY, 1997, p. 398.

camp system was quite limited. It took until the present millennium when scores of former political prisoners escaped from North Korea that enough information became available to detail the camp system and how it works. Notwithstanding, the bits of information that did leak out of North Korea in the 1970s, '80s and '90s are worth noting as they demonstrate both the duration and evolution of the prison camp system the regime persists in denying.

Scholarly Insights

Korea scholars have written about political imprisonment, often in conjunction with their study of the North Korean political leadership. They have documented waves of purges sweeping through the highest echelons of the government, the army, and the Korean Workers' Party. In their two-volume 1972 textbook, *Communism in Korea*, Professors Robert Scalapino and Chong-sik Lee noted that along with various prisons, two prison camps had been set up in the 1950s. They are named after the number of proclamations that brought them into existence: Camp 8 for perceived political wrong-doers and Camp 149 for both wrong-doers and their families.[63]

Early Non-Governmental Organization Documentation

In 1974, the situation of the North Korean prison camps became known in select international human rights circles when Amnesty International (AI) campaigned for the release of Ali Lamada, a citizen of Venezuela, and Jacques

---

63 Scalapino and Lee, *Communism in Korea, op. cit.*, p. 830.

Sedillot, a citizen of France, both of whom had been recruited to work in North Korea by the DPRK Ministry of Foreign Affairs to translate the collected works of Kim Il-sung into Spanish and French, respectively. Following the release of Ali Lamada, Amnesty published in 1979 his account of his imprisonment—perhaps the first English-language North Korean political-prisoner account to introduce the North Korean prison-camp system to an international audience. Lamada's story of his imprisonment from 1967 to 1974, except for his nationality, is remarkably similar to the stories of recently escaped North Koreans. Their cases are summarized herein because they demonstrate the longstanding nature of the ongoing phenomena of repression documented in this report.

A decade later, the first full length international human rights NGO report on North Korea, Human Rights in the DPRK (North Korea), was published in December 1988 by the Minnesota Lawyers International Human Rights Committee and Human Rights Watch/Asia. Primarily a legal analysis of the DPRK Constitution and legal system, it noted the camps cited by Professors Scalapino and Lee.

In the early 1990s, researchers at Amnesty International investigated and publicized three different categories of persons imprisoned on political grounds in the DPRK: 1) ethnic Koreans from Japan who voluntarily migrated from Japan to North Korea in the early 1960s; 2) North Korean loggers in Russia who attempted to escape their labor crews and were caught by North Korean police operating within Russia; and 3) other North Koreans who were forcibly repatriated from Russia and/or China to the DPRK. AI's investigations focused on five cases: two Korean-Japanese who migrated to the DPRK only to disappear into, AI believed, the labor camps;

The Cases of Ali Lamada and Jacques Sedillot, 1967 to 1974

Ali Lamada and Jacques Sedillot were recruited in 1967 by the DPRK Ministry of Foreign Affairs and placed in the Department of Publications to translate the writings of Kim Il-sung into Spanish and French respectively. Lamada was an active member of the Venezuelan Communist Party and his poetry and books were well known in the Spanish-speaking world. Both Lamada and Sedillot were arrested in September 1967. Sedillot was accused of being a French imperialist spy. No charges were initially brought against Lamada, who was simply arrested and coerced to confess to spying by means of solitary confinement in a 2 meter by 1-meter cell (7 feet by 3 feet by 10 feet) in the Ministry of Interior for a year on below-subsistence level food rations. During this time, he lost 22 kilograms (more than 50 pounds) and his body became covered with sores.

After a year, Lamada was returned to his residence in Pyongyang and placed under house arrest but was picked up two months later and sentenced to twenty years of forced labor for being a spy. He was driven some three hours from Pyongyang and thrown into a punishment cell in a prison camp, where, handcuffed for three weeks, he slept on the floor without a blanket or mattress in freezing temperatures. Transferred to the main prison-camp building, he was locked in unheated rooms and his feet suffered frostbite. His toenails dropped off, and his feet became covered with sores. From guards, he learned that the name of the prison camp was Sariwon, where some 6,000 to 8,000 prisoners worked twelve hours per day assembling jeep parts. A doctor told Lamada that there was a special section of the prison camp where 1,200 sick persons were held.

While imprisoned at Sariwon prison-labor camp, Lamada learned from guards and "orderlies," who were privileged prisoners, some of whom had been held previously in other prison-labor facilities, of approximately twenty other prison-labor camps holding, Lamada calculated, at that time roughly 150,000 prisoners altogether.

The government of Venezuela and the President of Romania intervened on behalf of Lamada, and both he and Sedillot were released in May 1974. Sedillot died in Pyongyang of prison-related illnesses before he could return to France. Lamada recuperated in Eastern Europe before returning to Venezuela, where he published his account of his experience in the North Korean prisons and the Sariwon prison-labor camp. (See Ali Lamada, A Personal Account of the Experience of a Prisoner of Conscience in the DPRK, AI: ASA 24/02/79) a North Korean, Mr. Kim Duk-hwan, who married a Russian woman while studying in Moscow, but who, upon return to North Korea, disappeared into detention; and two other North Koreans who were believed to have been forcibly repatriated from Russia to the DPRK. These cases are summarized herein, as they demonstrate the systemic and on-going continuity of the conditions about which we now have much more voluminous documentation.

Prisoners' Memoirs and Testimony

Prisoner testimony, initially only in the Korean language, started to emerge publicly in the mid-1990s, after two former prisoners from the "re-revolutionizing zone" of *Kwan-li-so No. 15* (Yodok), Kang Chol-hwan and An Hyuk, escaped to South Korea via China in 1992 and published their prison memoirs in Seoul.[64] In 1994, a former prison guard, Ahn Myong-chol, who had worked at four different prison-labor camps, defected to South Korea and was able to provide a great deal of first-hand information. In 1996, the Seoul-based Korea Institute of National Unification (KINU) began publishing an annual *White Paper on Human Rights in North Korea*, which contains reporting that draws on the extensive interviews conducted by the South Korean government with all North Koreans provided with asylum by the Republic of Korea.

In the late 1990s, as the production and distribution system in North Korea broke down, greater numbers of Koreans fled to China, primarily in search of food. Some of these had been imprisoned in either the *kwan-li-so* or the *kyo-hwa-so*.

A number of those who fled to China, particularly after 2000, made their way to South Korea and published accounts or interviews in South Korean journals or magazines.

The First Satellite Photographs of the Prison Camps

The first public satellite photographs of the prison camps appeared in December 2002 in the Far Eastern Economic Review, a now defunct but formerly influential weekly news magazine. It published satellite photographs of *Kwan-li-so* No. 22 at Hoeryong, North Hamgyong province. John Larkin, a Seoul-based, Korean-speaking correspondent for the Far Eastern Economic Review, was able to obtain coordinates of latitude and longitude of *Kwan-li-so* No. 22 from old Soviet-made maps of North Korea on which, in consultation with former guard Ahn Myong-chol, Larkin was able to precisely locate the sprawling encampment at Hoeryong. After Larkin obtained satellite photos from a commercial firm, Ahn was able to locate and identify buildings at the penal-labor colony where he had been a guard.[65]

---

64 In 2001, Kang Chol Hwan's memoirs, co-authored with Pierre Rigoulot, was published in English as *Aquariums of Pyongyang: Ten Years in the North Korean Gulag*, Basic Books, New York.

65 Apparently, both the United States and South Korean governments long had even better satellite photographs of the prison-labor camps. When Kang Chol-hwan first came to Seoul in 1992, he was shown satellite photos of the *Kwan-li-so* No. 15 "Yodok" and was able to pick out his former house in the images. But these intelligence agencies have never released their photographs to the press or public.

Korean Migrations from South Korea to Japan to the DPRK

Some 600,000 ethnic Koreans, overwhelmingly from the southern parts of the Korean peninsula closely adjacent to the Japanese islands, migrated or were transported to Japan during the Japanese occupation of Korea (1910–1945). According to a prominent scholar, Professor Tessa Morris-Suzuki, Australian National University, the Koreans were designated as "foreigners" by the Japanese government, had no legal right to permanent residence, and faced considerable prejudice and discrimination. In the mid-to late-1950s, ethnic Koreans in Japan, with the support of the North Korean and Japanese governments, began agitating to migrate to North Korea. At the time, Syngman Rhee's impoverished and authoritarian regime in South Korea had no desire to repatriate these ethnic Koreans, many of whom were leftist-nationalists in their political orientation. North Korea, sensing a propaganda and hard currency opportunity, offered the Koreans in Japan employment opportunities, free education, housing and medical care, and the chance to build and live in "the socialist paradise." The Japanese government was not unhappy to reduce the number of resident ethnic Koreans, some of whom were involved in leftist politics, and others with criminal groups or semi-legal enterprises.

Following ethnic Korean "repatriation" demonstrations in front of the Japanese Red Cross Society, which were observed by a visiting delegate from the Geneva-based International Committee of the Red Cross (ICRC), the National Red Cross Committees of Japan and North Korea arranged what was called a "repatriation" program, even though most of the Koreans were from what was then South Korea. Starting in 1959, some 93,000 persons migrated to the DPRK, including roughly 6,000 Japanese who had married Korean spouses. A few of the Korean migrants to the DPRK did very well. One woman became Kim Jong-il's wife. Many others fared poorly.

The Koreans migrating from Japan were ranked number 32 in the 51-category hierarchy of social classes (*songbun*) that the DPRK developed in the 1960s. Some twenty to forty percent ended up in the labor camps. (The forty percent figure comes from one of the Korean-Japanese interviewed for this report based on a statement by DPRK officials. When celebrating the 20th anniversary of the "repatriation" program North Korean officials noted that "forty percent" of the migrants needed "revolutionizing," the name of the zone within the labor camps to which many "returnees" were sent.) Perhaps as many as 150 of the migrants subsequently fled from North Korea to China and have resettled in either Japan or South Korea, reportedly 100 in the Tokyo area and another thirty to fifty in the vicinity of Osaka. Several Korean-Japanese who recently fled from North Korea were interviewed for this report. Their testimony appears on p. 73, 79, 80, 126, and 127.

Korean Laborers in Russia

According to AI, a 1967 agreement between Russian Prime Minister Leonid Brezhnev and Kim Il-sung set up North Korean work crews at logging sites in the Khabarovsk and Amur regions of the Russian Far East, and at construction sites in several Russian cities. Initially the North Korean labor crews in the USSR were thought to number around 20,000, but by the mid-1990s, the number was thought to have declined to somewhere between 2,500 and 6,000. These crews worked under the control of North Korean state enterprises and North Korean police. While it was recognized that these work crew jobs were highly sought after, AI was concerned about labor conditions, and about reports of political imprisonment within the labor sites for those who criticized the North Korean system or expressed a desire not to go back to the DPRK. But mostly, AI was concerned about the fate of North Korean laborers who escaped from the work sites, rather than returning to North Korea after their three-year contracts expired.

AI had received reports about North Korean police agents tracking down Koreans within Russia, and reports of Russian police turning over North Koreans for repatriation against their will to the DPRK. Following the collapse of the USSR, Russian journalists visited the lumber cutting sites and wrote a number of stories about the conditions of the North Korean labor crews. In 1993, a number of logging sites were visited by the Russian Parliamentary Human Rights Commission, headed by the noted former dissident, Sergei Kovalyov, who obtained copies of the cooperation protocols between the Russian and North Korean police agencies operating in Russia and declared the protocols to be illegal. These concerns and others, particularly the forced repatriation of North Koreans from Russia to the DPRK, are summarized in the AI report, "Pursuit, Intimidation, and Abuse of North Korean Refugees and Workers" (AI Doc # ASA/24/06/96). An appendix to this report contains the text of a 30 December 1994 appeal from North Korean refugees in Moscow seeking assistance and support from the UN, the ICRC, "the Church" and human rights organizations. See also AI, "Russian Federation/DPRK: Refoulment of Lee Yen Sen / Fear for Safety in the DPRK" (AI Doc # EUR 46/06/96, February 1996).

For the testimony of a North Korean refouled from Russia in 1999 and sent to *kwan-li-so* Camp No.15 (Yodok) who was interviewed for the present report, see Kim Eun-chol, page 63 below.

AI's Investigation of Shibata Kozo and Cho Ho-yong

Mr. Shibata Kozo (Korean alias, Kim Ho-Nam)

Born in Tokyo in 1930, Kozo, a Japanese citizen, married Shin Sung-suk, a Korean widow living in Southwest Japan in 1959. In late January 1960, Kozo, Shin and her two children from a previous marriage took the sixth boat transporting Koreans and their Japanese spouses to North Korea. Living in Pyongyang, Kozo worked on Korean-Japanese translations, and had a child with Shin. In 1964 Shin wrote Kozo's sister in Japan that he had been taken to a sanitarium. Knowing that some "returnees" had not fared well, Kozo's family doubted this, as he did not mention any health or medical problems in previous letters. In 1974 letters from Shin or their daughter stopped completely.

In 1992, a weekly news magazine, Bunshun, carried a story about a former North Korean, Huang Pyong-joo, who fled to China, and claimed he had shared a prison cell with Kozo at the Sungho-ri prison labor facility, which reportedly contained some 6,000 prisoners at that time. According to Huang, Kozo had been imprisoned as a spy from 1964 to 1984. The spying allegation was based on Kozo's admission that years before, while still in Japan, he had rented an apartment owned by a Japanese police official. Kozo had also supported the protests of several Japanese wives of "returned" Koreans, who were seeking the implementation of the previously promised guarantee that they could visit their families in Japan every three years. Additionally, according to Huang, a guard at Sunho-ri told him that Shin and the three children had been sent to the camps.

Mr. Cho Ho-yong

Cho Ho-yong and his Japanese wife, Koike Kideko, "returned" to North Korea in February 1962. Cho had been a physiology student at the Tohoku University graduate school and was convinced by Chongyron, the pro-DPRK Association of Korean Residents in Japan, that if he went to North Korea the government would send him to Moscow for further graduate study. Initially assigned as a physiology instructor at a medical college in Hamhung, rather than being sent to Moscow, Cho was re-assigned to an orchard as an agricultural worker. In 1967 he wrote to his family still in Japan that he was about to undertake "re-education." In 1973, after three years of silence his family received a letter from Koike that she and the children had been living alone for six years. Then all letters stopped.

Alerted by her family in Japan, in 1994, AI took up their cases as disappearances, and via the DPRK Ambassador to the UN and in a mission to Pyongyang in 1995, AI raised Cho and Kozo's cases with North Korea. The DPRK informed AI that the Kozo family had been killed in a train accident. It also reported that in 1973 Cho had been detained as a spy at the Chonnae Prison, but he escaped and two days later, he and his wife and children were shot by Korean border guards during an attempt to flee North Korea after killing a North Korean soldier while stealing a boat to make their escape.

AI found the North Korean explanations to be internally inconsistent and contradicted other information in AI's possession, which indicated that both were still in detention. These discussions and the background information on these cases were summarized in an AI Report, "Human Rights Violations Behind Closed Doors" (AI Doc # ASA/24/12/95) an appendix to which contains the names of fifty North Koreans of concern to AI, the majority of whom were Korean-Japanese.

Hidden Gulag (first edition)

As noted in the introduction, the first edition of *Hidden Gulag: Exposing North Korea's Prison Camps* (2003), was widely recognized as the first systematic and comprehensive account of political prisons, prison camps and the subsidiary systems of arbitrary detention in the DPRK. It was the first time that satellite photographs were used by an NGO report to precisely document the sites of human rights violations. *Hidden Gulag* was translated into Korean and Japanese, and published in Seoul and Tokyo.

Google Earth: Mapping the Fences

In 2006, as earlier noted, Google Earth's improved technology allowed detailed online viewing of satellite images of the Korean peninsula. Many of these images are of much higher resolution than the images previously available. Initially using the coordinates of the prison camps as published in *Hidden Gulag*, Google Earth enabled viewers to zoom in on the prison camps, and with its clearer resolution even trace the barbed wire fences surrounding the encampments, and additional facilities.[66] Former prisoners confirmed these markings as the fences and guard posts tracing the outside perimeters of the camps. (For prison camp satellite photograph identifications of more recently escaped political prisoners interviewed for this report, see pages 197-229.)

Contemporary Witnesses and Testimonies

Kwan-li-so Camp No. 14, Kaechon, South Pyongan Province

Operated by the *Bo-wi-bu* (State Security Agency) police, *Kwan-li-so* No. 14 is located in Kaechon-kun, (*kun* is a geographic area roughly equivalent to a county) in South Pyongan province, so the camp is referred to as "Kaechon." Located in a mountainous area, it is some 40-50 kilometers (25-31 miles) long and some 30 kilometers (19 miles) wide, and is estimated to hold 15,000 prisoners. It is located on the north side of the Taedong River. It is across the river from another prison camp, No. 18 at Bukchang-kun, South Pyongan.[67] Enterprises at Camp 14 include mining, clothing manufacturing, farming, and livestock-raising. The latter was considered as the occupation of choice, as the prisoners had the opportunity to steal animal food and even pick through animal droppings for undigested grains.

---

66 Two persons who have examined the satellite photographic images of North Korea including the prison camps in great detail have websites where images and/or information are placed online as they become available. See the websites of a Washington DC-based attorney, Joshua Stanton "OneFreeKorea," and "North Korea Economy Watch," by a Miami-based graduate student, Curtis Melvin.

67 A former prisoner from Camp 18, Mrs. Kim Hye-sook, whose testimony appears below, (p. 71) reports that following the discovery of valuable mineral deposits in Camp 18, just south of the Taedong River, the boundaries of Camp 14, which is run by the more powerful *Bo-wi-bu* political police agency, and Camp 18 were redrawn with Camp 14 acquiring the chunk of territory below the Taedong River with the mineral deposits, so that the mineral extractions would accrue to the more powerful political police agency.

WITNESS AND TESTIMONY:
Shin Dong-hyuk, *Kwan-li-so* No. 14 (1982–2005)

Shin Dong-hyuk spent 23 years at Camp 14, Kaechon, located on the north side of the Taedong River in South Pyongan province under very unusual circumstances. He was born there in 1982 to two model prisoners whom the prison guards had coupled together. According to Shin, some sections of Camp 14 had an unusual reward system for young prisoners, the most exemplary of whom would be allowed to have sex three or four times a year with another prisoner chosen for them by the prison staff. The term "you're married" was used, though the mated parents were not allowed to live together with the children, like Shin Dong-hyuk. The young prisoners welcomed these unions for obvious reasons, especially since women who became pregnant outside of these guard-chosen "marriages" were taken away and never returned to their previous work or residence units. Shin also believes that an additional motive for the arranged matings was a labor shortage in the prison camp owing to high prisoner death rates from malnutrition and work accidents.

Shin's father's family, his grandmother, grandfather, his father and two of his uncles were deposited in Camp 14 in 1965 following a pre-dawn raid during which the police descended on the household and just took the family and their furniture away by truck. Shin later learned that this was because two of his father's brothers had defected to South Korea. Shin lived with his mother until age 12, during which time he rarely saw his father who was held in another part of the camp. And he saw little of his mother, an agricultural laborer who worked in the fields from early morning until the nighttime work criticism session. Shin had an older brother, eight years his senior, who had already been transferred to a "singles barrack" by the time Shin reached primary school age. Shin met his brother only three or four times that he can remember. Shin had so little family life that, regrettably, he notes, he developed no bond of affection for his parents or brother.

The section of Camp 14 where Shin grew up had six areas or "villages," five for families and one "village" for singles, which could not be visited by people from the family villages. His prison home, called "main village," had forty houses with one hundred sixty households, as each house contained four households of women and young children. For the children of these Camp 14 couplings, there was an elementary school where the children learned reading and writing, addition and subtraction, but only that. Multiplication or division are not taught, he relates, having learned of these basic mathematical tools after he escaped from North Korea. At school, there were two or three classes per grade with about thirty pupils per class up through fifth grade, making for roughly four hundred children in all.

Camp life was harsh. Once, when he was nine, *Bo-wi-bu* police officers assigned as teachers, searched the children and found a small amount of wheat in the pocket of a girl. She was made to kneel and was beaten on the head for almost an hour until she fainted. Her classmates carried her home, but were told the next day that the girl died during the night. A year later, at age ten, during the rice-planting season, Shin, like the other children followed his mother into the fields to assist in planting. Unwell, his mother could not keep up the pace for her group's work quota. Instead of being allowed to have lunch, his mother was compelled to kneel with her hands raised above her head for an hour and a half. Without lunch, even weaker, his mother fainted in the field around three o'clock in the afternoon. Again that evening, at the mutual criticism session, she was compelled to kneel for another two hours while, her fellow workers were compelled to accuse her repeatedly of being lazy and not fulfilling her work quota.

At age 12, Shin entered what was dubbed "middle school." But there was no instruction; the "classes" were organized child labor squads for weeding, harvesting, carrying fertilizer, etc.

In 1996, Shin was handcuffed, blindfolded and taken by car to an underground interrogation and detention facility where he was held for some six or seven months. In the course of his interrogations, Shin was informed of the reasons for his father's initial detention at Camp 14: two of his father's brothers had fled to South Korea. Shin's detention in the punishment cells at the Camp was related to an apparent escape attempt or plan by his mother and older brother. Shin was tortured repeatedly—being suspended over a fire, burning his backside, while pierced in the folds of his stomach to stop his squirming from the flames at his back—to confess details of his mother's and brother's escape plot. His wounds festered badly, and he was placed in the adjacent cell of an elderly prisoner long held in the punishment cell within the prison camp, who nursed Shin back to reasonable health. Shin

accounts this as the one piece of human kindness he encountered in 23 years at Camp 14.

Shin was taken outside where he saw his father, who unbeknownst to Shin, had also been detained in the underground cells at Camp 14. Shin and his father were blindfolded and driven away. When the blindfolds were removed, father and son were at the camp execution site, where Shin had previously witnessed multiple executions every year. He figured that he and his father were to be executed. But they were placed in the front row as two wretched prisoners were dragged forward. At close range, to his shock, Shin recognized his mother and brother, though his brother was just skin and bones and his mother's face and body were swollen with bruises. They were denounced as enemies of the people. His mother was executed by hanging and his brother killed by firing squad. Shin looked at the ground or over at his father, who was also looking down at the ground with tears rolling down his cheeks.

Shin's father was sent off to a construction site elsewhere in the camp and Shin was returned to his middle school labor brigade. Between the spring of 1998 and the autumn of 1999, along with other young teenagers, Shin was mobilized to build a dam connected to a small electrical generator. There, he was struck by the number of children killed in work accidents while constructing the dam. Shin and other teenagers from the middle-school labor brigade were also sent deep into the mines at Camp 14 to load loose pieces of coal that the adult prisoners had dug up into carts that were pushed by hand up the inclined shafts.

Shin was later assigned to work in a sewing machine repair shop at a large garment factory within the camp where he estimated that some 2,000 prisoners, mostly young women, produced military uniforms. At one point, Shin dropped a sewing machine base he was carrying to the second floor of the factory. In punishment for damaging the machine, the guards cut off the tip of his middle finger at the first knuckle.

To avoid the kicking and beating for unmet work quotas, young women at the garment factory sought the jobs of cleaning prison officials' offices, even though the provision of sexual services could be part of the assignment. A young woman, who had been in the same classes as Shin, was among those cleaning women. When the girl became pregnant, Shin and some other former classmates tried to cover up her pregnancy. But her pregnancy was soon discovered. She was taken away and never returned. Fellow prisoners believed she had been executed to eliminate the evidence of the prison officials' sexual abuse of the female prisoners.

In 2004, another prisoner who was assigned to the garment factory became Shin's close friend. This prisoner had grown up in the outside world, and had even seen Pyongyang and visited China. Learning about the world outside Camp 14 fired Shin's imagination. Shin grew to hate the life he knew in the camp and became determined to escape and see the outside world he was learning so much about. Six months later, in early 2005 the two young men were assigned to gather firewood high in the mountain at the far border of the camp. Seeing the barbed wire fence, the two ran for it. His friend went through first but got caught in the electrified fence and slumped over the barbed wire. Shin scrambled through.

Sleeping in the forest or abandoned buildings and stealing food and clothes for a month Shin made his way north, to and across the China border. He worked for a year and a half tending cows in rural China, while trying to listen to South Korean radio broadcasts. He went into the South Korean consulate in Shenyang. After evacuation to South Korea, Shin was hospitalized for two months for depression and anxiety. His story was published in South Korea under the title, Escape to the Outside World. His biography in English, *Escape from Camp 14*, by former Washington Post reporter, Blaine Harden, will be published (Viking Press) in March 2012.

See pages 214 to 215 for the locations Shin identified on satellite photos of Camp No.14

WITNESS AND TESTIMONY: Kim Yong, *Kwan-li-so* No. 14 (1995–1996)

Kim Yong was born in 1950 in Hwanghae province. When he was seven years old, unbeknownst to him at the time, his father and older brother were accused of spying for the United States and executed. To spare him the collective guilt attributed by North Korean officials to the families of political wrongdoers, Kim's mother placed him in an orphanage under a false name. Kim grew up to become the Korean equivalent of a lieutenant colonel in the *Bo-wi-bu* (National Security Agency) police. Like other military departments and security police units, his unit set up income-generating businesses, and Kim became a vice president in the Sohae (West Sea) Trading Company, which operated three fishing vessels, exporting flounder and sole to Japan. As a hard-currency earner for the regime, Kim had access to foreign currency, goods and culture, and a chauffeur driven car.

Unfortunately, Kim's true parentage was discovered, quite by accident, after someone else turned up bearing his assumed name. He was arrested and interrogated for three months at the Maram *Bo-wi-bu* detention/interrogation facility in the Yongsong district of Pyongyang and at another *Bo-wi-bu* jail, called Moonsu, also in Pyongyang. The torture at Moonsu was particularly severe. Accused of deliberately infiltrating the security service, Kim was forced to kneel for long periods with a wooden bar placed behind and between his knees and calves. He was suspended by his handcuffed wrists from his prison-cell bars, and he was submerged up to his waist for long periods in tanks filled with cold water.

In 1995 and part of 1996, Kim Yong was imprisoned in *Kwan-li-so* No. 14 at Kaechon district, South Pyongan province, where he worked in a coal mine. In 1996 he was transferred, he believes through the intervention of his supervisor at his former trading Company, to the adjacent Labor Camp No. 18, located on the other side of the Taedong River, where unbeknownst to Kim Yong, his mother was imprisoned. (His testimony about his experience at Camp No. 18 resumes below on page 76.)[68]

___

68 In 2009, Kim Yong's biography (with Kim Suk-Young), *Long Road Home: Testimony of a North Korean Camp Survivor,* was published by Columbia University Press, New York.

At Camp 14, daily meals, according to Kim Yong, were limited to 20-30 kernels of corn and watery cabbage soup. When he first arrived at *Kwan-li-so* No. 14, he was assigned to coal mining at *Mujin II Gang*—No. 2 Cutting Face mine entrance. He was shocked by the skinniness and discoloration of the other prisoners, who looked to him like soot-covered stickmen.

For nearly two years, all Kim saw was the inside of mine shafts, and the adjacent barracks, which contained six rooms with fifty persons per room sleeping on three tiers of wooden bunks. Fortunately, as this was a coal mine, the barracks were heated. Next to the barracks was an eating room/washroom, a sawmill, and a pumping station. The mining work was divided among tunneling/digging teams, loaders, tracklayers, railcar operators, and sawmill workers. The leader of Kim's tunneling team was a former major general, Kim Jae-keun, who had been purged and sent to *Kwan-li-so* 14 for having sided with Kim Il-sung's stepbrother Kim Pyong-il against the succession of Kim Jong-il.

Men and women were segregated from each other. In fact, the only time Kim saw women during his two years of imprisonment at Camp 14 was when all the workers were taken outside the mine area for road construction.

In Kim Yong's section of Camp 14, guards executed some twenty-five prisoners. In one execution, a prisoner by the name of Kim Chul-min was executed for collecting, without authorization, ripe chestnuts that had fallen to the ground from a tree at the mine entrance. Another hunger-crazed prisoner, Kal Li-yong, died after having his mouth smashed by a feces-covered stick for having stolen a leather whip, which he soaked in water and then ate the softened leather.

More prisoners died of malnutrition and disease than from execution, and even more died from accidents in the mines.

See pages 209 to 213 for Kim Yong's identifications on satellite photographs of Kwan-li-so No. 14.

Kwan-li-so Camp No. 15, Yodok, South Hamgyong Province

Yodok is the most well known of North Korea's prison camps, primarily because it has sections known as "revolutionizing processing zones" (*hyeok-myong-hwa-koo-yeok*). Prisoners judged to have been "re-revolutionized" or "re-educated through labor" from being "counter-revolutionaries" to being again potential loyal participants in the "Kim Il-sung nation" are thus eligible for release. Once released from Camp 15, a number of the former prisoners concluded that they would always be under suspicion and surveillance and had no possibility of a good future if they remained in the DPRK, so they fled to China with the intention of going on to South Korea. The first edition of *Hidden Gulag* contained the testimonies of four such former prisoners. Their testimony covered the camp from 1977 through 1999. During the research for the second edition, five additional former Yodok prisoners were interviewed. Their testimony, in chronological order, provides information on this camp from 1970 to 2006.

According to former prisoner An Hyuk (below), Yodok, which is shorthand for Yodok district, an area of land measurement within a province that would be comparable to a district or county, is located in South Hamgyong province. Yodok-kun[69] contains twenty *ris*[70] (also sometimes transliterated as "li" or "ni"), five of which comprise Yodok. The re-revolutionizing zones include Ipsok-ri (or Yipsok-ri), Knup-ri (or Gnup-ri) for Korean families from Japan, and Daesuk-ri (or Taesuk-ri), and a newer section called Sorimchon or Kumchon-ri, where several former prisoners interviewed for this report were held in "singles" villages. Other sections include Pyongchang-ri, a punishment or detention area within the prison camp called Yongpyong-ri, a secluded killing area called Kouek, and other areas for prisoners imprisoned for life.

The whole encampment is surrounded by a barbed-wire fence measuring 3 to 4 meters (10 to 13 feet) in height. In some areas there are walls 2 to 3 meters (7 to 10 feet) tall, topped with electrical wire. Along the fence there are watchtowers measuring 7 to 8 meters (23 to 26 feet) in height, set at 1-kilometer (0.62-mile) intervals, and patrolled by 1,000 guards armed with automatic rifles and hand grenades. Additionally, there are teams with guard dogs. Inside the camp, each village has two guards on duty at all times.[71]

According to Mrs. Kim Young-sun, Yodok was opened in 1970 following a July 1969 speech by Great Leader Kim Il-sung on the need to "revolutionize" the Korean Workers' Party. Mrs. Kim was taken to Yodok during its first year of operation. The areas she was familiar with included Knup-ri and Ipsok-ri sections of the camp, of

---

69 "Kun" (or "Gun") is a larger North Korean administrative unit.

70 "Ri" (or "Ni" or "Li") is a smaller North Korean administrative unit.

71 These figures come from pages 48–59 in An Hyuk's Yodok List, translated into English in Life and Human Rights in North Korea, Volume 1, Autumn 1996, a publication of the Citizen's Alliance for Human Rights in North Korea, Seoul, pp. 18–19.

which the former had many persons who had held high-level positions in Pyongyang or who had studied abroad. However, she reports that many of the former high level officials were not well suited to agricultural or industrial production in the labor camps and quickly succumbed to malnutrition, illness and disease.

These sections were broken down into work units and each work unit into seven work groups. Each work unit was overseen by a *Bo-wi-bu* Lt. Colonel "security guidance officer" (*Bo-wi-ji-do-won*), who was called "teacher." From amongst the prisoners, the camp officials appointed a prisoner work unit leader (*jak-up-bun-jang*) as work unit record keeper (*tong gye won*) and often a livestock work group leader (*chuk-san-goon-jo-jang*).

Initially, Mrs. Kim and her family were assigned to Work Unit 3 at Knup-ri, which farmed corn. In 1971 she was transferred to Work Unit 1 of an "industrial battalion" (*kong-up-dae*) that had six "companies" (*so dae*) overseen by a supervising commissioner (*kwan-li-wi-won-hwe*). At first she worked in a wood drying plant next to a furniture factory. But she was shortly transferred to a construction company that built prisoner housing. Because her handwriting was very neat she was made the record keeper or statistician for the work unit. From her work as a record keeper, she believes that the population of the camp in the early 1970s numbered 20,000, some 60 percent of whom were the families of the presumed "wrong-doers."

In 1975 there was a re-registration of camp prisoners. At that time a "total control zone" (*wan-jeon-tong-je-kuyuk*) named Yongpyong-ri was constructed at Yodok.[72] And Mrs. Kim and several others from the Knup-ri section were selected to be work unit leaders at the total control zone section of Yongpyong-ri, which held some 5,000 prisoners, mostly the family members of other North Koreans who had fled to South Korea, including family members of Christian pastors and elders. For three years, until her release from Camp 15, Mrs. Kim resided in Yodok's "total control zone."

When asked if there were any arranged marriages or couplings at Camp 15, comparable to Shin Dong-hyuk's parents at Camp 14, Mrs. Kim scoffed. To begin with, she responded, there were very few men. And very few women, including herself, had not ceased menstruation cycles. To her, the idea of bringing a child into the hellish world of the prison-labor camps was preposterous.

Kang Chol-hwan, who entered Yodok in 1977, remembers a sign at the front gate of the colony reading, "Border Patrol Unit 2915." The colony is bound to the north by Mt. Paek (1,742 meters, or 5,715 feet, high), to the northeast by Mt. Modo (1,833 meters, or 6,014 feet, high), to the west by Mt. Tok (1,250 meters, or 4,101 feet, high) and to the south by Mt. Byoungpung (1,152 meters, or 3,780 feet, high). The valley is entered from the east by the 1,250-meter (4,101-foot) Chaebong Pass. The streams from the valleys of these mountains form the Ipsok River, which flows downstream into the Yonghung River, which flows into the sea near Wonsan City.

---

72 See page 197 for a satellite photograph overview of Yodok in which the Knup-ri, Ipsok-ri and Yongpyong-ri sections of Camp 15 can be seen.

During An Hyuk's year-and-a-half imprisonment, there were, he thought, some 30,000 prisoners in the lifetime area, and 1,300 singles and 9,300 family members in the re-revolutionizing zone along with some 5,900 Koreans, including Kang's family, who had voluntarily repatriated from Japan. They were later judged not to fit into the "Kim Il-sung nation."[73] By the time of Kim Tae-jin's release from Yodok in 1992, the number of persons in this re-revolutionizing zone had decreased to somewhere between 2,000 and 3,000 because of releases of prisoners to society and because of transfers of other prisoners to the lifetime-imprisonment zones.

According to Kang Chol-hwan, labor operations at the Knup-ri section of Yodok included a gypsum quarry and a re-opened gold mine (which was originally opened during the Japanese occupation of Korea), where some 800 men worked in groups of five. Assignments in these mines were considered the worst form of labor because of the frequency of work accidents. The section for ethnic Koreans who had voluntarily migrated from Japan also had textile plants; a distillery for corn, acorn, and snake brandy; and a coppersmith workshop. The prisoners raised rabbits for the lining of soldiers' winter coats, worked on agricultural teams, and were periodically organized to look for hard woods and gather wild ginseng in the forest hillsides.

During Kang's ten-year imprisonment there were somewhere between 2,000 and 3,000 persons in his village area, and about one hundred deaths per year from malnutrition and disease, particularly from severe diarrhea leading to dehydration.

---

73 Ibid.

While Kang's was a family village, sexual contact between men and women was not allowed, as it was thought this could result in another generation of counter-revolutionaries. Such contact did occur, but, with two exceptions in ten years, all pregnancies were forcibly aborted. The involved men would be physically punished and the women would be humiliated by being compelled to recount their sexual encounters to the entire village.

Kang's village was a "re-revolutionizing" area, so it included "re-education," which consisted of readings from *Rodong Shinmun*, the Workers' Party newspaper.

Described by Lee Young-kuk, the singles area in Daesuk-ri was a valley 4 kilometers (2.5 miles) long by 0.5 kilometers (0.3 miles) wide next to a small 600-700-meter high (1,969-2,297-foot) mountain. During Lee's imprisonment, the area held roughly 1,000 prisoners, of which only 50 were women. The women's cells were heated, but the men's were not, so male prisoners suffered from frostbitten ears and swollen legs during the winter months. Roughly 200 prisoners died each year during the four years when Lee was imprisoned, mostly from starvation and related disease. But there were always new arrivals each month.

Both areas within Yodok where Kang, Lee, An, and Kim were imprisoned—Knup-ri and Daesuk-ri—had public executions by hanging, shootings, and sometimes worse for prisoners who had tried to escape or who had been caught "stealing" food. Lee witnessed one public killing of an attempted escapee, a Mr. Hahn Seung-chul, who was tied and dragged behind a car in front of the assembled prisoners until dead, after which time the other prisoners were required to pass by and place their hands on his bloodied corpse. Another prisoner, a Mr. Ahn Sung-un, shouted out against this atrocity, and he was immediately shot to death. Kim witnessed a public execution by firing squad, after which the assembled prisoners were required to pass by and throw a stone at the corpse still slumped and hanging from the post to which the victim had been tied. Several women prisoners fainted as they were pressed to further mutilate the corpse. Kang witnessed some fifteen executions during his ten years at Knup-ri.

Nonetheless, according to Kang, prisoners who were brought to Yodok from other *kwan-li-so* said it was much better there than at their previous prison-labor camps. He reports that several prisoners committed suicide before they were to be transferred to other camps, where they feared they would just die a slow death.

Camp 15 itself evolved over the years. And our knowledge of it grows from additional former prisoners who have made their way to South Korea. From Former Prisoner # 27, we have learned of a long existing sub-section of Ispok-ri named Baeksan, where prisoners farm corn and engage in logging in nearby mountain slopes. From former prisoners Kim Eun-chol and Jung Gwang-il, we learned of a newer sub-section in one of the re-revolutionizing zones called Sorimchon to which "border-crossers," North Koreans who were forcibly repatriated from China were sent along with various government officials being punished for one reason or another. For reasons unknown, the name of this area of the camp was changed from Sorimchon to Kumchon or Kumchon-ri.

WITNESS AND TESTIMONY: Mrs. Kim Young-sun, *Kwan-li-so* No. 15 (1970–1978)

Mrs. Kim Young-sun was born in Shenyang, China in 1937. Her family had moved to Manchuria in the late 1920s following the Japanese occupation of Korea. After the Japanese occupation of Manchuria, the family moved deeper into China and her brother became a high-ranking anti-Japanese partisan in the "Yan'an faction" of the Chinese communist army fighting the Japanese under the command of Mao Tse Tung. In 1945, when Mrs. Kim was seven years old, her family returned to Korea, as her brother was a committed communist party member.

Back in Pyongyang, Mrs. Kim studied dancing at the Pyongyang Arts University. She was was a professional dancer for thirteen years at the Korean People's Military Art Center. One of her classmates and fellow dancers was Mrs. Sung Hye-rim, who later became Kim Jong-il's secret consort, then wife, and the mother of Kim Jong-il's first son, Kim Jong-nam. Following her retirement as a professional dancer, Mrs. Kim held a post at a foreign tourist shop in Pyongyang, where foreigners and Pyongyang's political and social elite were able to shop for high quality, often imported, goods not generally available to the North Korean public. Because of her family background, and her long friendship with Sung Hye-rim, Mrs. Kim traveled in Pyongyang's highest social circles. Her first husband was, like her brother, a high-ranking official in the

"Yan'an faction" of the Korean Workers Party. But they divorced when, following the Korean War, Kim Il-sung purged the "Yan'an faction" of the Korean Workers' Party, which was suspected of being amenable to Chinese influence.

In July 1970, her second husband, who worked at the publishing house of the Korean Encyclopedia, disappeared. To this day, she has no knowledge of his whereabouts or fate, but she assumes he was sent to another prison camp. One month later, in October 1970, the *Bo-wi-bu* State Security Agency came for her. She was detained and interrogated for two months by the *Bo-wi-bu* Preliminary Investigation Unit (Ye-shim) Department # 312. Even though she refused food for a week to protest her detention, she was not mistreated. But she was required to write out her life story in great detail, particularly her long friendship with the woman who had become Kim Jong-il's wife. After two months, five *Bo-wi-bu* officers came and told her they could not assume responsibility if her knowledge about Kim Jong-il's wife fell into the wrong hands.

In October 1970, she was taken to her home to pick up, in accordance with the *ycon-jwu-je* (the three generation guilt-by-association collective-punishment system), her two parents and four children (then aged 3,5,7, and 10) after which the whole family was deported *incommunicado* to Yodok, Camp 15, where she remained until 1978. During that time, her parents died of malnutrition and untreated diseases, and one of her three sons drowned at the age of eleven.

Her testimony provides a great deal of information on how Camp 15 operated in its early years.

And while most information on Yodok[74] comes from former prisoners from the *hyuk-myung-hwa-koo-yeok* "re-revolutionizing" sections of Camp 15, three of her years in the prison camp were spent in one of the *wan-jeon-tong-je-koo-yeok*, the "total control zone" areas of the camp, from which no prisoners were released. According to Mrs. Kim, Camp 15 was established following a 1969 speech by Kim Il-sung on the need to further revolutionize the Korean Workers' Party members. Upon her arrival, her family shared a two-room (one room with a separate kitchen) shack with another family. She was assigned to the 3rd work unit out of ten in the Knup-ri section of Yodok, where she worked in the wood drying section of a factory that made furniture for use in Pyongyang. She only had contact with three of the ten work groups, one of which was for single, unmarried, prisoners. The other two work groups, including hers, were for imprisoned families. In 1971, she was assigned to a construction work unit that built houses and a food factory within the camp. Because her handwriting was very neat she was made a statistical record keeper for the construction unit. This position gave her considerable knowledge of the organization and workings of the labor camp.

During this time she met other "high level" people she had known in Pyongyang. There were persons who had high-ranking positions, former diplomats, military officers, and others who had studied abroad. While not informed of specific "charges," some of the prisoners were accused during their pre-prison camp interrogations of mishandling portraits or busts of the Great Leader Kim Il-sung. Others had been over-

---

74 See p. 197 for satellite photographs.

heard or suspected of "complaining." According to Mrs. Kim, the three tiered *songbun* citizen classification system (loyal, neutral or antagonistic) with fifty-one subcategories, all based on the grandparents' political position and stance toward the Japanese occupation and the post liberation socialist regime, had been instituted in the late 1960s. There was dissatisfaction, even within relatively high standing ranks, that an insufficiently high *songbun* would limit the future aspirations of the family. Overheard, or reported to the police, such complaints about assigned socio-political status could, and did, lead to banishment to the labor camps.

In 1975, Mrs. Kim and ten other prisoners from the "re-revolutionizing zone" areas of Yodok were chosen to be work unit leaders in the "total control zone" area of Yodok, Yongpyong-ri No.7. Mrs. Kim and her family, and the families of the ten other so chosen "work leaders" were transferred to the area of the camp from where prisoners deemed to be incapable of "re-revolutionizing" would spend the rest of their lives doing a variety of forced labor: planting and harvesting food and tobacco and raising pigs, in this particular work unit.

This part of the "total control zone" area of Yodok in those years was filled with the families of the 2nd or 3rd generation of Koreans deemed hard core counter-revolutionaries. Generally, the male heads of these families were previously executed, or sent to another prison camp, or defected to South Korea. These generations included the families of former landowners and "rich" farmers, policemen during the Japanese occupation, pastors or elders in Protestant Christian churches, and the families of the "traitors to the nation" who fled south. Most of the prisoners in Yongpyong-ri No.7 had come from North

and South Pyongan, and North and South Hwanghae provinces.

These prisoners were all "skin and bones." Their clothes were rags and they were constantly dirty, not being allowed to wash very often. Persons whose pigs died were taken away. People whose paddies dried out were treated as beasts. They were told they were criminals who would, nonetheless, be kept alive even though they did not appreciate the blessings and mercy of the Workers' Party.

In late 1978, Mrs. Kim and her family, along with the families of the other ten families who had been previously selected to be work unit leaders in the total control zone, were released from Camp 15 after they had been fingerprinted and made to promise never to tell anyone about the prison-labor camp. This was a pledge Mrs. Kim kept as long as she remained in North Korea. Upon release from the camp, Mrs. Kim and her family were assigned to work in a gold mine located in the mountains near Chongjin. The work there was less arduous than in the labor camp. She was able to send and receive letters, and allowed to travel with the permission of local party officials. In 1979, she was allowed to travel to Pyongyang where she looked up her old friends, not one of whom had known where she had been sent nine years earlier, or why. In 1980, she was able to move to Hamhung where she worked in a tailor shop. In 1988 one of her sons tried to flee North Korea but was caught and executed. In 2001, she successfully fled to China, where she was a domestic worker for two and one-half years. In 2002, she left Harbin, in China's far northeast, starting a five month journey through southwest China and Southeast Asia before reaching Seoul in November 2003.

WITNESS AND TESTIMONY: Kang Chol-hwan, *Kwan-li-so* No. 15 "Yodok" (1977–1987)

Kang Chol-hwan was born in Pyongyang in 1968. His Korean–Japanese grandfather, who made a fortune in Japanese *pachinko* parlors (pinball/slot machine casinos), and his Korean-Japanese grandmother, a stalwart supporter of Kim Il-sung's Korean Workers' Party, had voluntarily migrated to Pyongyang to contribute to the building of socialism in North Korea. Gradually the bank accounts, cars, and furniture the family had brought with them to North Korea were seized.

One day, Kang's grandfather simply disappeared without a word or trace. Several weeks later, agents came to Kang's father's home, announced that the grandfather had committed an (unspecified) act of high treason, and took the entire family—except for Kang's mother—to *Kwan-li-so* No. 15 at Yodok. The mother, coming from a high level political family, was required to divorce Kang's father at that point. Initially the family had no idea where they were. The sign above the entry gate only said "Border Patrol of the Korean People, Unit 2915." Subsequently, they learned that they were in a guarded "village" surrounded by barbed wire and reserved for the families of ethnic Koreans from Japan who had voluntarily repatriated to North Korea. They also learned that they were in the rehabilitation section—the "revolutionizing zone"—of

a sprawling prison-labor camp. Three years later, they learned from a prisoner who had been transferred into Yodok *kwan-li-so* from Sungho-ri prison camp, some forty miles from Pyongyang, that Kang's grandfather had been imprisoned at Sungho-ri.

Kang was imprisoned from age nine to nineteen, in what is North Korea's most well known political prison-labor camp. After being released without explanation in 1987 (Kang suspects that his grandfather had died), Kang lived in several places in North Korea. He eventually met up with another former prisoner, An Hyuk, whom he had first met in Yodok, and the two of them fled North Korea. They went to to Yanji, Shenyang, Beijing, and finally Dalian, from where, in 1992, they went by boat to South Korea.

In Seoul, Kang co-authored with historian Pierre Rigoulot a superlative and ably translated prison memoir, *Aquariums of Pyongyang: Ten Years in the North Korean Gulag*,[75] the first detailed account of a North Korean prison-labor camp to be published in the West. The book describes the horrors and deprivations of life at Yodok without losing the sense of puzzlement with which a young boy, subsequently a teenager, attempted to comprehend the perniciously bizarre and cruel situation in which he grew up. Today, Kang is a reporter for Chosun Ilbo, a large daily newspaper in Seoul.

---

75 Kang Chol-hwan and Pierre Rigoulot. *Aquariums of Pyongyang: Ten Years in the North Korean Gulag* (New York, N.Y.: Basic Books, 2001); originally published in France as Les Aquariums de Pyongyang (Editions Robert Laffont, 2000).

WITNESS AND TESTIMONY: An Hyuk, *Kwan-li-so* No. 15 "Yodok" (1987–1989)

An Hyuk was born in Manpo City, Jakang province, in 1968 into a loyal party family. At the age of twelve, he received a government scholarship to a school for physical education. In 1986, when he was nineteen, after skiing in Hyesan near Mt. Paekdu on the Chinese border, An crossed into China largely out of curiosity. Arrested in China, he was repatriated to North Korea. He was detained for one year and eight months in solitary confinement in an undersized, underground cell in the Maram *ku-ryu-jang* (detention facility) at Yongsong, Pyongyang, and for another year and a half at the Daesuk-ri singles prison area at Yodok, one of the villages in the "re-revolutionizing" section of *Kwan-li-so* No. 15.

While at Maram, An was subjected to sleep deprivation and compelled to sit motionless for days. He saw only forty other detainees, but believes there were as many as 1,000. Among those in nearby cells were prisoners detained for spilling ink on or failing to adequately dust photographs of Kim Il-sung, charges that, according to An Hyuk, even the prison guards regarded as lacking seriousness. An relates that when he was transferred to Yodok, the guards there told him that he had been sitting down for too long and that it was time for him to do some work. During his year and a half at Yodok, there were some 2,000 prisoners in the Daesuk-ri section of the prison camp for unmarried prisoners.

At Yodok, An's first labor assignment was construction work at a water-driven electric power plant at the camp. His duties entailed breaking ice and wading waist-deep into a frozen stream to gather stones, and laying boards to re-channel the water. It was literally a "murderous" construction project, as scores died from exposure, and even more lost fingers and toes to frostbite. His next work assignment was cutting down and carrying rare hardwood trees from high mountains for export to Japan. Deaths resulted from injuries during this project as well. His last work project was gathering wild mushrooms in the mountains, also for export.

In 1992, An escaped to Seoul along with his former fellow prisoner at Yodok, Kang Chol-hwan. In 1995, Chongji Media in Seoul published his Korean-language prison memoirs, *Yodok List*.

WITNESS AND TESTIMONY: Kim Tae-jin, *Kwan-li-so* No. 15 "Yodok" (1988–1992)

Kim Tae-jin was born in 1956 in China, where his father worked in the Chinese military. He returned with his mother to North Korea in 1961. After reaching adulthood, he worked in a leather factory in South Pyongan province. In 1986, he went to visit relatives in China and stayed for eighteen months before being arrested, in July 1987. In mid-August he was repatriated to the Musan-kun *In-min-bo-an-seong* (People's Safety Agency) detention center in Chongjin, where he was tortured during interrogation. After four months, he was transferred to the *Bo-wi-bu* (State Security Agency) police *ku-ryu-jang* interrogation facility in Chongjin. He was again tortured during interrogation and accused of treason, even though he had gone to China only to visit his family. He was beaten, deprived of sleep, and forced to kneel or sit motionless for hours on end. Because Kim was not permitted to wash, he found the fleas and lice in the jail cells as bad a problem as the torture and freezing cold temperatures.

In March 1988, Kim was sent to the *hyuk-myung-hwa-koo-yeok* re-revolutionizing process zone of Daesuk-ri section at Yodok, where he was imprisoned for four years and six months, until April 1992. At Yodok, he farmed corn, cut trees into firewood, and worked in a furniture factory.

After having spent eight months in confinement in provincial jail cells, Kim thought Yodok an improvement in that he was at least allowed to move around. But food rations were meager, consisting of steamed salty corn dishes—this was before famine conditions afflicted North Korea. To stay alive, he ate plants and grasses, rats, snakes, and frogs. Kim saw deaths from malnutrition and related diseases "every week." He also personally witnessed five public executions of persons who attempted to escape. While at Yodok, he was beaten and forced to endure a sit-down-stand-up punishment until he could barely sit up. Even though Yodok was a "living hell," he still regarded these as the "golden years" for prisoners at Yodok compared with what longer-term prisoners told him about previous conditions.

After four and a half years, Kim was released. His wife divorced and denounced him. After five years, he became convinced things would never improve for him in North Korea and fled to China. He came to Seoul in June 2001 via Mongolia. He now heads a Seoul-based NGO of former North Korean political prisoners.

WITNESS AND TESTIMONY: Lee Young-kuk, *Kwan-li-so* No. 15 "Yodok" (1995–1999)

Lee Young-kuk was born in 1962 in Musan, North Hamgyong province, into a politically loyal family. During his ten years of compulsory military service, from 1978 to 1988, he became a bodyguard to Kim Jong-il and got to know the "Dear Leader" personally. After returning to his hometown in 1988, Lee reports that he was struck by the discrepancies between the lifestyles of the privileged in Pyongyang and the living conditions of the people of Musan. From 1991 to 1994, he was sent to the Central Military College in Pyongyang, after which time he was posted to a senior party position in Musan District. Because of his privileged status, he had a radio capable of receiving KBS (South Korean radio) broadcasts. Soon he became disillusioned with the political indoctrination he had been taught at the Military College, and from the KBS broadcasts, he came to believe that South Korea had become a real democracy with real freedom.

In 1994, Lee fled to China hoping to defect to South Korea. However, he was discovered missing, and because of his personal association with the "Dear Leader," North Korean security agents chased after him. Entrapped in Beijing and wrongly thinking he was talking to a South Korean diplomat who could assist with his defection, Lee confessed his true opinions about the North Korean regime. Under the impression that he was being escorted to the South Korean Embassy, he was whisked instead into the Embassy of North Korea, where he was bound, drugged, and put on a plane to Pyongyang.

Lee was held in Pyongyang for six months in an underground detention cell by the *Bo-wi-bu* (National Security Agency) police. He was subjected to kneeling torture (made to kneel motionless, not even turning his head, for hours at a time) and waterboarding torture (held down by five or six agents who poured water into his mouth and nose until he gagged and nearly suffocated) and was severely beaten on the shins, eyes, ears, head, and mouth. Six of his teeth and one of his eardrums were broken. Years later, he still suffers double vision in his left eye and his shins are still black and blue. Lee believes his torture was solely intended as punishment for having fled to China. While in Beijing, he had freely expressed unfavorable opinions about the regime, leaving no further information for the North Korean police to beat out of him.

Because other members of his family continued to serve Kim Jong-il—one of his cousins was one of Kim's chauffeurs—Lee's family was not punished along with him. In March 1995, Lee alone was sent to a singles camp in the *hyuk-myung-hwa-kyoo-yeok* (re-revolutionizing process) section of Yodok, where he quarried stones for fourteen hours each day for four years. Before his capture in Beijing, he weighed 94 kilos (207 pounds). While at Yodok, he also cut logs, cleared rocks, and farmed. Released from Yodok in January 1999, Lee weighed 58 kilos (128 pounds).

In April 1999, Lee again fled to China and reached South Korea in May 2000, smuggled aboard a ship from Dalian with three other North Koreans. Nearly two years passed before Lee was willing and able to tell his story. He had arranged during that time for an ethnic Korean in China to go to Musan to tell his parents that he was in Seoul, but his parents could not be found, so Lee decided to tell his story.

WITNESS AND TESTIMONY: Former Prisoner # 27, *Kwan-li-so* No. 15 "Yodok" (1999–2000)

Former Prisoner # 27 was born in North Pyongan province in 1966.[76] In the mid 1990s, he earned money selling used cars in China. Along with his wife and son, he was among a small group of North Koreans seeking to defect to South Korea who were caught by the Chinese police in Kunming, near the Chinese-Vietnamese border area. Former Prisoner # 27, along

---

76 As noted above, former prisoners who requested not to be identified by name for fear of jeopardizing family members remaining in North Korea, are designated numerically in the order of their original interview.

with his wife and son, was sent all the way back to the Tumen River area in northeast China. He was forcibly repatriated to North Korea at Onsong, and sent to the Chongjin *Bo-wi-bu* office where he and his wife were detained for eight months, while their four-year-old son was sent to an orphanage (*gu-ho-so*).

At the beginning of his detention, Prisoner # 27 was interrogated daily and later weekly. In order to force his confession, interrogators beat him in the face, causing him to lose his front teeth. And they handcuffed him to the cell bars so that he could not sit or lie down. Because food rations at the *Bo-wi-bu* interrogation facility were so scant, prisoners kept the corpse of a prisoner who died in detention within the cell to get the deceased prisoner's food ration.

Unusually, Prisoner # 27 was processed by what he described as a *Bo-wi-bu* "prosecutor" and "judge." He was accused of violating Articles 46 and 47 of the Criminal Code for "betrayal of the nation." And he was originally "sentenced" to ten years of imprisonment, though this was dropped to one year because, he says, his relatives were "higher ups," who knew he was detained by the Chongjin *Bo-wi-bu*. While others in his group of repatriates were sent to *Song Pyong Kuyok, Song Gok Dong* "Susong *Kyo-hwa-so*," or what he informally called Chongjin political prison (*jung-chi-bum kyo-hwa-so*) No. 25., Prisoner # 27 was sent to the Baeksan sub-section of the Yipsok-ri "re-revolutionizing" Section of Camp 15, where he logged and grew corn.

The Baeksan section of Yodok had existed for 20 years and was originally only for females. However, during his stay, it functioned as a location for both single men and single women.

Of the 180 people held there, only twenty some were women. People in the Baeksan unit area stayed a maximum of three years.

Prisoner # 27's barrack cell room at Yodok was shared by 20-25 men. He recalls that most of the prisoners who had been incarcerated with him were higher-level government employees. Many women at Baeksan were also government workers though some had worked overseas as dancers and singers. Because this section of the camp had a small hydroelectric dam and a generator, there was electricity. These prisoners were even able to watch North Korean TV at night, following the self-criticism and re-education sessions.

But otherwise, conditions were "really horrible." Because there was not enough food, he witnessed fifteen hunger related deaths among the 180 prisoners. Stealing food after being warned resulted in transfer to the "total control zone" (life-time incarceration) area of Camp 15. Prisoner # 27 saw three persons so transferred. Within the year he spent there, one woman and two men were publicly executed for attempting to escape.

He was released from Camp No. 15 in 2000. He arrived in South Korea in November of 2003 after traveling through China and Thailand.

WITNESS AND TESTIMONY: Kim Eun-chol, *Kwan-li-so* No. 15 "Yodok" (June 2000–August 2003)

Mr. Kim Eun-chol was born in March 1980 at Musan-gun, North Hamgyong province of North Korea. In 1999 he fled to China "to survive" where he met South Koreans who told him he could go to South Korea from Russia. So he made his way to Ussuriysk, about eighty kilometers north of Vladivostok. However, on the first day he was arrested along with six other North Koreans for illegal immigration. Held in Russia for twenty days, he was visited by staff of the UN High Commissioner for Refugees (UNHCR) from Vladivostok whom he hoped would provide some sort of travel documents for the group. He was also visited by North Korean consular officials who rebuked him, asking how he and the others could turn their backs on their motherland, which under the warm care of its loving leader, had given Mr. Kim eleven years of education. However, they were told that if they went back to North Korea they would be forgiven. Russian authorities sent the group of North Koreans back to Milsan, China en route to return to North Korea. While still in China, they all tried to run away to avoid repatriation to the DPRK. Six others were caught, but Mr. Kim hid in a temple where Falun Gong practitioners were also hiding out. Later, Mr. Kim decided to return to North Korea to see his father. The Falun Gong practioners gave him eighty yuan (about twelve US dollars), which he used to return to North Korea at Musan.

While going to see his father he was arrested by *An-jeon-bu* police, but after two days he was turned over to the Musan *Bo-wi-bu* police where he was held for 6 months. During interrogation, Mr. Kim was beaten with wooden sticks and metal rifle cleaning rods. He lost 2 teeth and has scars on his head, ear and knees. Mr. Kim was repeatedly asked what he did while in China, if he participated in any religious activities, met South Koreans, watched South Korean video and TV, or complained about the North Korean system. Mr. Kim initially denied all of the charges, but to stop the beatings he confessed that he had met South Koreans.

Mr. Kim did not receive what he regarded as a trial, but he did have a "session" with a *Bo-wi-bu* "prosecutor" (*komsa dam hwa*). In the session, the prosecutor reviewed the interrogation documents and asked if they were correct. Afraid of more beatings Mr. Kim said that they were. The prosecutor told him, "under the care of our Leader, you will be placed under three years of 're-revolutionizing process.'" Transported to Camp No. 15, walking through the entry gates, Kim doubted the length of his sentence thinking he would never get out of the camp.

At Yodok, Mr. Kim was assigned to a construction team in a small section of the re-revolutionizing zone called Sorimchon where from June 2000 to August 2003 he was assigned to a construction work unit where 19 men constructed farm houses for pigs and chickens, and also some homes for the *Bo-wi-bu* prison camp officials. There were about two hundred persons in this section of the camp, each work unit sharing a cell with wooden beds like in military barracks. There was, however, a wood burning stove for heat, and even occasional TV privileges. The women prisoners in this singles section of Camp 15 did farm work.

Mr. Kim was given two sets of used clothes, one for summer and another for winter, formerly worn by *Bo-wi-bu* guards. People who brought clothes with them from China bartered the clothes for food because everyone was so hungry. Mr. Kim said he was constantly hungry and that there were a number of deaths in detention from starvation and malnutrition-related diseases.

Most prisoners in this section of the camp did not know for how long they would be held, but some prisoners were told the length of their imprisonment during political dialogue sessions (*jeong-chi-dam-hwa*). Only a few of the prisoners in the Sorimchon section were imprisoned for "border crossing," although these included all of the seven who were repatriated together from Russia. Other prisoners included students who had studied abroad, and government officials and bureaucrats. In February 2002, two prisoners who attempted to escape were executed by firing squad. One of those executed was a 26-year-old man called Kim Ho-seok. Other prisoners were forced to watch the execution.

Just outside the Sorimchon section there was a punishment facility for "rule violators." Rule breakers were sent to this prison within the prison camp for 10-45 days and almost everyone died shortly after release. Mr. Kim described this as "killing people by drying them out" because these prisoners lost so much weight they could not even walk. He knew three persons sent to the punishment cells, one person for "stealing" honey, another for eating raw corn intended for the animals, and one woman who had sex with another prisoner. All three died upon release from the punishment cells.

Mr. Kim thought Sorimchon was the only "re-revolutionizing zone" in Yodok when he was there. He was aware of prisoners at the "total control zones" at Yodok, but never met or talked to any of them. During his imprisonment he met another former prisoner interviewed for this report, Mr. Jung Gwang-il (see below).

After release, Mr. Kim worked as a miner in Musan for 2 years. When Mr. Kim attempted to escape to China again, he was caught and sent to a Musan mobile training brigade (*ro-dong-dan-ryeon-dae*) for 3 months. However, the Musan mobile labor brigade did not have enough sleeping facilities for all the detainees, and Mr. Kim escaped while awaiting transfer to a larger facility. He again fled to China, made connections for travel onward through Vietnam and Cambodia, and arrived in South Korea in March 2006.

WITNESS AND TESTIMONY: Mr. Jung Gwang-il, *Kwan-li-so* No. 15 "Yodok" (April 2000–April 2003)

Mr. Jung Gwang-il was born in Yanji, China. His family moved to North Korea when he was seven. Following military service in the North Korean army, Mr. Jung was involved in exporting high quality mushrooms to China, where he sold the mushrooms directly to South Korean businessmen, rather than going through a Chinese middleman. Because of his direct business contacts with South Koreans, he was accused of spying for South Korea. He had made the mistake of making remarks critical of the Kim regime to a dinner companion in China who turned out to be a North Korean police informant.

In July 1999, he was picked up by the Hoeryong *Bo-wi-bu* State Security Police for interrogation at a large underground detention facility. For some six or seven months, he was beaten and tortured to confess to spying for South Korea. He was beaten with a wooden stick, which broke many of his teeth and scarred the back of his head. Much more painful was the so-called "pigeon torture" which pinned the arms behind the back and attached the prisoner to cell bars in ways that made it impossible to either sit down or stand up and caused paralyzing pain in the shoulders. During these torture sessions he was not allowed to go to the toilet, and had to urinate and defecate in his pants. During his time in the underground cells, two fellow prisoners died in detention.

He was also deprived of food, and his weight dropped from 75 to 38 kg (165 to 84 pounds). Driven by hunger, he agreed to confess in exchange for some food. After eating he recanted his false confession, for which he was again beaten severely. Shortly thereafter he was visited by what he described as a "prosecutor," who asked him if the spying charges he confessed to were true. At first, he claimed that he confessed falsely under duress, but the charges were accepted as true. Like other prisoners, he also hoped that even a false confession would result in a transfer to a *kyo-hwa-so* prison or *kwan-li-so* labor camp where at least he would be able to walk around.

In late March or early April, 2002 Jung was transferred to a "re-revolutionizing" area of Yodok, in a sub-section called "Sorimchon," which had been set up in October of 1999 following the closing of the "singles" section of Baeksan "village" area. Before deportation to Yodok, *Bo-wi-bu* police stopped off at his home to pick up bedding, clothes, eating utensils and other belongings. So his family knew he was being taken somewhere, but they were never told where or why.

This small "village" within the sprawling camp held some 230 prisoners, about thirty of who were women. Mr. Jung was assigned to agricultural labor and construction, most notably at a fish farm. He could see people working in the adjacent "total control zones" within the Yodok camp, though there was barbed wire between the various sections and people in the different zones were not allowed to talk to one another.

Sorimchon was administered by Bureau Seven, the "enlightenment" or "re-education" bureau. He witnessed beatings by the guards, but not systematic torture. He believes, however, that there was systematic torture at the *ku-ryu-jang* punishment facilities of Camp 15's central *Bo-wi-bu* headquarters because the prisoners sent there for infractions of camp rules came back "in such very bad shape." Notwithstanding such leniencies as watching television every other Sunday, Mr. Jung witnessed twenty-six fellow prisoners die and another six taken away which he believes was for execution in this relatively privileged re-education section during his three years of detention. Of the twenty-six known deaths, twenty-three were from malnutrition, two were from public execution, and one as a result of torture.

Released from Yodok in April 2003, Mr. Jung again fled to China and made his way to South Korea via the long escape route through Southeast Asia, arriving in South Korea in April of 2004. Gifted with a remarkable memory, he provided a Seoul-based NGO of former North Korean political prisoners a listing of 121 names and descriptions of fellow prisoners in the Sorimchon section of Yodok. This publication provided a snapshot of the *wrong-doing, wrong-thinking* or *wrong-knowledge* that sent these North Koreans to the labor camp for "re-revolutionizing."

Thirty-four were imprisoned for "border crossing" after being forcibly repatriated from China or Russia, or for suspicion of departure. Thirty-six were imprisoned for "reactionary discourse"—criticism of the party or government. Another six were imprisoned for talking about matters deemed secret. Thirteen were detained for other political or religious problems. Four had been students studying in East Germany during the collapse of the socialist regime. Another had been posted abroad in Eastern Europe during the collapse of the socialist bloc and was taken to Yodok directly from the airport upon return to North Korea. Among the prisoners for wrong-doing related to religion were two "lightly punished" couples who had been part of a Bible study group, whose leader had been executed, while other group members had been sent to the "total control zone" area within Yodok.

See pages 197-208 for satellite photographs of this section of Yodok during Mr. Jung's time of imprisonment.

WITNESS AND TESTIMONY: Former Prisoner # 28, *Kwan-li-so* No. 15 "Yodok" (1999–2006)

Former Prisoner # 28 was born in Onsong-kun, Sambong-ku, North Hamgyong province in 1970. She went to China in 1998 and was in a group of nine defectors caught in December 2002 trying to enter Mongolia en route to South Korea. She was detained for 20 days in Mongolia and the group was sent to Tumen detention facility in China and detained for another 20 days.

She was repatriated to the Onsong *Bo-wi-bu* where she was detained for six months. Since the Onsong *Bo-wi-bu* guards knew her family, initially, she was not treated harshly. But another person in the group confessed that they were trying to go to South Korea. After this confession, Pyongyang *Bo-wi-bu* sent interrogators for more questioning.

She told the interrogators from Pyongyang that she left North Korea to earn money. But those *Bo-wi-bu* agents responded that they knew her group was trying to defect to South Korea. During interrogation, they beat her in the face with wooden rulers and books. In between interrogations they made her kneel motionless from 5 am to 10 pm, which made her legs swell badly. Alternatively, she was compelled to do stand-up and sit-down exercises three hundred times. When she failed to complete this punishment, the jailers hit her fingers and made her butt her head repeatedly against the iron bars. The Onsong *Bo-wi-bu* detention-interrogation facility was extremely crowded. There were, she believed, perhaps as many as five hundred men and women spilling out of the cells and sitting in the hallways of the building. When prisoners were allowed to sleep, people lay down on each other's hips because there was no room to stretch out.

After confessing that she was trying to enter Mongolia, *Bo-wi-bu* officers came from her hometown to transport her to Camp 15. She was not told what particular law she had broken, but she was told that she would be detained in Yodok for three years. Her father was called to bring her some clothing. When he did, her father did not know if he would see his daughter again, as persons sent off to the camps were not expected to return.

The area she was sent to within Yodok was the "re-revolutionizing zone" section, previously called Sorimchon, but renamed Kumchon-ri. About 200 people were there in the singles' barrack, many of whom were "border crossers." However, after 2003, most prisoners sent to this section were "high level people," including, she reports, former *An-jeon-bu* police who had made comments against the system or regime. There were also a number of former professional singers. Her barrack had 7 cells, 1 cell for women, 5 for men and a separate cell for former "higher ups."

No marriages or children were allowed in the camp. Two women had babies from male prisoners but the babies were abandoned in the mountains. Prisoner # 28 witnessed guards bury one baby in the ground. The women prisoners who got pregnant were imposed an additional six

months in prison and their male lovers an additional two months. However, one of the men was later transferred to the "total control zone." Prisoner 28 could see people in the "total control zone," but was not allowed to talk with them. Sexual abuse of the female prisoners by prison guards took place. Fortunately, a prison staff member who tried to take advantage of Prisoner # 28 was transferred.

She was assigned to farm corn and beans for prisoners and staff. There was also a livestock farm for pigs, goats, ducks, dogs and sheep. She was always very hungry because all she got to eat was three or four spoons of corn for each meal. Even this small amount was reduced when she could not meet her work quota. About ten people out of two hundred in her barrack died of malnutrition. Even the sick people were compelled to work and some prisoners died while working.

Normally she worked from 6 am to noon and 1 pm to 7pm. There was a *saeng-hwal-chong-hwa* (study on political ideology) once a month for the whole barrack, and smaller after dinner study sessions every 10 days for smaller groups. Oil lamps were lit at night for the political ideology sessions because there was no electricity at that time.

There was an execution site under a bridge and a *ku-ryu-jang* (punishment cell) for the singles' work area. The *ku-ryu-jang* and execution sites were for the people who tried to escape, steal food, etc. Some people never came back from the punishment cell, and others who returned, particularly men, died soon after release from the *ku-ryu-jang* cell because they were so weakened.

Keumchun-ri Prisoner Dormitory
Kwanliso No. 15 "Yodok", South Hamgyong Province

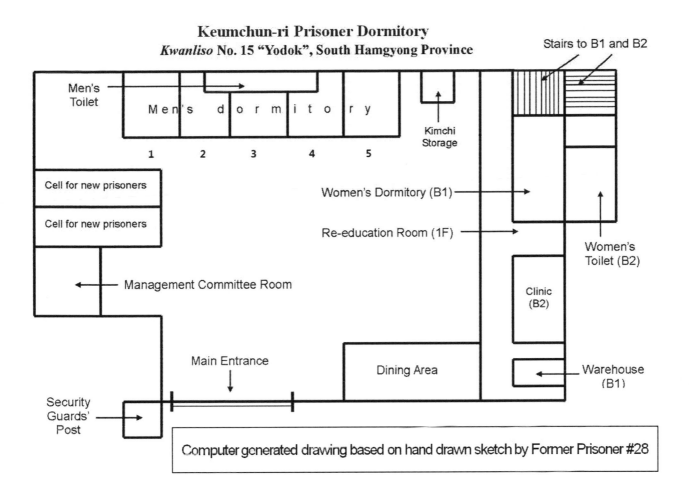

Computer generated drawing based on hand drawn sketch by Former Prisoner #28

Prisoner 28 was released from Yodok in 2006, her length of imprisonment having been extended from three to five years. She was taken back to Onsong *Bo-wi-bu* where her brother came to the police station to guarantee that she would not flee again. However, she feared that, as a former *kwan-li-so* prisoner, she would always face persecution. So she and her father fled to China despite knowing that they would be under surveillance.

She confirmed the prisoners' barracks and guards' dormitories on satellite photographs. See page 199.

See pages 197-208 for satellite photographs of Kwan-li-so No. 15 Yodok.

Kwan-li-so Camp No. 18, Dukchang-ri, Bukchang-kun, South Pyongan Province

Located on the other side of the Taedong River from *Kwan-li-so* No. 14, *Kwan-li-so* No. 18 is something of an anomaly among the *kwan-li-so*. It is run by the *In-min-bo-an-seong* People's Safety Agency police (still generally referred to as *An-jeon-bu*, the former name for the regular police) rather than by the *Bo-wi-bu* (State Security Agency) police.[77] It is a somewhat less strict and less severe prison-labor colony. According to former prisoners, the camp holds some 27,000 prisoners including the families of the presumed wrongdoers imprisoned in *Kwan-li-so* No. 14. Camp No. 18 is somewhat unusual in that civilians from outside the camp, employed as camp administrators called *dae-ne-min*, run various subsections of the camp.

Like Camp No. 15, Camp No. 18 had a "re-revolutionizing zone" for prisoners that were eligible for release back into society. Camp No. 18 also had a "liberation zone" with some 3,000 persons, called *hae-je-min* (literally "lifted people" or "cleared people") who had been released from imprisonment, but continued to live at the camp. The "cleared people" can seek employment outside the camp. They have access to small plots of land for growing crops outside the camp, and are able to send and receive mail, go to the local markets, and obtain travel permits for domestic travel. The *hae-je-min* even received a gift of liquor on the occasion of Kim Il-sung's birthday, apparently in recognition of their restored citizenship. According to one of the former prisoners from Camp No. 18 interviewed

for this report, these persons were allowed to leave the prison camp entirely if they could find some other locality where they could register and be assigned work and housing. (It is suggested in the Conclusion to this report that the *hae-je-min* section of Camp 18 could be instructive for the dismantlement of the entire labor camp system in the DPRK.)

Extraction and manufacturing work at *Kwan-li-so* No. 18 included coal mining, brick making, and cement making, along with work in a glass factory and a distillery. Prison laborers were paid varying token amounts in won. One former prisoner interviewed for this report received 30 won a month—barely the cost of a pack of cigarettes. Families were allowed to live together, and privileged prisoners were allowed to marry and have children. And unlike the guard-arranged couplings at Camp 14 across the river, young prisoners at Camp 18 were allowed to choose their own marriage partners. At some points during the forty years of imprisonment at Camp No. 18, there were also radio broadcasts, and copies of *Rodong Shinmun and the Workers' Daily* posted at the entrances to worksites (according to the four former prisoners whose stories are presented below). Some prisoners were allowed outside the gates to collect herbs.

Sizeable numbers of prisoners at Camp No. 18, like the other prison camps, died of malnutrition, disease, and work accidents. And there were public executions, as elsewhere, usually for escape attempts.

---

77 And thus is not considered a *kwan-li-so* by some.

WITNESS AND TESTIMONY: Mrs. Kim Hye-sook, *Kwan-li-so* No. 18 (December 1974–February 2001)

Born in 1962, Mrs. Kim Hye-sook had been sent as a young child to live with her maternal grandmother in Pyongyang. While living with her maternal grandmother, for reasons unbeknownst to her at the time in 1970, the rest of her family—mother, father, sister, brother and paternal grandmother—were deported to Camp No. 18. For several years, Mrs. Kim's maternal grandmother successfully harbored young Hye-sook, but in December of 1974, when she was thirteen years old, Hye-sook was also taken away to Camp No. 18. (Decades later, following her release from the camp, Mrs. Kim learned that her paternal grandfather had fled to South Korea, the presumed reason for the family's banishment and incarceration— all three generations, according to the *yeon-jwa-je* "guilt by association" system of collective punishment.)

When she got to Camp No. 18, she learned that her father had been previously taken away by *Bo-wi-bu* police within the camp. The family did not know, and never found out, his whereabouts, or even if he was dead or alive. At Camp No. 18, Kim Hye-sook attended *Duk-chang-in-min* school from ages 13 to 15 and *Shim-san* high school, where she was taught rudimentary reading, writing and math, from ages 15 to 17. But mostly, Mrs. Kim relates, the Camp No. 18 schools served as gathering points for mobile child labor brigades, often cutting trees or gathering wood. However, unlike the prison-camp schools attended by Shin Dong-hyuk and Kang Chol-hwan at Camps Nos. 14 and 15 respectively, the pupils were provided with Korean school uniforms every three years.

During her two-and-a-half decades at the camp, Mrs. Kim resided in the Suksan-ri, the Shim-san and the Bong-chang-ri sections of the camp. For most of her time in the camp, Hye-sook, like other girls and their mothers in the Shim-san area, were assigned to gather coal in the Hong-je mine. Men and boys dislodged the coal with picks and shovels, and the women and girls picked up the coal pieces and transported coal in buckets, wheelbarrows and coal trolleys which they would then carry, push or pull up ramps leading to the surface of the mine-face. There were many accidents in the mines, with the injured prisoners then being assigned to construction brigades or other work. Most of the workers doing forced labor in the mines contracted what is now called "black lung disease," a condition for which Mrs. Kim is currently being treated in hospitals in South Korea.

According to Mrs. Kim, most families at Camp No. 18 lived in residence units that contained four rooms, though a few barracks had up to 20 rooms. There was one family per room, each of which had rudimentary kitchen facilities, but no bathroom or toilet. All family members slept on the floor, sharing one blanket between them. After Mrs. Kim married another prisoner, he moved into the one room shared with the rest of her family. A few of the units had tile roofs, but most of the roofs were wooden and leaked when it rained. The prisoners lived mostly on thin "corn porridge" with occasional small amounts of salt or bean paste. For vegetables, people ate grass or plant leaves they could gather whenever they got the opportunity.

Mrs. Kim and the other members of her family were released from Camp No. 18 in February 2001. Her brother and sister remained at Camp No. 18, though they were free to leave. Mrs. Kim re-settled in Sunchon, South Pyongan province, where she resided as a nurse and housekeeper in the home of an elderly woman. Subsequently, the house was destroyed in a flood. Homeless, Mrs. Kim fled to China and found work in a restaurant. To supply the restaurant in 2007, Mrs. Kim returned to North Korea to purchase piglets that were being raised and sold surreptitiously by a group of North Korean soldiers. While waiting in Musan for some of the piglets to finish weaning, Mrs. Kim was picked up by the police.

The soldiers from whom she bought the piglets threatened her against revealing their illegal side-business. So she remained quiet and faced the police on her own. The police took her back to Camp No. 18, but having officially "released" her several years earlier, the Camp No. 18 officials refused to re-imprison her. She was then sent to the formerly industrialized, but now impoverished and destitute city of Chongjin where she was supposedly "registered." But Chongjin officials, having no residence or job to which to assign her, also refused to accept her. So she was again sent back to Camp No. 18, where they again refused to re-admit her. While temporarily at Camp No. 18, she re-established contact with her brother and sister who had remained at the camp even after they were officially released. But they were desperately impoverished and unable to help her. Having no future in North Korea, but resourceful nonethe-

less, Mrs. Kim made her way back to China where she made the connections to travel on to South Korea.

With more than two decades of incarceration at Camp No. 18, Mrs. Kim provides valuable testimony on its operation. As previously noted, unlike the other *kwan-li-so* political penal labor colonies, which are run exclusively by the *Bo-wi-bu*, the political police agency, the *An-jeon-bu* regular police play a major role in running Camp No. 18. There are *Bo-wi-bu* police officials present around the camp, although Mrs. Kim describes their function mostly as the surveillance of the *An-jeon-bu* police. The operating office for Camp No. 18 is called the *an-jeon-song*.

By all four accounts from the former prisoners at Camp 18 interviewed for this report, Camp No. 18 is a less "strict regime" than the other labor camps for suspected political undesirables and their families. Those who broke prison camp regulations were sometimes subjected to mobile labor brigades rather than the torturous miniscule punishment cells common to the *Bo-wi-bu*-run encampments. In some sections of the camp, men at age 30 and women at age 28 were allowed to marry. And unlike the privileged sexual "couplings" described by Shin Dong-hyuk at Camp No. 14 across the river, the men and women were allowed to choose their own mates and live together with the children born to them within the camp. There were no wedding "ceremonies," but the couples could register themselves as couples with the camp authorities. As noted above, school age children would occasionally be given school uniforms, as is the practice in Korean primary and secondary education.

Most significantly, there are three categories of persons at Camp No. 18. The largest category, containing some 27,000 persons, are prisoners euphemistically termed "moved people" or "migrants" (*e-ju-min*). The sections of the camp for the *e-ju-min* are surrounded by electrified barbed wire. The second category includes civilians from neighboring towns who were hired for administrative duties within the camp, titled *dae-nae-min*. According to Mrs. Kim, these civilian camp administrators would, on occasion, quietly approach the prisoners and apologize for the way they were being treated.

Lastly, there was a category of *hae-je-min*, "cleared people" whose restrictions are removed. In fact, they were free to leave the camp if they could find a place to go. The *hae-je-min* often had small farming plots in the mountains outside the camp to which they could come and go. They could also obtain travel passes, often three to five days duration, to travel more widely outside the camp. But mostly, they lived and ate the same as the restricted, imprisoned *e-ju-min*. As noted above, after Mrs. Kim's brother and sister were released, they remained at Camp 18 as *hae-je-min*. There were statues of Kim Il-sung and Kim Jong-il within the *hae-je-min* areas, in front of which the prisoners had social events, even dances, on national holidays. On Kim Jong-il's birthday, the *hae-je-min* would assemble in front of the statues to receive small gifts (fruit, candy, or liquor) from the Great General, as is the general practice throughout the DPRK.

While Camp No. 18 is a less "strict regime" prison camp than the other *kwan-li-so* forced labor encampments described in this report, the brutality of the place is plainly evident in Mrs.

Kim Hye-sook's list of priorities of what should be provided to those imprisoned there:

1. Food and nutritional supplements, bearing in mind, Mrs. Kim says, that the prisoners never eat "regular" or "real" food.

2. Respiratory medicines for "black lung disease."

3. Rib fracture treatments for prisoners whose ribs are damaged from the severe coughing associated with black lung disease.

4. Amputee doctors and medicines for people who have lost toes or feet to frostbite (as they do not have proper shoes) or lost hands and arms to mining accidents.

5. Shoes and clothing.

6. Soap.

7. Anti-intestinal worm treatment.

Mrs. Kim's grandmother, mother and father, husband, and one brother died in detention at Camp No. 18.

WITNESS AND TESTIMONY: Lim Jung-soo, *Kwan-li-so* No. 18 (1967–1987)

Imprisoned by virtue of guilt-by-association, Mr. Lim was thrown into Camp No. 18 in 1967 and spent two decades there. His father had been a South Korean soldier in the Korean War who was captured by the North early in the war, who then subsequently served for three years in the North Korean army. His mother was from a formerly well to do family that benefitted from association with Japan. Mr. Lim's maternal grandfather, who earlier studied photography at Waseda University in Tokyo, had been publicly executed because of his association with Japan.

During the 1970s and 1980s, there were many repatriated Japanese-Koreans who were sent to Camp No.18. Mr. Lim recalled a Japanese-Korean man named Jung Bong-sun who was well known within the camp because he taught karate to security guards. However, he was publicly executed when he tried to escape in May 1982.

The major industry of Camp No. 18 was mining. Men worked in the mines and women were organized into work units, laboring from 5 am to 9 pm, collecting coal or doing other construction work. Mr. Lim describes four categories of residents in the camp. The first two categories were termed *cola-min* (political prisoners) and *e-ju-min*, a euphemism literally meaning migrant or immigrant. They were people who had done harm to the socialist system or economy by mistake. These two groups were the lowest level of prisoners in the labor colony. They lived in houses or barracks without the portraits of the Great Leader. Children from these two groups went to primary schools that also had no portraits, where the education was minimal, and where the children also had work assignments every day. The absence of portraits was an indication that these people were not going to be released back into North Korean society, though some of the *e-ju-min* were subject to "re-revolutionizing" and eventual release.

The ethnic Koreans who "repatriated" from Japan and who were subsequently sent to Camp No.18 were classified as *cola-min*. Mr. Lim's family was treated as *cola-min*, but after his father worked very hard in the coal mines for more than 10 years, they were reclassified as *e-ju-min*. Mr. Lim himself was released after 20 years in the camp.

He describes a separate detention facility within the *kwan-li-so* to imprison persons within the prison camp who disobeyed internal rules or did not work hard enough. Mr. Lim called the prison within the prison camp a *chong-hwa*.[78] Mr. Lim witnessed multiple public executions of people who were caught while attempting to escape. Most public executions included three or four persons at a time, but Mr. Lim witnessed larger public executions where fifteen to twenty persons were put to death. He estimates the number of executions yearly to have been fifty to sixty people.

Mr. Lim also recalled the sexual harassment of women and the ban on sexual relationships between men and women in the lower ranking sections of Camp No. 18. The prisoners in his section of the camp were not allowed to mate. Mr. Lim witnessed the death of a Japanese-Korean man with the family name of Yoon. He fell in love with a daughter of the chief of the labor squad at the mine and she became pregnant. When authorities at the camp found out, they tied the man naked behind a bicycle and made him run through the entire camp multiple times a day. Other prisoners were ordered to curse him and stone him. After ten days, the man died from exhaustion and wounds from the

---

78 Literally meaning "political indoctrination."

stoning. All women prisoners were considered property of the authorities who could take whatever advantage of them they wanted.

This testimony was presented at a December 7, 2008 conference in Tokyo attended by the present author. Mr. Lim's story and testimony in Korean and Japanese is available on the website of the Japanese NGO "NO FENCE."

WITNESS AND TESTIMONY: Former Prisoner # 29, *Kwan-li-so* No. 18 (1977–1983)

Former Prisoner # 29 was a twelve-year-old student in 1978 when the police came for him at his school in Pyongyang and told him to come with them, as he would be moving to a nice place. Returning home with the police, he saw his mother crying while the family belongings were being packed into a truck. When his mother told him not to say a word, he realized that something was very wrong and that they were not going to a nice place.

Departing around lunchtime, the truck arrived around midnight at what appeared to be an apartment complex at Seok-son-ri, Bukcheong, South Pyongan province for the night. The next morning his mother and three siblings were taken to what looked like a beggar's hut as it had holes in the walls and where another family

of four was already living. That night, Former Prisoner # 29's family was joined by the father, who had been picked up earlier and transported separately to the camp. For six months they shared the "beggar's hut." For the next five years, his dwindling family would reside in the "re-revolutionizing zone" in Camp No. 18.

His father had been born and raised in China, but had moved to Sinuiju where he met and married a soloist in an artists group with a particularly beautiful voice. His mother was appointed as a soloist for a newly formed orchestra, so the family moved to Pyongyang where his father then worked as a Korean-Chinese translator for a military company that imported Chinese machinery for the Pyongyang subway system. His father had come under suspicion because he missed three of the compulsory ideological seminars that all male North Koreans were required to attend. But his greater error, Former Prisoner # 29 believes, was to have purchased a tape recorder from a Korean-Japanese, who had brought the recorder to North Korea. His father wanted to record his wife's singing so it could be presented to Kim Il-sung. But somehow, the purchase of a tape recorder made him a decadent capitalist and he and his immediate family were sent off to Camp No. 18 for "re-revolutionizing."

This small "re-revolutionizing area" at Camp No. 18 had, in those years, about five hundred families in it. His father was assigned work as a digger in the coal mine, the major production and occupation at Camp No. 18, while his mother was made a singer in a morale building propaganda unit within the camp. His father was in a three person digging unit. He made the mistake of saying to his two co-workers that he missed his mother and father in China, and that coming to North Korea had been a mistake. One of his two co-workers reported this disloyalty. *Bo-wi-bu* police agents, who ran a *ku-ryu-jang* punishment/detention facility within the generally *An-jeon-bu* administered camp, came to take his father away, never to return. The agents told the family that their father was a traitor to the nation.

Former Prisoner # 29 was assigned to a school in the mornings, and had to do various work assignments in the afternoon. If there was no productive work available, the children were required to dig holes, only to fill them up again.

He was constantly hungry, saying that there were more days when he didn't eat than days when he did. In the winter he was constantly cold, as the family had bartered away all the clothes they brought with them from Pyongyang for food. He lost fingernails to frostbite, and his front teeth to beatings. In his five years in the camp he was compelled to watch ten executions by firing squad, eight for escape attempts and two for "destructive behavior," that is, sabotage of camp machinery.

In some respects however, the "re-revolutionizing zone" was better than life in the "total control zone" areas of the camp. While there were no newspapers from the outside, there was an occasional two page internal camp newsletter. It mostly contained production statistics from the various coal faces and pits within the camp. It was occasionally possible for the residents of the "re-revolutionizing zone" to watch television sets that were set up near the coal mine entrances.

In November 1983, he and his mother were called in with a group of forty others and told that under the consideration of the Great Leader and the Party they were being returned to society. "From now on, never forget this blessing and always be loyal to the Party," they were told. Former Prisoner # 29 was assigned to be a miner at the Culsan iron ore mine in Bukchang County, South Hamgyong province. This was the site, he said, of former *Kwan-li-so* No. 17. But he was never allowed to return to Pyongyang.

During the decade, he mined iron ore. Knowing his father had relatives in China, he tried to contact them since he could send and receive letters by mail. In 1993, he received a response to a letter he sent two years earlier. After several exchanges of letters, in 1997, owing to the severe food shortage in North Korea, he traveled to Musan to get help from his relatives in China. Shortly thereafter he fled to China, and arrived in South Korea in October of 2000.

Kim Yong Testimony about *Kwan-li-so* No. 18 (1996–September 1998)

(Continued from his testimony on Camp 14, page 51 above)

As noted above, in 1996, Kim Yong was transferred from Camp No. 14 to the adjacent Camp No. 18, located on the other side of the Taedong River in Dukchang-ri, Bukchang-kun, South Pyongan. Mr. Kim believes he was transferred through the intervention of his boss at the Asahi Trading Company, which as noted above, was a foreign currency raising enterprise within the *Bo-wi-bu* police agency. At Camp No. 18, he was assigned to repair coal trolleys. There, to his surprise—as he did not know if or where she was imprisoned—he was reunited with his mother, with whom he was allowed to live.

Subsequently, Kim's mother was severely beaten by camp guards for returning late to the camp after gathering edible weeds outside the prison gate. Arguing that they were both just going to die in the camp anyway, she encouraged him to escape, even if it meant risking his life. And so he did, in September 1998, by hiding in a coal train bound for the coal-fired electrical generating plant to which most of the coal mined at Camp No. 18 was sent. He soon crossed the Tumen River into China and, in October 1999, went to South Korea via Mongolia.

See pages 216-221 for satellite photographs of Kwan-li-so No. 18. [79]

---

79 Subsequent to the completion of research for this report, several former residents of South Pyong-an province arrived in South Korea. Some of these new arrivals reported to South Korean human rights activist colleagues that large portions of Camp 18 at Bukchang have been effectively dismantled. Some parts of Camp 18 may have been incorporated into Camp 14, which is just across the Taedong River. Or possibly, some prisoners were transferred to other prison camps or detention facilities. But apparently, large numbers of former prisoners were essentially "cleared," and large portions of the former prison camp changed to the *"hae-je-min"* areas for cleared or released persons described above in the testimony of Mrs. Kim Hye-sook (p. 70-73). That is, the former prisoners continue to live and work in the same places as before. However, they are no longer imprisoned behind gated walls and barbed wire fences, and apparently have the same limited and constrained rights, freedoms and privileges as other North Korean citizens. It is suggested in the recommendations of this report (p. 168-175) that this should be considered by the North Korean authorities as a model for disabling and dismantling the rest of the prison camp system.

Kwan-li-so No. 22, Hoeryong, North Hamgyong Province

WITNESS AND TESTIMONY: Former Guard, Ahn Myong-chol, *Kwan-li-so* No. 22 (and Camps Nos. 11, 13, 26)

Unlike the witnesses just described, who were released or escaped prisoners, Ahn Myong-chol was a *kwan-li-so* guard. Ahn was born in 1969 in Hongwon-kun, South Hamgyong province. Ahn came from a good Korean Workers' Party family. For his compulsory military service, he became a *Bo-wi-bu* (State Security Agency) police guard assigned, consecutively, to four different *kwan-li-so*: No. 11, at Kyungsun, North Hamgyong province, from May to August 1987; No. 13, at Jongsong, North Hamgyong province, from August 1987 to the winter of 1990, except for four months during this time when he was sent to the much smaller prison No. 26 in Pyongyang; and No. 22 at Hoeryong, North Hamgyong province, from late 1990 to mid-1994. Of the four places, as of 2011, only *Kwan-li-so* No. 22 remains operational.

Ahn's father had worked at a public distribution center. During the 1990s famine, he was caught giving extra food to one of his neighbors and was labeled a "reactionary element." When he learned of his father's situation, Ahn fled with his wife across the Tumen River into China. After he reached Seoul, he was interviewed by the monthly magazine *Chosun Wolgan* (*Chosun*

Monthly). Portions of the resulting article were published in English in *Political Prison Camps in North Korea*, by the Center for the Advancement of North Korean Human Rights, Seoul. Ahn's Korean-language memoir, *They Are Crying for Help*, was published by Chungji Media, Seoul, but the book is out of print, and the publisher closed. In 1998, Ahn testified before the U.S. Congress. In December 2002, he was able to identify the buildings and grounds on several satellite photographs of *Kwan-li-so* No. 22 for publication in the *Far Eastern Economic Review* (December 12, 2002).

Ahn's guard duties included making deliveries by truck to various parts of *Kwan-li-so* No. 22. This assignment gave him unusual mobility within the camp, even for a guard. He learned much from his conversations with other guards while making deliveries to various sections of the camp. His work at four of the *kwan-li-so* camps over a period of seven years provided him with comparative insight into the functioning of the *kwan-li-so* system.

His guard training and indoctrination provides insight into the operation of the prison camp system. Ahn reports that the prisoners were referred to as "emigrants." Great stress was placed on the harm and threat that "factionalists" posed to the revolution: how factionalism produces class enemies; how factionalists and class enemies have to be destroyed like weeds, down to their roots through the *yeon-jwa-je* three-generation family-incarceration system; and how guards have to exercise their control duties so as to reveal the "dictatorship of the proletariat" to the class enemies. Like some of the former prisoners, Ahn recalls the shock he felt upon his first arrival at a camp, where he likened the prisoners to walking skeletons, dwarfs, and cripples in rags.

Identified as Hoeryong, after the name of the nearby city, the official designations for *Kwan-li-so* No. 22 are "Chosun People's Security Unit 2209" or "Paeksan-ku Ministry of State Security." No. 22 covers an area, according to Ahn, some 50 kilometers (31 miles) in length and 40 kilometers (25 miles) in width. There are roughly 1,000 guards and 500–600 administrative agents for as many as 50,000 prisoners, including the families of alleged wrong-doers.

Ahn reports that the annual agricultural production quotas for *Kwan-li-so* No. 22 were as follows: 400 tons of corn, 100,000 tons of potatoes, 50,000 tons of lima beans, and 10,000 tons of red peppers per year. The camp also grew Chinese cabbages, radishes, cucumbers, and eggplants, and had a distillery that produced soy sauce and whiskeys. Camp No. 22 mined coal that was shipped to the Chongjin Thermal Power Plant and the Chongjin and Kimchaek Steel Mills.

Notwithstanding the agricultural production, Ahn estimates that 1,500 to 2,000 prisoners at *Kwan-li-so* No. 22, mostly children, died from malnutrition yearly during his years as a guard there. Executions were not public but were carried out at a site named "Sugol." He estimates that there were ten executions per year, mostly in October, of people who had been caught eating from recently harvested food stocks. People were fed corn and potatoes, almost no vegetables, and no meat. The only meat in their diets came from the rats, snakes, and frogs they could catch. There were also deaths from beatings of prisoners who had not been meeting their production quotas. In fact, Ahn says, there were so many deaths from beatings that at one point, the guards were urged to be less violent.

Only a few privileged prisoners were allowed to conjugate. Otherwise, sex was prohibited. Ahn is aware of one pregnant woman who was executed as a punishment for her pregnancy. *Kwan-li-so* No. 22 had a notorious detention barrack for prisoners who disobeyed camp regulations. Ahn was a guard nearby and heard the screams of the prisoners as they were beaten.

The prisoners at *Kwan-li-so* No. 22 were paid approximately 500 won per year. Youth at the colony received basic schooling in elementary reading, writing, and arithmetic. The camp had nine holidays per year.

See page 222 for satellite photographs of Kwan-li-so No. 22.

Other *Kwan-li-so*

Reputable South Korean sources such as the National Human Rights Commission, the Korean Bar Association and the Korean Institute for National Unification (KINU), and leading scholars, such as Prof. Heo Man-ho of Kyungpook University, report additional political penal labor camps.

The (South) Korean Bar Association's 2008 *White Paper on Human Rights in North Korea* identifies Camp No. 16 at Hwasong, North Hamgyong province,[80] and Camp No. 25 at Susong-dong, Chongjin, North Hamgyong province. The KINU 2009 *White Paper* also notes *Kwan-li-so* No. 16 and *Kwan-li-so* No. 25

for offending prisoners.[81] The National Human Rights Commission study also notes these same two prison camps.[82]

Professor Heo Man-ho of Kyungpook National University, Daegu, reports that *Kwan-li-so* No. 16 at Cochang-ri, Hwasong-kun (located in North Hamgyong province), contains about 10,000 "anti-revolutionary and anti-Party elements." They are held on charges of opposing the succession to Kim Jong-il, and he adds that former Vice-Chairman of State Kim Dong-gyu is imprisoned there. Professor Heo further notes a Susong Center in Sunam district, Chongjin City, run by the *Bo-wi-bu* (National Security Agency) police. Reportedly, the center holds about 3,000 detainees and their families, including pastors and church leaders from South Hwanghae province, and Mr. Heo Taek, a Korean repatriate from Japan.[83] The National Human Rights Commission Survey Report estimates the number of prisoners at Camp No. 16 at 20,000, and the population at Camp No. 25 at 5,000.

Former *kwan-li-so* prisoners interviewed for this report have mentioned that there is at least one former prisoner from Camp No. 16 currently in South Korea, although he declines to be interviewed by journalists or other researchers. No former prisoners or guards were accessible to provide first-person accounts or eyewitness confirmation during the preparation of this report, so these camps are not further discussed herein.

---

80 2008 *White Paper on Human Rights in North Korea*, Korean Bar Association, Seoul, p. 539.

81 Ibid. p. 130.

82 Survey Report on Political Prison Camps in North Korea, Seoul, 2009, p. 38.

83 "Political Detention Camps in Relation to Socio-Political Change in North Korea," paper presented at the 4th International Conference on North Korean Human Rights and Refugees, 2003, Prague, Czech Republic.

However, a Washington DC-based attorney has scoured Google Earth sateillite photographs looking at prison camp sites. In so doing, he ascertained the barbed-wired perimeters of many sections of the prison camps discussed above and found a penitentiary-like structure just north of Chongjin city. A South Korean human rights NGO showed satellite photos of this structure and its surrounding areas to several former residents of Chongjin, two of whom identified the structure in the photographs as Camp 25. One of the former Chongjin residents had gone out to the prison camp to visit a friend who was a guard there. The other former resident had driven a truck to the prison camp to pick up a shipment of the bicycles made there by the prison laborers.

Satellite photos of Camp 25 can be seen on pages 223-224.[84]

Closed *Kwan-li-so*

South Korean sources also list five additional political prison labor camps that were closed between 1989 and 1991. Persons interviewed for this report witnessed three of these closed camps.

---

84 The Washington-based attorney, Joshua Stanton, operates a website, OneFreeKorea, which has several displays of prison-camp satellite photographs. The South Korean human rights NGO, North Korea Database (NKDB), has published several studies referred to earlier in the present report.

Closed Camp No. 11, Kyongsong, North Hamgyong Province

WITNESS: Yoshio Kinoshita

Yoshio Kinoshita is the Japanese name of a second generation Korean-Japanese who "returned" to North Korea in 1961. He studied engineering at a technical college in Chongjin. He was one of over 2,000 workers assigned in 1990 to close *kwan-li-so* Camp No. 11, in order to convert the area into a villa for Kim Il-sung. He worked there for seven months to disassemble a brick and furniture factory in the camp. He reported that it took a total of two years to convert the prison camp to the palace property, part of which involved the construction of an underground railroad leading to and from the villa.

He was able to provide details about the camp. It had held some 20,000 prisoners and was divided into three sections or settlement areas: one for the more serious offenders; one for the less serious offenders; and one for the families of those placed in the first two sections. Upon closing, some prisoners were transferred to Camp No. 15 and the others to Camp No. 22. The section for the more serious offenders was some 2,000 meters high in the mountains. There were rows and rows of tiny (1.2 meters wide, 2 meters long and 1.5 meters high) houses built half above ground, half below ground, with each row holding about 400 prisoners. There were adjacent pigpens that were exactly the same size as the

---

Testimony About Yoshio Kinoshita's Sister

Mr. Kinoshita was interviewed in Tokyo in 2009 about his sister who "disappeared" in *Bo-wi-bu* custody in Chongjin in April 2002. His younger sister had gone from North Korea to China to receive money sent by other relatives still in Japan. While in China she wrote a return letter to her relatives in Japan describing the poverty and destitution in North Korea and her harsh judgment of Kim Jong-il. She mistakenly gave the letter to another North Korean to take to the post office, who gave it to North Korean police instead. Upon return to Chongjin, she was called to the police office for "some questions." That was the last her family ever saw of her. The family went to the *Bo-wi-bu* office repeatedly for information, but they were told that the police had no information about her. Later, *Bo-wi-bu* officers came to the house to collect food, clothing and medicine for Kinoshita's sister. Her children took the food and clothing to the police station but were not allowed to see their mother. Other *Bo-wi-bu* officials came to the house for more food and clothing. The family again went to the police station inquiring about the reasons for the ongoing detention. They were told they would never see their mother/sister again, as she had died of illness and had been "disposed of in house" (*shil-nae-cheo-ri*). Another former detainee later told the family that Kinoshita's sister had been sent to Camp No. 22 as she had damaged the honor of Kim Jong-il. Mr. Kinoshita fled North Korea and returned to Japan in 2007.

---

prisoner houses that held about 1,200 pigs, he reported. There were also other facilities for storing corn and potatoes, all surrounded by barbed, electrified wire.

WITNESS: Former Guard Choi Dong-chul

Choi Dong-chul is the son of Lee Soon-ok, whose story appears below.[85] At the time of his mother's arrest, Choi was a student at Kim Il-sung University in Pyongyang. Prior to his mother's arrest, when the family was still in very high standing within the Korean Workers' Party, Choi fulfilled a portion of his compulsory military service, from February 1985 to June 1986, as a guard at *Kwan-li-so* No. 11 for families of political wrongdoers, located in Kyongsong, North Hamgyong province. This is the same encampment of 15,000–20,000 inmates where Ahn Myong-chol was a guard in 1987.

Though *Kwan-li-so* No.11 was closed in 1989 and its inmates transferred to other political penal-labor colonies, Choi's testimony, along with that of Ahn, provides an additional glimpse into the operation of North Korea's *kwan-li-so*.

---

85 See p. 103.

Both Ahn Myong-chol and Choi Dong-chul were guards at *Kwan-li-so* No. 11 at Kyongsong, North Hamgyong province, from May to August 1987 and from February 1985 to June 1986, respectively. In this camp, some 20,000 family prisoners engaged in potato farming and logging.

Ahn Myong-chol was also a guard at *Kwan-li-so* No. 13 at Jongsong, North Hamgyong province, from 1987 to 1990. No. 13 held some 30,000 prisoners, he estimates. According to the KINU *White Paper* on Human Rights in North Korea, *Kwan-li-so* No. 13 was closed at the end of 1990 because it was too close to the Chinese border, tempting prisoners to try to escape.

For one four-month period while he was a guard at *Kwan-li-so* No. 13, Ahn was briefly transferred to guard the much smaller political prison No. 26 at Hwachon-dong, Sungho-ri, Pyongyang. The KINU White Paper on Human Rights notes that No. 26 closed in January 1991.

The KINU *White Paper* also notes that *Kwan-li-so* No. 12 at Changpyong, Onsong, North Hamgyong province, was closed in 1989, also because of its proximity to the border with China. Further, *Kwan-li-so* No. 27 at Chonma, North Pyongan province, was closed in 1990 for unknown reasons.

One of the anonymous former prisoners from a *kyo-hwa-so* prison discussed in the next section of this report was transferred to a *kwan-li-so* at Danchun, South Hamgyong province in the mid-1980s. He reports that this camp closed in the late 1980s.

The 2009 KINU *White Paper* identifies additional closed Camps: No. 12, Changpyong, Onsong-kun, North Hamgyong province, and Camp No. 13, Jongsong, Eunsung, North Hamgyong province, closed in May 1987 and December 1990 respectively. They were too close to the border with China. Camp No. 26, Hwanchun-dong, Sungho District, Pyongyang, where former guard An Myong-chol worked briefly, was reportedly closed in January 1991. And Camp No. 27, Chunma, North Pyongan province was reportedly closed in November 1990 for unknown reasons.[86]

---

86 2009 *White Paper on Human Rights in North Korea*, KINU, Seoul, p.131.

PART THREE

THE *KYO-HWA-SO* LONGTERM PRISON-LABOR FACILITIES (FELONY LEVEL)

Introduction

The Korean word transliterated phonetically as *kyo-hwa-so* literally translates as "a place to make a good person through education." North Korea has *kyo-hwa-so* prisons in every province, holding both political prisoners and persons convicted of criminal offenses as are commonly understood. *Kyo-hwa-so* is the term used for prisons in South Korea. The term is sometimes translated into English as an "enlightenment center," "edification center," "re-education center," or "re-socialization center." In light of the testimony below, these are but cruel euphemisms given the conditions and practices in the North Korea *kyo-hwa-so*. Some of the former prisoners interviewed for this report used the term *ro-dong* (labor) *kyo-hwa-so,* indicating "re-education through labor." There is also a variation of *kyo-hwa-so* termed *kyo-yang-so,* which is literally translated as "a place to make a good person through nurturing." On the basis of available data, there does not appear to be substantial differences between these two facilities.

Viewed in satellite photographs, these *kyo-hwa-so* appear as compounds with several buildings surrounded by high walls, often with clearly visible guard towers, not unlike what felony level penitentiaries in the United States look like in aerial photography. The first edition of *Hidden Gulag* also referred to *kyo-hwa-so* as "prison camps." To distinguish them more clearly from the *kwan-li-so* encampments, the present second edition, simply refers to these facilities as prisons or penitentiaries.

Translated literally, *kyo-hwa-so* means "a place to make a good person through education." However, the literal translation bears no relation to the *kyo-hwa-so* described by the former North Korean prisoners interviewed for this report. The education component of the imprisonment, according to the former prisoners, consists mostly of: 1) forced memorizing of Kim Il-sung's speeches or the New Year's Day Joint Editorials (carried in North Korean newpapers to set forth the regime's priorities and political line for the coming year), and 2) organized "self-criticism" sessions, mostly in regard to work teams and production quotas. These "education" sessions are conducted in the evenings, and the exhausted prisoners are not, they report, allowed to return to their cells to sleep until they can recite the speeches or editorials. During the self-criticism sessions, prisoners kneel in front of their work-units and face the prison officials. The prisoners doing self-criticism frequently falsely confess to imaginary mistakes, which the prison officials or prison group leaders can then criticize, so that the work unit can conclude the sessions and go back to their often overcrowded cells.

Kyo-hwa-so are run by the *In-min-bo-an-seong* (People's Safety Agency) police, formerly called the *Sa-hoe-an-jeon-bu* (Social Safety Agency) and still commonly referred to in North Korea as *An-jeon-bu*. Some of the *kyo-hwa-so* resemble large penitentiaries: a large compound surrounded by high walls and barbed- or electrified-wire fencing and containing several buildings for manufacturing various products, prisoner housing, and offices for guards and prison officials. Other *kyo-*

hwa-so are barbed-wire-enclosed facilities, located in rural areas where prisoners toil in mines or cut lumber in nearby mountains.

In many aspects of day-to-day prison life, the *kyo-hwa-so* resemble the *kwan-li-so* described in the previous section of this report. The prisons are harsh "strict-regime" places (virtually no prisoner privileges) where prisoners are forced to do hard, often heavy and dangerous labor while being provided food rations insufficient to sustain even sedentary life. The combination of hard labor and below-subsistence-level food provisions results in rapid weight-loss, industrial or mining work accidents, malnutrition-related diseases, and death. The so-called prison "hospitals" or "clinics," that, according to former prisoners, rarely have doctors or medicines, are essentially places where the sick and injured, who can no longer work, are sent to await death. Loss of life occurs at such high rates that many of the *kyo-hwa-so* are perceived by prisoners as death camps, as they expect to die before the completion of their sentences.

There are several substantial differences between *kyo-hwa-so* prisons and *kwan-li-so* prison camps. As noted, the *kyo-hwa-so* contain persons imprisoned for criminal offenses as well as political offenses. The *kwan-li-so* are only for political offenders. In the *kyo-hwa-so* system there is no imprisonment of the families of the perceived or convicted wrongdoer. Many, though certainly not all, persons imprisoned in the *kyo-hwa-so* have been subjected to some form of judicial process and given a fixed term sentence. Incarceration is not incommunicado. The families of the imprisoned persons know where their relative is being detained. In an important respect, *kyo-hwa-so* prisons and prison camps are, by

design, correctional facilities for persons convicted of "heavy crimes," the equivalent of what would be felony offenses in the United States.

But some of those sentenced to the *kyo-hwa-so* prisons are convicted of offenses that would not normally be criminalized: private economic transactions not undertaken within an officially appointed workstation or offenses that are, in essence, political crimes. For example, some interviewed for this report were driven to engage in private economic transactions such as transporting goods across the North Korea-China border to survive following the breakdown in the state-run production and distribution systems. Another was arrested for singing a South Korean song. And still another was arrested for getting caught up in a power struggle between Workers' Party functionaries staffing the production/distribution facilities and police units that were dissatisfied with their share of goods and/or bribes.

This section includes testimony by former *kyo-hwa-so* prisoners who admitted that they were justly convicted of what would be criminal offenses in most countries around the world as well as the testimony of former prisoners who were sent to the *kyo-hwa-so* for what are essentially political offenses or economic transactions that according to international human rights standards, should not be criminalized. The former prisoners convicted of legitimately criminal offenses report that there were "political prisoners" incarcerated along with the common criminals.

Some persons sent to the *kyo-hwa-so* felony-level penitentiaries are arrested in North Korea, interrogated, charged, and convicted. Many others, including persons whose stories are told below, enter the DPRK penal system via forced repatriation from China. They are usually interrogated, and very often beaten or tortured, at one or more police *ku-ryu-jang* interrogation-detention facilities before being consigned, with or without trial, to the *kyo-hwa-so* penitentiaries. The system and process of forced repatriation from China and the brutal punishments perpetrated against the repatriated North Koreans are described in Part Four of this report. However, if the repatriated North Koreans end up in *kyo-hwa-so* penitentiaries, their stories are told below in order to detail the *kyo-hwa-so* prisons and their role in the overall North Korean system of political imprisonment. However, their pre-*kyo-hwa-so* detentions are described also. Since, it should be noted, the brutalizations and inhuman treatment endured in the *kyo-hwa-so* prisons are preceded by months and months of pre-trial, pre-sentence brutality at one or more of the local police detention facilities.

his parents died in the famine, his two sisters fled to China in 1997. A year later, he also crossed the North Korean border to meet his sisters in the Jilin area of China to get food, money, and clothes. Having no work in North Korea, and sensing the opportunity to earn a living, he began trading curios, gold and wild animal meats back and forth across the China-North Korea border.

After three or four border crossings, Former Prisoner # 37 was arrested by North Korean police in September of 2002. He was detained at the Onsong *Bo-wi-bu* office for a month, and then transferred to the Onsong *An-jeon-bu* office where he was confined and interrogated for 6 months. After a very short trial for form's sake, he was given a sentence of 15 years to be served at the Chongo-ri *Kyo-hwa-so* No. 12. However, due to severe illness, he was released after three years.

Kyo-Hwa-So Witnesses and Testimony

WITNESS: Former Prisoner # 37

Kyo-hwa-so No. 12, Chongo-ri, North Hamgyong Province (April 2003–March 2006)

Former Prisoner # 37 was born in Onsong-kun, North Hamgyong province in July 1971. After

TESTIMONY:

Onsong *Bo-wi-bu* Interrogation/Detention Facility

Bo-wi-bu authorities came and arrested Former Prisoner # 37 at his home, saying that they had things to "check with him." Detained at the police station for a month, he was ordered to write down everything he had done wrong in his life and was beaten with wood sticks for no apparent reason, which resulted in severe damage to his left eardrum. Former Prisoner # 37 saw authorities confiscate medicines that families had brought in for their imprisoned relatives. Prisoners, he noted, are given medicine only when they are "barely breathing."

Onsong *An-jeon-bu* Interrogation/Detention Facility

When Former Prisoner # 37 was transferred to Onsong *An-jeon-bu* in October 2002 for six months, he was again interrogated and beaten with wooden clubs, particularly when he asserted that he had not done anything wrong. These beatings damaged his right eardrum. He saw others at the *An-jeon-bu* facility with broken teeth and torn eyelids from these beatings. During his detention, through March of 2003, he was confined in a small room, barely two meters by three meters, with ten other persons. During his detention, he barely saw the sun.

Meager amounts of food left the detainees malnourished almost to the point of starvation. Former Prisoner # 37 was given boiled cornhusks, corn powder gruel and some soybeans in a dirty plastic bowl. Guards cut the handle of spoons so that prisoners could not use them to commit suicide. Prisoners secretly drank unsanitary water from the toilet when they were not provided with drinking water. While he was detained at the *An-jeon-bu ku-ryu-jang*, he heard about, but did not personally witness, forced abortions and violence against pregnant women, particularly if the fathers were suspected of being Chinese.

During his interrogation, Former Prisoner # 37 was again asked about meeting South Koreans or attending church while in China. More importantly, he was shown a list written by a then un-identified person that included Mr. Kim and his sisters' names. Later it turned out that the list was created by a person whose home he had visited on his trips to China. The *An-jeon-bu* authorities decided he was guilty of smuggling and "kidnapping" his sisters.

See page 144 for Former Prisoner # 37's sketch of Onsong An-jeon-bu and Bo-wi-bu Police Interrogation-Detention complex.

Former Prisoner #37's "Trial"

As the police had already decided Former Prisoner # 37 was guilty of smuggling and kidnapping, he was assigned to stand trial publicly in the main market square in Onsong, where several thousand persons were gathered to witness the hour-long proceeding. Former Prisoner #37 was assigned a lawyer who told him that he had recommended to senior officials a reduction in Former Prisoner # 37's fifteen-year sentence but his appeal was rejected. He believes the trial was very unfair. However, Former Prisoner # 37 felt relief at the thought of leaving behind the beatings and extremely cramped confinement in the *ku-ryu-jang*, and going to a prison where he would have a work assignment and a little more mobility.

Kyo-hwa-so No. 12, Chongo-ri

Former Prisoner # 37 was confined in Chongo-ri[87] *kyo-hwa-so* from 2003 to 2006. He was originally sentenced to 15 years in prison because authorities thought he would flee North Korea again unless he was sent to prison for a long time.[88]

---

87 In the first edition of *Hidden Gulag*, *Kyo-hwa-so* No. 12 was transliterated into English as "Jeonger-ri."

88 While he was staying at Chongo-ri *kyo-hwa-so*, Mr. Kim noted that there were 10-15 people who were caught on their way to South Korea and received lifetime sentences.

Kyohwaso No.12
Chongo-ri, North Hamgyong Province

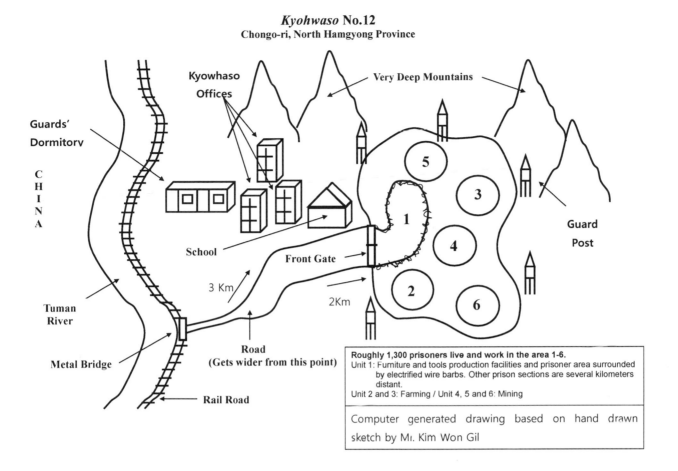

Roughly 1,300 prisoners live and work in the area 1-6.
Unit 1: Furniture and tools production facilities and prisoner area surrounded by electrified wire barbs. Other prison sections are several kilometers distant.
Unit 2 and 3: Farming / Unit 4, 5 and 6: Mining

Computer generated drawing based on hand drawn sketch by Mr. Kim Won Gil

There were about 1,700 male prisoners at Chongo-ri. These prisoners worked 14 hours a day in a copper mine, on a potato farm, or in workshop factories to make furniture. The antiquated machines used for making furniture caused many accidents. There was an accidental death every several days, as the prisoners seldom got more than five hours of sleep per night. In the evenings, after working all day, the prisoners had to memorize *kyo-hwa-so* rules and engage in "mutual criticism" virtually every night.

Falling logs at his work site injured Former Prisoner # 37. Both eardrums were already broken in the *ku-ryu-jang* before he was sent to

kyo-hwa-so. Unable to work, he was sent home to "recover." Outside, he obtained false medical documents contending ongoing illness, and he bribed the *An-jeon-bu* "sick-leave control agent" so that his improved health was not reported to the authorities.

He learned that his sisters had gone from China to South Korea. Former Prisoner # 37 concluded he could not live in North Korea anymore (pending a return to prison, if authorities saw through his ruse of continuing illness). His sisters hired a "broker" on the China-North Korea border who assisted him in fleeing North Korea. A series of brokers assisted him to transit

China, and pass through Vietnam and Cambodia. After 4 months of escaping North Korea, he arrived in South Korea in 2009.

He drew this sketch of Chongo-ri. See also satellite photograph on page 227.

Fortunately, Former Prisoner # 28 was pardoned after serving only eight months (December 1998 through July 1999). In August 1999, he fled to China, making his way to Mongolia, where he joined a group of five North Koreans, who made their way to Seoul in October 2001.

WITNESS: Former Prisoner # 28

Kyo-hwa-so No. 12, Chongo-ri, North Hamgyong Province (December 1998–July 1999)

A young man in his early twenties from Chongjin City, North Hamgyong province, Former Prisoner # 28 has a straightforward story. As the food situation in North Korea deteriorated in the 1990s, he took to buying and selling goods between North Korea and China to stay alive and to provide food for the family with whom he was living. Arrested in December 1997, he was held in a local jail for three months and then transferred to an *An-jeon-bu* (People's Safety Agency) *ka-mok* [89] in Onsong. He was held at the ka-mok for another eight months before being sentenced to three years, including time served in ka-mok, to *Kyo-hwa-so* No. 12 at Chongo-ri, North Hamgyong province, for violating, he says, Penal Law 117, Article 2: illegally crossing the North Korea–China border and illegally transporting money and goods.

---

89 As noted, some former North Koreans use the term *ka-mok* (jail) and *ku-ryu-jang* (interrogation-detention facilities) interchangeably.

TESTIMONY: *Kyo-hwa-so* No. 12, Chongo-ri, North Hamgyong Province

Sometimes also called Onsong-kun *kyo-hwa-so*, although it is not located there, *Kyo-hwa-so* No. 12 at Chongo-ri holds some 1,300 to 1,500 men, who mine copper and iron, cut logs, make bricks, and farm. The most salient features of *Kyo-hwa-so* No. 12 were the deplorable conditions and the high rate of deaths in detention. Out of twenty-three other prisoners who entered on the same day as Former Prisoner # 28, only two survived. The rest died within eight months of arrival, from hard labor and sub-subsistence level food rations—small mixtures of corn and beans, with rice added only on holidays. Former Prisoner #28 believes that eight hundred prisoners died while he was there—so many, according to what another prisoner told him, that the guards had to burn the corpses.

There were no "self-criticism" sessions for him at *Kyo-hwa-so* No. 12. However, each night, the prisoners had to gather at the gates around nine in the evening, at which time the guards would order one of the prisoners to recite the prison rules. Rule-breakers were beaten. Former Prisoner # 28 witnessed two public executions of other prisoners who had tried to escape.

See page 228 for satellite photographs of kyo-hwa-so No. 12 at Chongo-ri.

Oro *Kyoyangso* Penitentiary for Women
Hamhung, Youngwang-kun
Dongjung-ri, South Hamgyong Province

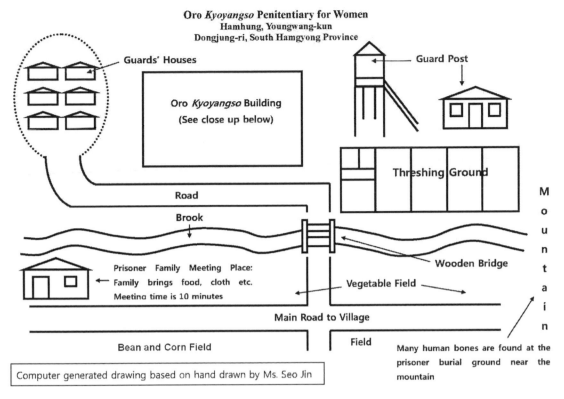

Guards' Houses

Oro *Kyoyangso* Building
(See close up below)

Guard Post

Oro *Kyoyangso* Building

Threshing Ground

Road

Brook

Wooden Bridge

Prisoner Family Meeting Place:
Family brings food, cloth etc.
Meeting time is 10 minutes

Vegetable Field

Main Road to Village

Bean and Corn Field

Field

Mountain

Many human bones are found at the prisoner burial ground near the mountain

Computer generated drawing based on hand drawn by Ms. Seo Jin

Main Building, "Oro" *Kyoyangso* Penitentiary
Dongjung-ri, South Hamgyong Province

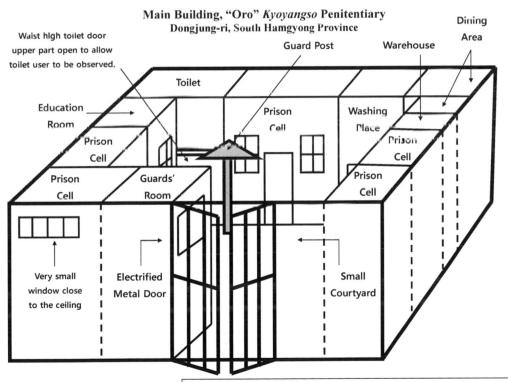

Waist high toilet door
upper part open to allow
toilet user to be observed.

Toilet

Guard Post

Warehouse

Dining Area

Education Room

Prison Cell

Washing Place

Prison Cell

Prison Cell

Guards' Room

Prison Cell

Very small window close to the ceiling

Electrified Metal Door

Small Courtyard

Computer generated drawing based on hand drawn sketch by Ms. Seo Jin

89

WITNESS: Ms. Seo Jin

Kyo-yang-so No. 55 "Oro" South Hamgyong Province, (June 2004–July 2005)

A Malnutrition Death in Korea; Trafficked in China

Ms. Seo was born at Myongchon-kun, North Hamgyong province in 1970. During the famine, she was too malnourished to breast-feed her five-month-old baby, who died of starvation. Despondent, Ms. Seo fled to China. Almost immediately, she was kidnapped by traffickers who sold her for roughly US $1,500 to a Chinese farmer, with whose family she lived and worked for four years until she had "paid off" the amount of her purchase. The farmer's family was also worried, she relates, about being punished for harboring illegal North Korean immigrants if this commercially arranged "marriage" was discovered during Chinese police sweeps, often termed "strike-hard" campaigns.

Ms. Seo then worked for three years in a restaurant in Yanbian prefecture to earn enough money to flee to South Korea. But she was caught trying to enter Mongolia in May of 2003, and taken by Chinese police to a detention facility in Tumen for illegal immigrants where she was held for six months. All of the money she had saved and carried with her to flee to South Korea was confiscated, and she was unable to wash during her six-month detention. She commented that prisoners there were an abnormal color due to severe malnutrition.

TESTIMONY: Forced Repatriation: Brutalization at Three Interrogation/Detention Facilities

In December 2003 Ms. Seo was repatriated to the Onsong *Bo-wi-bu ku-ryu-jang*. Guards stripped her naked and made her do a "squat-down-stand-up-run around" routine to see if she was hiding any money in her rectal and vaginal cavities, even though all her money had already been confiscated by the Chinese police. She was interrogated relentlessly, beaten during interrogation, and given very little food.

After fifteen days she was transferred to the Musan *Bo-wi-bu ku-ryu-jang*, where there were about fifty women and ten men detained. She was kicked and again beaten with wooden staves so that she could hardly walk. That was not as bad, she says, as the "sitting-motionless-torture," which was extremely painful. She was overwhelmed by fear and bitter cold, as it was January and the detention facility was barely heated. She continued to be unable to wash.

Ms. Seo saw pregnant women being sent out one by one from the Musan *ku-ryu-jang*. She was not sure where they were taken, but the common understanding was that after their abortions, the women were sent to a labor training center/mobile labor brigade called "Kop-ba-koo" and that some of the women were able to escape from the hospital where the abortions took place.

After about 40 days she was transferred to the Musan *An-jeon-bu ku-ryu-jang.*

Upon arrival at the *An-jeon-bu* police station, female guards made Ms. Seo stand up, bend over, and touch the ground with her hands for a vaginal inspection to find hidden money. When she resisted the examination, she was cursed and hit by the female guards, which Ms. Seo considered insulting, as the guards were much younger women. The humiliations continued. When Ms. Seo had diarrhea she had to cry and beg the guards to let her use the toilet. Guards followed her to the toilet, which had a very small door providing little privacy. She was required to raise her hands above her head while using the toilet, and guards checked her stool for hidden money. While held for 50 days in the *An-jeon-bu* police station, two elderly women died from illness and malnutrition. She also heard the guards curse the pregnant detainees for carrying "the Chinese seed."

During her months of interrogation and detention, she never admitted her intent to defect to South Korea, even though Chinese police at the Mongolian border had apprehended her. Frustrated by her refusal to confess, a police official cursed her saying "You go to Oro!" as if he had been saying, "Go to hell." With that, and without any trial or judicial proceeding, in June of 2004 she was transferred to *Kyo-yang-so 55.*

TESTIMONY: "Oro" *Kyo-yang-so* No. 55

Dongjoong-ri, South Hamgyong Province (June 2004–July 2005)

There were, Ms. Seo said, about 1,000 men and 250 to 300 women. She worked about twelve hours a day sometimes cutting grass but usually transporting bags of sand and stone. Evenings were taken up with "ideological struggle" and "mutual criticism" sessions. The prison guards hit her on the back or kicked her legs when she did not work fast enough.

Ms. Seo was very ill for two months with a high fever, but she was never treated with any medication. She just lay on the cold floor. Ms. Seo often saw an oxcart that carried the corpses of dead prisoners. The dead bodies were all put in a large box together and were dumped into a pit in the ground. She could see human bones washed away from the burial ground following rainstorms.

Ms. Seo hunted for rats living in toilets to supplement her meager food rations. She shared the rat meat with the weak people because they could not move well enough to collect any extra food for themselves. Prison hygiene was problematic. There was no toilet paper and the women who had not stopped menstruation cycles, had to rip up their clothing to make sanitary napkins.

In June 2005 she was released, and returned to her hometown. But appalled by the ongoing lack of food, ten days later, she again fled to China. She worked for a year to earn money, and returned to North Korea to give her savings to her family. She again went to China for work, but used her earnings to pay for a broker who assisted her to flee to South Korea via Thailand. She arrived in South Korea in April 2007.

WITNESS: Former Prisoner # 31

Chung-san *Kyo-hwa-so*, South Pyongan Province (May 2004–July 2005)

Former Prisoner # 31 was born in 1978 in Kyounsong-kun, an area near Chongjin City, North Hamgyong province, where her Korean-Chinese parents had previously migrated in order to escape Mao's Cultural Revolution in China.

At the height of the late 1990s famine in North Korea, at age 19, she went to China. She lived in China for five years before she was arrested and repatriated to Onsong *Bo-wi-bu* in 2003, where she was held for six months before being transferred to a *ro-dong-dan-ryeon-dae* mobile labor brigade at Kyongsong for a month. Upon release in November 2003, she returned to China to rejoin her Korean-Chinese mother who had moved back to China.

But she was caught by Chinese police immediately after crossing the border and was again forcibly repatriated to Onsong *Bo-wi-bu*. As this was her second attempt to leave North Korea, even though it was to join her mother in China, her punishment was more extensive. She was held at Onsong *Bo-wi-bu* for three months, and then sent to a mobile labor brigade at Onsong for a month. In 2004, she was sent to the Kyongsong *Bo-wi-bu* for two months, followed by ten days at the Sungnam *Bo-wi-bu*, before being returned to the Kyongsong *An-jeon-bu ku-ryu-jang*

for three months. She was not given a trial, but told she would "have to suffer for a year," and they took her by train to the Chung-san *kyo-hwa-so* for one year and two months.

At the Onsong *Bo-wi-bu* in 2003, female guards subjected her to a naked body search and the male interrogators twice whipped her with a belt, but she was not asked the usual interrogators' questions about meeting South Koreans or going to church. At that time, there were about 80-90 prisoners: 50-60 women and about 20 men. Some women had their young children with them. Some of the women were in advanced states of pregnancy. One aborted during interrogation due to the stress. Some women gave birth in the jail, but most were sent to the hospital. She heard of one case of forced abortion, very early in a pregnancy. However, she did not know the fate of the pregnant women taken to the hospital while she was being detained.

TESTIMONY: Chung-san *Kyo-hwa-so*, South Pyongan Province (May 2004–July 2005)

Chungsan *kyo-hwa-so*, (also transliterated as "Jungsan") which she also called a "*kyo-do-so*," is a sprawling largely women's penitentiary closely resembling a prison camp. There are some ten or eleven separate agricultural areas each of which hold about 500-600 prisoners, about 50-60%, or even more of whom are "border crossers." Other women prisoners were incarcerated for theft, prostitution, spreading superstition (a reference to fortune-telling), or for unauthorized selling of North Korean materials in China. The sprawling plots, almost due west of Pyongyang, adjacent to the West Sea (sometimes labeled on maps as the Yellow Sea), are bounded in the east by several reservoirs. A few of the plots seem to have been maintained as short term labor training sections (what this report terms mobile labor brigades), although most of the agricultural plots were worked by laborers imprisoned for periods of several years. Scattered on the field were settlements in which the prison officials and guards lived. Virtually all of the agricultural output was sent to the Ministry of Public Security in Pyongyang.[90]

In the farming seasons, the women grew rice and corn. Outside of the planting and harvesting cycles, the women made fertilizer by mixing dried straw with human feces, and made rope out of the rice plant stalks. In spite of being a prison farm, food rations were abysmal. Former Prisoner # 31 reports that she lost half of her body weight. She believes that a third of the prisoners died that year from combinations of malnutrition, disease, and forced labor. There was also a lack of heat and hot water. Former Prisoner #31 had only the clothes in which she was arrested, until a guard gave her a blanket she used as a coat.

Prisoners were often beaten if they did not work hard enough. Too weak from malnutrition to work hard enough, she was beaten on the legs and hips with an iron bar. Her wound got infected, and she was treated, though without an antiseptic, in the prison clinic. Very ill, she was released in July 2005 to die elsewhere, she

---

90 "Rimjim-gang: News from Inside North Korea," edited by Ishimaro Jiro, AsiaPress, Osaka, Japan, contains interviews with two other former inmates from Chungsan prison, who were interviewed inside China.

related. Women who died at the prison camp were buried without coffins or grave markers on a hill the women termed the "flower mountain."

It took Former Prisoner # 31 five months to recover her strength, but in December 2005, she again fled to China and reunited with her mother for the first time in ten years. In March 2006, she arrived in Seoul after traveling through Ulan Bator.

WITNESS: Mrs. Bang Mi-sun

Kyo-hwa-so No. 15, Hamhung, South Hamgyong Province (June 2000–December 2001)

Trafficked Three Times

Born in Musan County, North Hamgyong province in 1954, Mrs. Bang's husband, a miner by profession, died of starvation during the mid-1990s famine in North Korea. Unable to maintain communications with a daughter who was studying dance and acting in Pyongyang, and fearful of losing the rest of her family to famine or disease, Mrs. Bang fled to China in 1998 with her nineteen year old daughter and sixteen year old son. Apprehended by a gang of traffickers who threatened to turn over her children to the Chinese police for repatriation to North Korea, Mrs. Bang agreed to a "brokered marriage" and was sold to a handicapped Chinese farmer for 7,000 Chinese yuan (roughly US $1,000).

Shortly thereafter, while her "husband" was out in the field, she was kidnapped by another gang of traffickers and sold a second time. She ran away but was again apprehended by traffickers who sold her "like livestock" she says for a third time to a thirty-four year old bachelor who was still living with his parents. He demanded that Mrs. Bang, then forty-eight years old, bear him a child, a prospect she thought preposterous to begin with. She told her third "husband" that she had received an intra-uterine contraceptive device in North Korea following the birth of her third child. Her "husband" and his friends held her, spread-eagled on the floor, while a "doctor" of some sort "rolled up his sleeves" and manually removed the "ring." Bleeding profusely she became infected, and could not walk or stand up. She spent a month on the floor recovering, mostly in tears, she relates, at the "cruelty and shamefulness" that enveloped her.

Forcibly Repatriated

Upon recovery, she again ran away to the Yanbian Autonomous Prefecture in Yanji province in China to search for her children. But this time she was caught by the Chinese police during an identity card check in Nampyon. She was forcibly repatriated back to North Korea into the custody of the Musan county *Bo-wi-bu* State Security Agency police.

Musan *Bo-wi-bu* Interrogation/Detention Facility (October 1999)

At the Musan *Bo-wi-bu ku-ryu-jang* detention facility in October of 1999, there were some thirty detainees, mostly women, and perhaps ten men. The women detainees were required to strip naked with their hands tied behind their backs, and do the "sit-down/stand-up/run-around" exercises in front of female guards in order to dislodge valuables that may have been hidden in vaginal or rectal cavities. During interrogation she was asked the usual questions: "Where, why, and how did she get to China?" "Did she meet any Christians or South Koreans? Did she see South Korean movies or TV?" After three days of questioning, she convinced her interrogators that her "border crossing," occasioned by the starvation of her husband, was innocent of political motivations or implications.

Musan *An-jeon-bu Ro-dong-dan-ryeon-dae* Mobile Labor Brigade (November–December 1999)

It was deemed a serious offence, nonetheless, as she had taken her children with her.[91] So she was taken to the Musan County *An-jeon-bu* (People's Safety Agency) *ro-dong-dan-ryeon-dae* labor-training center, a mobile labor brigade, where she was held for two months in November and December 1999. Upon arrival there was more of the sit-down/stand-up/run-around routine. At that

---

91 Nothing in the Universal Declaration of Human Rights or International Covenant on Civil and Political Rights indicates that the right to leave and return to one's country of origin is compromised or negated if a parent exercises the right to leave in the company of his or her children.

time in this labor training center, the detainees, constituting an unpaid, corvee labor force, were tasked with preparing fields for farming in the spring. As at many of the labor training centers, the detainees either jogged or marched briskly to and from their work sites, often singing patriotic "praise songs" to the Great General, Kim Jong-il. Still weak from her vaginal ring removal infections, Mrs. Bang was unable to keep up. Falling down, a guard beat her on the head and leg with a wooden stave. Her leg became infected to the bone, a kind of osteomyelitis resulting in deep scars, which caused her to limp pronouncedly ten years later.

See page 147 for sketch of Musan Mobile Labor Brigade Facility.

Musan *An-jeon-bu* Pretrial Detention *Ku-ryu-jang* (January–June 2000)

Following treatment at a local hospital, in January 2000, she was taken to the Musan county *An-jeon-bu* People's Safety Agency detention center (*ku-ryu-jang*), where she was detained six months awaiting trial for "border crossing." Most of her fellow detainees were also held for "border crossing." This detention center was built in a semi-circle (see chart) of ten cells—six for women and four for men—that could easily be monitored by guards at the center point. The small cells were crowded to the point of overflowing. Mrs. Bang felt that she might suffocate. Prisoners were required to sit motionless for days on end, with prisoners forced to hit other prisoners who moved, even a little.

See page 147 for sketch of Musan An-jeon-bu Police Interrogaiton-Detention Facility.

Forced Abortion and Violence against Women

In early 2002, at Musan *An-jeon-bu*, there was a group of ten pregnant women who were going to be taken to the local hospital to abort their "half-Chinese" babies. One twenty-one year old, who was seven months pregnant, refused to go to the hospital to give up the baby growing inside her. The guards put her on the floor on her back and placed a board over her swollen womb, and pistol-whipped two male prisoners until they agreed to jump up and down on the board. After five minutes or so, the baby was aborted, and the woman was taken to the hospital where she died. Mrs. Bang learned of her death when she was taken to the hospital for more treatments for her infected leg.

"Trial"

Mrs. Bang was brought to trial at the Musan-kun (county) Court. Eight men sat behind a long table. Two or three were dressed in Kim Jong-il style jump suits, the others in regular shirts and jackets. Using *An-jeon-bu*-prepared paperwork, the man in the center of the long table read the charges against her: illegal border crossing and taking other persons (her children) with her across the border. Another man asked her if the charges were true. She was told that one of the eight men was her lawyer, but she did not know which one he was, though she believes it was the one who asked her if the charges were correct. She was sentenced to five years at the women's *Ro-dong Kyo-hwa-so*[92] labor penitentiary No.15

---

92 Literally, "a place to make a good person through education

near Hamhung, South Hamgyong province, minus the time already served in her various pretrial detentions. Her trial took ten minutes.

TESTIMONY: *Kyo-hwa-so* No. 15

Near Hamhung, South Hamgyong Province (June 2000–December 2001)

A prison farm located in Sungwon-ri, Hyesan district, South Hamgyong not far from the industrial city of Hamhung, Penitentiary No. 15 held some five hundred women organized into five groups (*ban*) of prison laborers. Group 1 grew vegetables. Groups 2 and 3 grew corn. Group 4 cut wood. And Group 5 did construction and repair. At the time of her entry in June 2000, the prison was still under construction, and her dormitory cell was covered only in tree branches. When it rained, they all got wet. Upon entry she turned in her civilian clothes and was given old clothes from former prisoners and prisoners who had died. Mrs. Bang was in Group 3. There were fifty-three women in her group, ranging in ages from twenty-one to seven. Most were in their thirties or forties. Four-fifths of the women in her group were there for "illegal border crossing." The same held true for the entire prison, where, according to Mrs. Bang, only some ten percent were incarcerated for "ordinary crimes."

The prison day began, except in the dead of winter, at 4:30 AM, with farm work from 5:00 to 9:00 AM; breakfast from 9 to 9:30 AM; farm work from 9:30 AM to 12:30 PM; lunch from 12:30 to 1:30 PM; farm work from 1:30 to 7:00

and labor."

PM; 7 to 10PM "re-education" and mutual self-criticism, which could result in reduced food rations if the criticism of prison work was severe. The "education" utilized a prison newspaper that carried stories of the Great General Kim Jong-il, stories about exemplary Korean Workers' Party members, about prisoners who were doing well on the outside upon release, and stories about model prisoners currently in the penitentiary.

Without variation, each meal consisted of fourteen beans per meal mixed with powdered corn. For the year and one-half she was detained (before early release), she was always hungry. Her body constantly craved salt and protein. After one month she was reduced to "skin and bones"—her body weight dropped from fifty-four to forty kilos (roughly 119 to 88 lbs.). Her skin turned black and wrinkled. Like other women, while doing farm work, she constantly searched for snakes, frogs, and insects that could be eaten raw. The women prisoners constantly tried to hide seeds and food in their clothing. The prison guards constantly searched under their clothes for hidden food, with kickings or beatings with rifle butts when hidden food was found. Out of her work group of fifty-three persons, ten women died during the year and one-half remained at Women's Penitentiary No. 15. It was the same, she said, for the other Work Groups.

Fearful of reduced food rations, Mrs. Bang worked as hard as she could, but with her damaged leg she could hardly bend over to work the short handled hoe. After five months she could not move her leg. So she was confined to the dorm cell, blanket-less, where her leg wounds continued to fester. She did sewing for

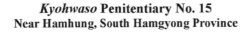

Kyohwaso Penitentiary No. 15
Near Hamhung, South Hamgyong Province

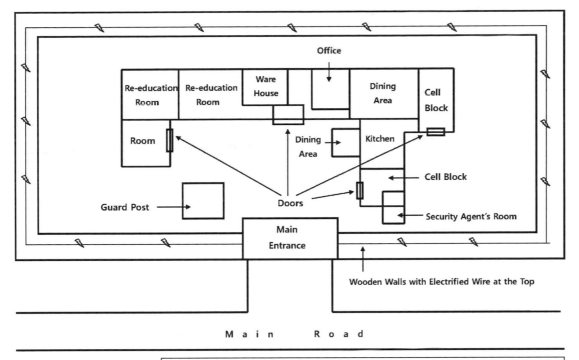

Computer generated drawing based on hand drawn sketch by Ms. Bang Mi Sun

Unit 3, *Kyohwaso* Penitentiary No.15
Near Hamhung, South Hamgyong Province

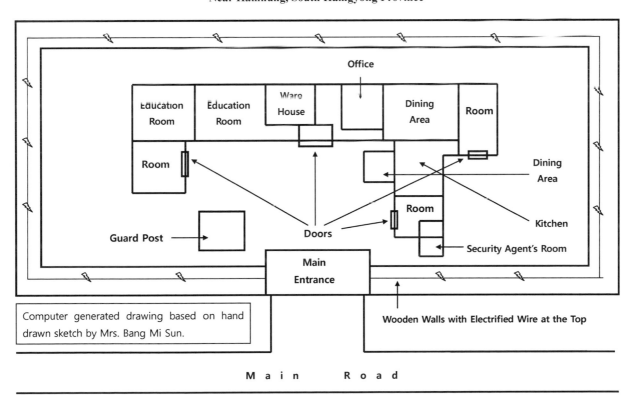

Computer generated drawing based on hand drawn sketch by Mrs. Bang Mi Sun.

the prison guards to avoid beatings for not working. A year later, on October 10, the anniversary of the founding of the Workers' Party, she was told that because she had observed prison rules and because of the Great General's grace (*eunhye*), she was granted amnesty.

Upon release, she went back to Musan to recover at the home of her deceased husband's parents. In March, a Korean-Chinese man came to the house looking for her. During the time of her post-repatriation imprisonment, her son had made it from Yanbian China to South Korea. Using his government resettlement grant and employment income, he hired a Korean-Chinese agent to search for his mother, and bring her to Seoul. Mrs. Bang could not yet walk, but with her son's money she bought food and medicine to restore her health. By October, she was able to travel. On October 27, she bribed a border guard and crossed again into China. In November 2003, she sought refuge in the South Korean Embassy in Beijing. On January 8, 2004 she came to Seoul. At the Hanawon orientation center for North Korean refugees newly resettled in South Korea, she met another defector whom she married. Reunited with her children, she now lives just outside Seoul with her new husband. She is hoping to form an NGO to assist North Korean women trafficked in China.

WITNESS: Yoo Chun-shik

Kyo-hwa-so No. "Two-Two," South Hamgyong Province

Mr. Yoo Chun-shik was born in November 1963 in Onsong, North Hamgyong Province. Following completion of his military service, in which he held the rank of platoon commander, he worked for a construction company in Onsong. His long string of encounters with the North Korean prison and detention system began in 1996.

After food distribution ceased at his place of employment, Yoo went to Kangwon Province to buy fish to sell to Koreans in China. He made "good money" and also began buying personal effects and selling them in China. Caught by the North Korean police, he was sentenced in January 1996 to six months' hard labor at the Onsong *An-jeon-bu* People's Safety Agency *ro-dong-dan-ryeon-dae* labor training camp. His sentence was for not working at his designated workplace, for unauthorized buying and selling, and for an old assault they dredged up from his military record. (Mr. Yoo thinks he would have been given a longer sentence if not for his military service record.)

In May 1995, with one month left to go in his six-month sentence, Yoo was given a temporary holiday release. But he became inebriated during the holiday festivities and was late returning to the labor-training camp. For this infraction, he was hung upside-down for three hours. All of the other one-hundred-odd prisoners at the labor-training center/mobile labor brigade had to march past and hit him while he was hanging. Following his collective beating, Mr. Yoo was taken to an *An-jeon-bu* detention center and then sent in a group of nine prisoners to *Kyo-hwa-so* No. 22 (called "two-two" by the prisoners) in Oro-kun, South Hamgyong province, for a one-year prison term. All eight of the other prisoners in his entering group died of malnutrition and beatings from guards and other prisoners during Yoo's yearlong sentence.

Released from *Kyo-hwa-so* No. 22 in September 1997, Yoo fled to China that October. He worked in Shenyang for a South Korean company until February 2000, when he was caught by Chinese police and held in Shenyang for six weeks and then in a detention center in the town of Dandong, near the North Korean border, for another month. The Dandong police turned him over to the Sinuiju *Bo-wi-bu* State Security Agency police, who held him in an interrogation-detention facility for six weeks of questioning. Mr. Yoo was accused of working for a South Korean company; fearing execution, he initially denied the accusation.

While in the Sinuiju *ka-mok*, Yoo was kicked, beaten, and, along with five or six other prisoners in his cell, made to sit motionless under a surveillance camera for the whole day, except during meals. If the prisoners moved, they were beaten on their fingers. If observed talking, they were forced to slap each other. Only a few of the guards allowed the prisoners to stretch. Yoo described the sitting-motionless torture as being more painful than the beatings.

Mr. Yoo reports that the majority of prisoners at the Sinuiju *Bo-wi-bu* interrogation facility were women, most of whom were later sent to other detention facilities in their hometowns. While he was detained in Sinuiju in mid-2000, seven newly repatriated women were brought in, four of whom were pregnant and shortly after taken away. He later met one woman from this group in China; she told him that the four who had been taken away were subjected to forced abortions.

Yoo finally admitted to his jailers that he had worked in China for a South Korean-owned company. He also convinced them all that the other employees were Chinese or Korean-Chinese, which seemed to matter to his jailers. He was taken to Pyongyang *Bo-wi-bu* State Security Agency center for additional interrogations, where, he reports, other imprisoned persons were high-ranking officials and where there was no torture.

After enduring two weeks of interrogation in Pyongyang, he was sent to a State Security Agency detention facility in his hometown of Onsong for the month of August. He was then transferred to the Onsong *An-jeon-bu* police jail for twenty days, before being sent in October to the *ro-dong-dan-ryeon-dae* labor-training center No. 55 in Youngkwang-kun, South Hamgyong province. This was for a one-year sentence of hard labor. Yoo became so ill that in January 2001, he was released on temporary home sick leave.

Upon recovery, he was supposed to return to the labor-training camp/mobile labor brigade to complete his term, but he slipped across the Tumen River and fled to China instead. Mr. Yoo recovered in Shenyang for two months and then made his way to Mongolia. He was caught by the Mongolian border police and held for three days without food, but was then released.

He went to Ulan Bator, and with the help of South Koreans at the consulate there, was able to board a plane to Seoul on May 20, 2001.

TESTIMONY: *Kyo-hwa-so* No. "Two-Two," Oro-kun, South Hamgyong Province

Work in 1996 at *Kyo-hwa-so* No. 22 consisted mostly of carrying rocks to a nearby river and constructing stone embankments that would allow a hydroelectric station to generate electricity. Eight hundred to 1,000 men and up to 100 women labored there while serving unusually short (for *kyo-hwa-so* prisoners) sentences of one to two years.

As at other *kyo-hwa-so*, there was, Mr. Yoo reports, a very high turnover rate at *Kyo-hwa-so* No. 22, owing to the high rate of deaths in detention. Yoo entered prison in a group of nine prisoners. Within the year, he was the only one of the nine who had not died from malnutrition, forced labor, and beatings by guards and other prisoners. The prisoners were organized to beat each other, most commonly by prison work-group or sub-group leaders, who would beat other prisoners if they worked too slowly or walked too slowly to or from their worksites.

Prisoners were provided several spoonfuls a day of powdered corn mixed with wheat, along with salted cabbage-leaf soup. Those who died of malnutrition were mostly prisoners whose families did not visit them to bring extra food.

Of twenty persons in Cell No. 7 at the *kyo-hwa-so,* four died of malnutrition within a year. Other overcrowded cells held up to sixty or seventy prisoners, often with two persons sharing one blanket. The cells were categorized by offense or the number of convictions. Prisoners at *Kyo-hwa-so* No. 22 had been sentenced for theft, assault, fraud, gambling, or opium addiction, as well as "border crossing." There were no public executions at *Kyo-hwa-so* No. 22 during Yoo's year long there, although there were suicides and attempted suicides by prisoners seeking to end their suffering.

WITNESS: Ms. Ji Hae-nam

Kyo-hwa-so No. 1, Kaechon, South Pyongan Province (July 1993–September 1995)

Ms. Ji Hae-nam was born in 1949 in Namun-ri, Hamhung City, South Hamgyong province. At one point, she worked as a Korean Workers' Party propaganda cadre, visiting factories to explain party policy and exhort factory workers, sometimes through patriotic work songs, to meet their production quotas. But after the 13th Party Congress in 1989, her faith in the Party began to waver. A decade of hardship began shortly thereafter.

At the time, a North Korean TV show mocking former South Korean President Park Chung-hee featured one of Park's concubines singing an apparently popular South Korean pop song, "Don't Cry for Me, Younger Sister (*Hong-do*). Ms. Ji was taken with the song and its melody and memorized it. On a lunar calendar holiday coinciding with Christmas day, December 25, 1992, Ji and four other women had an evening song party in Hamju-kun, South Hamgyong province. At this party, she taught the song to the other women. Overheard by neighbors, she was reported to the authorities, and arrested for singing a South Korean song. First, Ji was taken to the *An-jeon-bu* (People's Safety Agency) jail in Hamju-kun for fifteen days, and then to the *An-jeon-bu* police jail in Myungchon-kun, North Hamgyong province. During her pre-trial detention, she was beaten and sexually abused by a detention-facility guard. Mortified at her mistreatment by the young guard, who was in his early twenties, Ji tried to commit suicide by swallowing pieces of cement.

The other four women at the song party were sentenced to eight months of forced labor. During the investigation of Mrs. Ji's role as the song leader, the charge of falsifying documents to get more food rations was added to the charge of "disrupting the socialist order"—"Article fifty-something," she recalls. She was sentenced to three years of rehabilitation-through-labor at the woman's prison *Kyo-hwa-so* No. 1 at Kaechon, South Pyongan province (for her Testimony about No. 1, see below).

After serving two years and two months of her three-year sentence, in September 1995, Mrs. Ji, along with fifty other "light crime" prisoners, was released on the occasion of the fiftieth anniversary of Korea's liberation from Japanese occupation. She returned to Hamju-kun, but as a former prisoner, felt that doors were closed

to her. As the economy deteriorated, she was unable to make ends meet as a peddler and resorted to selling her blood at transfusion centers. Hungry and disillusioned about her future prospects, she fled to China in September 1998, but she was almost immediately caught by a trafficker and sold to a physically deformed Chinese man who locked her up as a "sex toy" for seven months before she was able to escape. She then made her way to Weihai, where she worked in a restaurant and saved what little money she could. She eventually teamed up with six other North Koreans in China and stole a boat to try to get to South Korea by sea, but the engine broke down. The boat filled with water on rough seas and had to be towed back to shore by Chinese fishermen. Shortly thereafter, Ji and her fellow Korean escapees stole another boat and again set out to sea, but this boat was intercepted by the authorities and the amateur sailors turned them over to Chinese border guards.

Taken to the Dandong detention center in China, Mrs. Ji was forcibly repatriated to North Korea and sent to the *Bo-wi-bu* (National Security Agency) police jail in Sinuiju, where there were twenty-five women and thirty men—all *tal-buk-ja* ("escaped North persons"). While in this *Bo-wi-bu* jail, she was beaten with broomsticks, forced to kneel for hours at a time, and made to do the "stand-up-sit-down" exercise to the point of collapse, usually after thirty to forty minutes. Some of the younger women were kept in solitary confinement and sexually abused, Ji reports. After a month, she was sent to the Sinuiju *jip-kyul-so* (detention center). But a week later on December 25, 1999, she was released as part of a larger pardon for persons repatriated from China.

Fearing she would be constantly watched and possibly re-arrested, Ji made her way to

Musan. In January 2000, she crossed the frozen Tumen River back into China. This time, her luck turned. She found work in a company managed by a South Korean. She then met a South Korean pastor who assisted a group of North Korean refugees, including Ji, in making their way to South Korea. The group went from Weihai to Beijing to Kunming in southern China. Caught by the Chinese police near the Vietnam border, they successfully passed themselves off as Korean-Chinese and walked overnight over a mountain path into Vietnam. By train, by motorbike, and on foot they made their way down through Southeast Asia and on to Seoul, where they obtained asylum.

During her interview for this report, which lasted all afternoon in a human rights NGO office in Seoul, Ji spoke in rapid anger as she described the conditions of *Kyo-hwa-so* No. 1 at Kaechon. She laughed as she recounted her misadventures on the high seas in stolen, leaky boats that had almost no chance of actually crossing the West Sea (also called the Yellow Sea) to South Korea. And she fought back tears as she referred to the sexual harassments and violations she endured in custody and as a trafficked person. For the last question of the interview, the Korean-English translator asked Mrs. Ji if she ever again sang the song, "Don't Cry for Me, *Hong-do*." Straightaway she replied, "Oh yes, and now without fear."

TESTIMONY: *Kyo-hwa-so* No. 1, Kaechon, South Pyongan Province

Surrounded by a 4-meter (13-foot) wall topped with barbed wire, *Kyo-hwa-so* No. 1 held roughly 1,000 women prisoners who made clothing and leather goods during Ji's imprisonment. (Shortly before her arrival, hundreds of women had been transferred to another prison, she was told by other inmates.) The prisoners were divided into nine work divisions and smaller work units. Two work divisions made shoes and leather bags. Men from another prison were brought in to prepare the leather. As the leatherwork was the worst work, it was the repeat offenders and prison rule-breakers—some seventy to eighty women—who were assigned to the leather divisions. Ji's offense was essentially political, but many other prisoners had been convicted of theft, fraud, murder, adultery, and prostitution.

While most women worked in sewing lines, other work units were organized for cooking, construction, cleaning, maintenance, farming outside the prison compound, and a mobile "day-labor unit." Each work unit was given a production quota that required hard, fast work. Talking was not allowed on the sewing lines, and "on a daily basis," the women guards or wardens would kick or beat women prisoners who worked too slowly in front of the other prisoners. Minor rule-breakers were given less desirable jobs or reduced rations. Worse offenders were placed in tiny punishment cells where they were unable to lie down or stand up.

Working hours were from eight in the morning until six in the evening, followed by hour-and-a-half unit-wide self-criticism sessions, both *saeng-hwal-chong-hwa* (daily-life criticism) and *sang-ho-*

bi-pan (mutual criticism). There were incentives and rewards for the prisoners to spy and tattle on each other, and the prisoners did so. According to Ji, the theory of the prison was that with their strength and spirit broken by hard labor, the prisoners would repent through self-criticism and change their way of thinking.

The most salient characteristic of this prison was the inadequate food rations. Each day, prisoners were given a palm-sized ball of cornmeal and some cabbage-leaf soup. According to Ji, seventy percent of the prisoners suffered from malnutrition, and during her two years of imprisonment, a fifth of the prisoners—namely those without nearby families to bring them extra food—died of starvation and malnutrition-related disease.

WITNESS: Mrs. Lee Soon-ok

Kyo-hwa-so No. 1, Kaechon, South Pyongan Province (1987–1994)

Mrs. Lee Soon-ok was born in 1947 into a privileged and stalwart Korean Workers' Party family. Her grandfather had fought in Kim Il-sung's Manchurian army against the Japanese occupation of Korea. Her son was enrolled in Kim Il-sung University in Pyongyang, open only to children of the elite. Trained as an accountant, Mrs. Lee rose to become a supervisor in the No. 65 Distribution Center in Onsong, North

Hamgyong province, which distributed Chinese-manufactured fabrics to party and state officials. She was arrested in 1986 in what she believes was a power struggle between the Workers' Party, whose members run the nationwide distribution system, and the public security bureau police, who were not satisfied with the amount of goods being provided to them by the distribution centers. She was charged with theft and bribery and held for seven months in the Onsong *Bo-wi-bu* State Security Agency jail, where she was tortured severely because she refused to confess to the allegations against her. Then, upon her expulsion from the Party, she was transferred to a People's Safety Agency provincial interrogation center, where she was held for another seven months and further tortured.

To escape even further torture and threats against her family members, Mrs. Lee ultimately agreed to sign a confession. Afterwards, she was given a public trial and sentenced to fourteen years at *Kyo-hwa-so* No. 1, located at Kaechon, South Pyongan province, where, among other things, the prisoners manufactured garments. Though she originally worked in the ordinary sewing lines, she was eventually transferred because of her accounting and managerial experience to the administrative office of the prison. Here, she had the opportunity to observe and learn a great deal more about how the forced-labor penitentiary was run.

After her release, in February 1994, Mrs. Lee and her son fled from North Korea to China, eventually arriving in South Korea in December 1995 via Hong Kong. Once in South Korea, she wrote a prison memoir, *Eyes of the Tailless Animals:*

Prison Memoirs of a North Korean Woman,[93] which names numerous persons who died under torture in the jails of Onsong and from various mistreatments at Kaechon prison labor camp.

Mrs. Lee's testimony for this report was drawn from her published prison memoir as well as from a personal interview.

TESTIMONY: *Kyo-hwa-so* No. 1, Kaechon, South Pyongan Province

Located in the corner of a valley surrounded by mountains in Kaechon, South Pyongan province, *Kyo-hwa-so* No. 1 is a prison complex holding, at the time of Mrs. Lee's imprisonment, about 6,000 prisoners. A high wall with an electrified wire fence surrounds the complex. It includes prisoner dormitories, a large two-story factory, and office buildings for guards and prison officials.[94]

The other prisoners, at the time of Mrs. Lee's imprisonment, included convicted criminals, citizens convicted of not obeying government rules, and Mrs. Lee reports, some 250 Korean women who had voluntarily "repatriated" from Japan in November of 1987. Some women, reportedly, were housewives convicted of stealing food for their families as the North Korean production and distribution system started its decline.

93 Published in Korean by Chunji Media, Seoul, in 1996, and in English by Living Sacrifice Book Company, Bartlesville, Oklahoma, in 1999.

94 Mrs. Lee Soon-ok was imprisoned at the same place as Mrs. Ji Hae-nam, whose testimony precedes Mrs. Lee's in this report, and only several months apart. The two women were interviewed separately and did not know each other. Lee's figures for the prison population at *Kyo-hwa-so* No. 1 include both male prisoners from a nearby prison and women prisoners.

Prisoners were supposed to get rations of some 700 grams (25 ounces) per day consisting of corn, rice, and beans. Instead, the guards ate the rice and beans, leaving each prisoner with only some 100 grams (3.5 ounces) of corn per meal, or a meager 300 grams (11 ounces) per day. Constant and severe hunger was the norm, and the dehumanizing environment led the prisoners to fight each other for scraps of food.

The primary prison-labor occupations at *Kyo-hwa-so* No.1 during Lee's imprisonment were garment and shoe manufacturing. Shoemaking was considered by the prisoners to be the worse of the two occupations because of the hard labor involved in cutting and sewing leather and because of the toxic glue used in the shoes. The garment factory initially made army uniforms. Later, it produced bras for export to the Soviet Union, doilies for export to Poland, hand-knit sweaters for export to Japan, and paper flowers for export to France.

The women's garment factories were organized into various departments: fabric cutting, sewing lines, machinery maintenance, and facility services. Most departments had some 250 to 300 members, and each department had a supervisor, record-keeper, and messenger. The departments were organized into units of fifty to sixty prisoners, and each unit divided into work teams of five to seven prisoners, with one prisoner assigned to be the work-team leader. Each work team did everything as a group: eating, sleeping, even toilet breaks. Newcomers had difficulty adjusting to the group toilet-break regimen. Initially unable to contain themselves, these prisoners would have to remain sitting at their sewing line workstations in their soiled clothing.

The whole group would be punished for the infraction of one of its members, a common infraction being the failure to meet individual or group production quotas. The most common and immediate punishment was reduced food rations. Frequently the threat of reduced food rations drove the women prisoners to work through constant pain. In winter, hands and fingers numb from cold were prone to accidents from the sewing needles and scissors. Mindful of their production quotas, prisoners continued at their workstations, doubly fearful that their dripping blood would soil the garments.

WITNESS: Former Prisoner # 6

Kyo-hwa-so No. 77, Danchon, South Hamgyong Province (Late 1980s)

Former Prisoner # 6 was born in 1960 in South Pyongan province. While in the North Korean military, he was a low level participant in a scheme within his military unit. It diverted the profit from goods that had been imported to North Korea from Japan and then re-exported to China to personal gain. Dismissed from the army after almost a year of military detention, he was convicted by a civilian "People's Judiciary" in Dukchun and sentenced for two years to *Kyo-hwa-so* No. 77 near Danchon, South Hamgyong province. The camp was a gold-mining labor camp where some 2,000 out of

roughly 7,000 to 8,000 prisoners died of mining accidents, malnutrition, and malnutrition-related diseases during the two years Former Prisoner # 6 was imprisoned there, in the late 1980s.

Former Prisoner # 6 mined gold for three months and then spent six months in the prison "health clinic" before serving the remainder of his sentence working in the prison cafeteria. He was released in 1987. He later fled to China, where he lived for several years before arriving in South Korea in 2001.

TESTIMONY: *Kyo-hwa-so* No. 77

According to Former Prisoner # 6, there was a large prison-labor *Kyo-hwa-so* No. 55 at Chunma, South Hamgyong province. However, that camp was so overcrowded that a number of prisoners there were transferred to *Kyo-hwa-so* No. 77, a *kyung-jae-bum* (economic criminal) re-education prison-labor campsite. The camp was located in the mountains between Daeheung and Geomtuk in South Hamgyong province. During the time when Former Prisoner # 6 was imprisoned, *Kyo-hwa-so* No. 77 held some 7,000 to 8,000 prisoners, all male, most of whom were serving three-year sentences.

The *kyo-hwa-so* was divided into units of 800 to 1,000 prisoners, and these units were divided into sub-units of 60 to 100 prisoners. In the unit of Former Prisoner # 6, some 15 to 20 prisoners were persons imprisoned for going to China, but most were prisoners convicted of what would be criminal offenses in any country. About half of the prisoners who came into this unit were already malnourished and ill from below-subsistence-level food rations while under pre-trial and pre-sentence detention. At *Kyo-hwa-so* No. 77 the prisoners were fed daily only a small coffee-cup-sized ball of mixed corn, rice, and beans along with a watery salted-cabbage soup. (These below-subsistence-level food rations preceded the mid-1990's famine in North Korea.) The prisoners slept in wooden dormitories holding between 60 and 70 persons.

Most prisoners at *Kyo-hwa-so* No. 77 mined gold. Some of the mineshafts dated back to the early days of the Japanese occupation of Korea in the early 1900s. Accessing the veins of mineable gold required descending and, later, ascending a wooden staircase 500 meters (1,640 feet) in length, using gas lanterns for light. Deaths from mining accidents were a daily occurrence, including multiple deaths resulting from the partial collapse of mineshafts.

Huge numbers of prisoners were so severely malnourished that after a short period of hard labor, they could no longer work in the mines and were sent to the clinic or "hospital" section of the prison camp. At times, this section would hold up to 1,000 prisoners. Some prisoners intentionally injured themselves to get out of the mines. Prisoners stayed at the clinic from one to six months, but the clinic was mostly a place to await death. During the detention of Former Prisoner # 6, nearly a third of the prisoners died within their first month at the clinic. Sometimes, if a prisoner was near death, he would be released to die at home, in an effort to reduce the extremely high number of deaths in detention. Thirty to fifty new prisoners were brought in every week to keep the mine going.

The prisoners themselves considered *Kyo-hwa-so* No. 77 to be a death camp, in that they did not expect to live until the completion of their (typically) three-year sentences. Nonetheless, the sub-units had a lecture and self-criticism session once a week, on Saturday or Sunday before the evening meal, when prisoners would confess their wrongdoings and shortcomings. During these sessions, the entire sub-unit would stand, except for the confessing prisoner, who would kneel in front of the group, facing the guards. Once every month there was a unit-wide criticism session to discuss production shortcomings.

There were public executions in front of the entire camp of persons caught trying to escape, steal from the prison warehouse, or inflict injuries on themselves. During public executions, the guards were very heavily armed.

WITNESS: Former Prisoner # 3

Kyo-hwa-so No. 3, Sinuiju, North Pyongan Province (late 1980s and early 1990s)

Former Prisoner # 3 was arrested as a young man for assault and battery. After what he described as a fair trial, he was convicted for a crime he admits he committed and was sentenced to ten years of imprisonment. He served from the early/middle 1980s to the early/middle 1990s at three separate prison facilities, including *Kyo-hwa-so* No. 8 at Yongdam, Kangwon province; and *Kyo-hwa-so* No. 3 in Sinuiju, North Pyongan province.

At Yongdam *Kyo-hwa-so* No. 8, some 3,000 prisoners manufactured bicycles, but most of the prisoners were transferred to a Danchon, South Hamgyong province to mine kiln-fire stones to be used in steel-making furnaces. At Danchon, prisoners died daily from the fumes emanating from the kilns and heated stones. After two years, when additional stockpiles of stones were no longer needed, many prisoners, including Former Prisoner # 3, were transferred to a prison-labor camp in Sinuiju, *Kyo-hwa-so* No. 3, where the prisoners made clothes.

After his release from the Sinuiju *kyo-hwa-so* in the early/middle 1990s, Former Prisoner # 3 carefully planned an escape from North Korea. He fled to China in 1998, slowly made his way down through Southeast Asia, and arrived in South Korea in August 2000.

TESTIMONY: *Kyo-hwa-so* No. 3, Sinuiju, North Pyongan Province

In the early 1990s, roughly 2,500 male prisoners were being held in *Kyo-hwa-so No. 3* in Sinuiju, North Pyongan province, a city on the North Korean border with China sometimes featured in the news as the site of a future "free-enterprise zone." The inmates made prison uniforms and mined stones and gold. Some of the inmates were arrested for border crimes—visiting and/or transporting goods to and from China. However, most were ordinary convicted criminals. Rations were meager: only some 450 grams (16 ounces)

per day of rice mixed with beans. Many prisoners died in the winter from malnutrition, scabies and other skin diseases, and paratyphoid. Prisoners were beaten by guards. Other infractions and mistakes resulted in longer prison sentences. Those who attempted and failed to escape, or who initially succeeded in escaping but were caught, were brought back for public execution, after which their corpses would be displayed for a day.

WITNESS: Former Prisoner #12

Hoeryong *Kyo-hwa-so*, North Hamgyong Province (1991–1995)

Former Prisoner # 12, a forty-three year old native of Chongjin, North Hamgyong province, was a truck driver when he was involved in a fistfight in 1991. A day after the altercation, the other person involved died from injuries sustained during the fight. As a result, Former Prisoner # 12 was tried, convicted, and sentenced to six to ten years imprisonment in a *ro-dong-kyo-hwa-so* (labor-prison) located in a mountainous area, roughly 40 kilometers (25 miles) from Hoeryong in North Hamgyong province. Prisoners mined copper, logged, manufactured furniture, and did farming work. Because of his previous occupation, Former Prisoner #12 was made a truck driver and repairman. It was a prison job that provided much greater mobility within the prison camp than that afforded to most other prisoners.

Former Prisoner # 12 did not protest his trial or conviction. While he had not intended to fatally injure the man he had fought, he admitted he had committed a crime for which he should be punished. He was imprisoned for four years, from 1991 to 1995. According to his testimony, so many prisoners died of malnutrition and related diseases in 1993 that prison officials allowed gravely ill prisoners home-leave in 1994 and 1995, to cut down on the number of deaths in detention. Former Prisoner # 12's weight declined from 80 kilograms (176 pounds) in 1991 to 35 kilograms (77 pounds) in 1995. He admits that, knowing of the sickness-release policy, he did not engage in the frantic search for anything edible that characterized most prisoners' experiences.

After returning to his home for two months to regain his strength, he fled to China where he lived among Korean-Chinese in Harbin for five years, before going to South Korea by a dangerous ship route in 2000.

TESTIMONY: Hoeryong *Kyo-hwa-so*, North Hamgyong Province

Hoeryong *kyo-hwa-so* is located in a mountainous area of North Hamgyong province and associated with the town of Hoeryong, even though it is some 40 kilometers (25 miles) away. Former Prisoner # 12 used the term *ro-dong-kyo-hwa-so* when describing the prison because the roughly 1,500 prisoners there were required to do hard labor: primarily copper mining, but also logging and furniture making. Convicts reportedly labored from five in the morning until five in the evening, mining not all that much copper but suffering many accidents to get it. Every day after work there was a self-criticism session, which Former Prisoner # 12 described as extremely petty, and at which time prisoners always had to find some mistake to confess.

Most prisoners at the camp were convicted criminals sentenced to anywhere from one to fifteen years, although in 1992, a number of "political prisoners" arrived. Some sixty prisoners shared a sleeping dormitory. The prison camp also had 1.5-meter by 1.5-meter (5-foot by 5-foot) "punishment cells," where scantily clad prisoners were placed on one-quarter food rations for one week or more. Confinement in the tiny punishment cells was extremely painful.

Prisoners were also organized and compelled to beat other prisoners who committed various infractions. The highlight of prison-camp life was the rare occasion when prisoners would be taken outside the prison walls for exercise walks, at which time they were able to eat plants and grass. The most salient feature of Hoeryong *kyo-hwa-so* was its death rate. Below-subsistence-level food rations coupled with harsh living conditions and hard labor resulted between 1991 and 1995 in the deaths of one-quarter to one-third of the inmates. So many prisoners died in 1993 that near-dead prisoners were allowed home-leave in 1994 and early 1995 to reduce the number of deaths in detention. Others were released in 1995 as part of an amnesty in honor of Kim Jong-il's birthday.

WITNESS: Former Prisoner #19

Kyo-hwa-so No. 4, Kangdong-kun, South Pyongan Province (Late 1996)

Former Prisoner # 19 grew up near Danchon, South Hamgyong province. In the mid-1990s, when North Korea's production/distribution system broke down and he was without employment or income, he set up a stall to make and sell what he called "Chinese style" rice and corn liquor. Arrested in late 1996, he was tried, convicted, and sentenced to a six-year term at *Kyo-hwa-so* No. 4. After working for three months at a limestone furnace, he contracted a lung disease and was transferred to the prison-camp clinic. In those three months, his weight had dropped nearly 30 kilograms (66 pounds). Believing that he would not survive his six-year sentence and observing that, to reduce the number of deaths in detention, extremely sick prisoners were being sent home to recuperate, he drank dirty water. He developed chronic diarrhea as a result and was given a temporary sick release. Away from the limestone furnace, his lungs recovered, and after regaining fifteen kilograms (33 pounds), he fled to China instead of returning to prison.

TESTIMONY: *Kyo-hwa-so* No. 4

Kyo-hwa-so No. 4 is located in Samdung-ri, Kangdong-kun, in South Pyongan province. During Former Prisoner # 19's detention there, some 7,000 convicts mined limestone and made cement in a factory originally built by the Japanese during their occupation of Korea. The prison camp was roughly two kilometers (1.24 miles) long by 1.5 kilometers (0.93 miles) wide and was surrounded by a barbed-wire fence.

All of the prisoners at *Kyo-hwa-so* No. 4 were men, most of them sentenced to anywhere from five to twenty years. The prisoners considered their sentences a cruel hoax, as they did not expect to live long enough to serve their time. Some prisoners mined limestone in the adjacent mountain. Others crushed the rocks or fired the lime in large kilns. Work started at seven in the morning and lasted until five in the evening, except in the crushing and heating units, where work often continued until ten at night. All aspects of the work were hard labor in dangerous conditions, with prisoners frequently suffering chest ailments and lung diseases from limestone dust.

Once a week there was an evening criticism session in groups of up to 500 men where the prison officials would criticize the prisoner called to stand in front of the group of prisoners. There were also lectures on Kim Jong-il and his policies. Infractions were punished with reduced rations, nominally extended sentences, and detainment in miniature punishment cells. During the eight months that Former Prisoner # 19 was held at *Kyo-hwa-so* No. 4, there were eight public executions in the prison. He did not recall the particular offenses of these eight executed persons. However, he did cite the four types of persons who would be executed at the prison camp: prisoners caught trying to escape, prisoners caught after they escaped, persons who committed crimes while on "sick leave," and prisoners who had committed capital crimes elsewhere and were brought to *Kyo-hwa-so* No. 4 for execution.

Food rations consisted of a mere 50 grams (under 2 ounces) per meal of mixed corn and wheat, plus cabbage-leaf soup. Former Prisoner # 19 weighed 76 kilograms (168 pounds) upon his entry into the prison camp. After three months, his weight had plummeted to somewhere around 45 kilograms (99 pounds). He was sure that most prisoners weighed less than 50 kilograms (110 pounds).

Prisoners slept head to toe on wooden floors in groups of 50 to 100. The unsanitary living conditions—there was no bathing or changing of clothes, and Former Prisoner # 19 says he was able to wash only his face two to three times a month—led to *Kyo-hwa-so* No. 4's particular idiosyncrasy: the cement dust in the prisoners clothing, commingled with dirt and sweat, would cause the tattered fabric to harden, resulting in skin abrasions and infections.

The most salient prison characteristic, however, was more common: exorbitantly high death rates. In Former Prisoner # 19's eight months there, of the eighty persons in his work unit, three prisoners died in work accidents, ten died of malnutrition and disease, and twenty were sent home on "sick leave" in order to reduce the high numbers of deaths in detention.

See page 226 for the satellite photograph of Kangdong Kyo-hwa-so No. 4. The satellite photograph was located by Curtis Melvin of North Korea Economy Watch using the prisoner's sketch below.

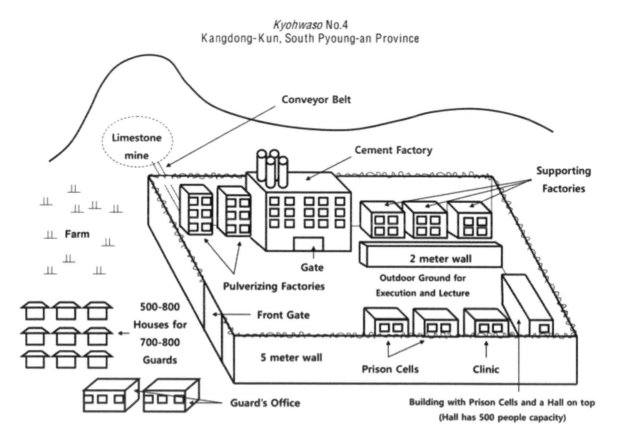

Kyohwaso No.4
Kangdong-Kun, South Pyoung-an Province

PART FOUR

DETENTION FACILITIES AND PUNISHMENTS FOR NORTH KOREANS FORCIBLY REPATRIATED FROM CHINA: VIOLENCE AGAINST WOMEN

Part Four examines in greater detail testimony from North Koreans who were forcibly repatriated from China back to North Korea. After being handed over to North Korean police, the repatriated persons are detained and interrogated in one or more police facilities generally known as *ku-ryu-jang*. Following interrogation and detention, which frequently includes beatings and systematic torture, many of the forcibly repatriated Koreans are assigned, often without judicial process, to short-term forced labor. This occurs in frequently brutalizing detention facilities known as *jip-kyul-so* (provincial or sub-provincial detention facilities) or to mobile corvee labor brigades known as *ro-dong-dan-ryeon-dae* (labor training centers). Other repatriated persons, whose cases are deemed more serious and often involve a political dimension, are sent to the longer term, felony level, forced-labor penitentiary-like *kyo-hwa-so* prisons, or "re-revolutionizing areas" of the *kwan-li-so* political penal labor colonies.

In recent years, young women have comprised a substantial portion of repatriated persons.[95] Their testimonies report sexual humiliation, trafficking and violence, and the unconscionable abuse of racially motivated forced abortion and infanticide.

This section will first provide a description of North Koreans who cross into China and their situation there, followed by testimonies of those forcibly repatriated and arbitrarily detained in North Korea for having exercised their human right to leave their country.

Why They Go: The Flow of North Koreans to China

For several reasons, over the last fifteen to twenty years, large numbers of North Koreans have been going to China. The largest number of North Korean "border crossers" were people simply seeking to survive,[96] by searching for food or employment to help sustain their families in North Korea, particularly during the acute famine in the 1990s. In the late 1990s, estimates of the number of North Koreans who fled to China ran as high as 200,000 to 300,000 persons. Almost all observers estimate the current number to be considerably lower.

Additionally, many North Koreans crossed, and continue to cross, the China border to engage in small-scale import-export commerce – bartering or trading Korean goods, often food or forest products of one sort or another, for processed food or consumer goods manufactured in China.

Other North Koreans, having a well-founded fear of persecution should they remain within North Korea, cross the border to seek asylum.

---

95 By some accounts, women comprise some 70 to 75 percent of forcibly repatriated persons in recent years.

96 See *The North Korean Refugee Crisis: Human Rights and International Response*, HRNK, Washington DC, 2006; *Perilous Journeys: The Plight of North Korean Refugees in China and Beyond*, International Crisis Group, Brussels, 2006; *Acts of Betrayal: The Challenge of Protecting North Koreans in China*, Refugees International, Washington DC, 2005.

These asylum-seekers include persons who previously went to China for food or employment, but were apprehended by Chinese police and repatriated to North Korea. Upon completion of their post-repatriation imprisonment and forced labor, they conclude that they will always be under suspicion, surveillance, and persecution in their country of origin, so they again flee to China. But now, they are in search of asylum, ultimately in South Korea.

To these "push factors" should be added "pull-factors" such as family reunions. North Koreans who have already found refuge and asylum in South Korea use their resettlement grants from the South Korean government, or their employment income, to finance the escape and transit of their family members still in North Korea.

To an extent, these outward flows of persons from North Korea are the Northeast Asian manifestation of global labor migrations from poorer, often rural areas, to more developed, often urbanized areas, where there is a demand for industrial or service workers. These labor migrations operate irrespective of domestic or international borders. Young Chinese from rural areas of Northeast China migrate to the manufacturing cities and sites along the Chinese coast. Ethnic Koreans in northeast China migrate to South Korea to work in construction trades or as waitresses and domestic workers. And young North Koreans, particularly from North and South Hamgyong provinces, where industrial production and the state-run public food distribution system substantially collapsed, migrate to Northeast China in search of food or employment.

However, labor flows in Northeast Asia involving North Korea differ from this global phenom-

> *"Upon completion of their post-repatriation imprisonment and forced labor, they conclude that they will always be under suspicion, surveillance, and persecution in their country of origin, so they again flee to China."*

enon in two ways. First, unlike most countries that export labor and welcome the hard currency remittances from its citizens who work in foreign countries, the DPRK often confiscates (sometimes brutally, as can be seen in the testimonies below) such earnings when it can. Second, even more fundamentally, North Korea prohibits its citizens from leaving the DPRK. This is a direct violation of Article 13(2) of the Universal Declaration of Human Rights, which asserts, "Everyone has the right to leave any country, including his own, and to return to his country." It is a direct violation of the same provision in Article 12 of the International Covenant on Civil and Political Rights to which the DPRK, as a ratifying State Party, has a legal obligation to respect.[97] There is, it should be noted, no corresponding "right to enter" an adjacent state, as control over immigration remains within the sovereignty of states. However, the DPRK is unique in criminalizing emigration. The severe punishments inflicted on North Koreans who have exercised their "right to leave" their country of origin are described below.

---

97 Thus, the UN Human Rights Committee, which oversees the implementation of the International Covenant on Civil and Political Rights, has long recommended the DPRK to rectify its domestic laws in conflict with this provision of the Covenant.

Notwithstanding the risks of severe punishment, North Koreans continue to exercise their "right to leave." They do so by surreptitiously wading across the shallow areas of the Tumen River that constitute the border between North Korea and China, or by crossing the frozen river on foot during the winter. Border crossing often includes bribes to the border guards.

The Situation of North Koreans in China

Having entered China without visas or formal travel documents, irrespective of the validity of their claims for protection (see below), the North Koreans are officially regarded as illegal immigrants. They are subject to deportation if apprehended by Chinese police. As the North Koreans seek food, employment, shelter and temporary asylum, they strive to blend into the communities of the approximately two million ethnic Koreans long resident in China, along with the Han ethnic majority in the area of Northeast China formerly known as Manchuria.[98]

There is also a great deal of cross-border commerce between North Korea and China, some of which is officially organized by and through North Korean state enterprises or state import-export companies. But when the North Korean production system broke down in the 1990s and people were no longer being compensated for their assigned work, large numbers of North Koreans resorted to buying and selling various goods across the border. Technically, private cross-border buying and selling by North Koreans does not have legal standing as the North Koreans have crossed into China without DPRK permission or authorization.

Three social phenomena in the northeast provinces of China directly affect the situation of North Koreans residing, working or doing business there. First is the ease of encountering South Koreans and South Korean culture such as TV or radio programs, movies, newspapers and magazines. Second is the coming into contact with ethnic Korean-Chinese religious believers and their churches, which often help the border crossers. Third is the likelihood of North Korean women being lured or caught by traffickers and forced into prostitution or sold as brides, often to rural Chinese farmers in areas where women are in short supply.

Border crossing to China without authorization from state or party officials is considered a criminal offense. Furthermore, contact by North Koreans with Chinese-Korean churches, contact with South Korean (or Korean-American) citizens, or exposure to South Korean culture are regarded by DPRK authorities as political offenses as well as a technical violations of North Korean law.

"Border crossing to China without authorization from state or party officials is considered a criminal offense."

---

98 The Yanbian Korean Autonomous Prefecture is located in Jilin province. There are also numbers of ethnic Koreans in Liao-ning and Heilongjiang provinces, and Korean communities in the Chaoyang district in Beijing.

Encountering South Koreans or South Korean Culture

Northeast China hosts large numbers of visiting South Koreans working, studying or traveling in the three northeast provinces of Liaoning, Jilin, and Heilongjiang: businessmen and women, students, famine relief and refugee workers, ministers and missionaries, journalists and tourists. (Mt. Paektu, a famous mountain considered the source of Korean civilization, straddles the Chinese-DPRK border, and large numbers of South Koreans visit Mt. Paektu from the Chinese side).[99] With an existing large ethnic Korean-Chinese population, and substantial numbers of visiting or transient South Koreans, South Korean TV shows, movies, radio programs, pop-music videos and recordings are all easily accessible in northeast China, as are internet cafes with easy access to Korean language, South Korean-based websites.

Along with encountering South Koreans and South Korean radio, pop songs, TV or movies, it has become commonplace for North Koreans arriving in China to seek out Korean-Chinese churches. In the late nineteenth century and throughout the twentieth century, Protestant Christianity was embraced by many Koreans, including ethnic Koreans in China, and particularly in the northern part of the Korean peninsula. In northeast China, as in South Korea, it is the practice of the Protestant Christians to afix a simple red neon cross to their church buildings and to the otherwise secular or commercial buildings in which they rent rooms to hold worship services. Upon arrival in China, hungry, fearful, or lost North Koreans have long known to seek out the buildings with the red neon crosses to find people who will help them find food, shelter or employment.

Trafficking of North Korean Women

North Korean women are particularly vulnerable to trafficking. Persons leaving North Korea know well the severe punishment that awaits them if they are caught in China and forcibly repatriated to the DPRK. Forced repatriation is a powerful, coercive lever used by traffickers against North Korean women who are in China without North Korean travel documents. Second, the gender imbalance due to China's one-child policy and the fact that rural Chinese women are leaving Northeast China to get factory jobs in the southern coastal cities drive demand for women as "wives" for rural Chinese men. Lastly, women are lured from North Korea with false promises of gainful employment.

At grave risk if turned over to the Chinese police and repatriated to North Korea, the women are preyed upon by traffickers. They have no protection against being sold as brides. These women accept this fate as preferable to immediate forced repatriation, hoping either that they can make a go of their commercially brokered, involuntary marriages in China, or else flee when the chance arises.[100] However, even when the North Korean "brides" accept their forced, involuntary marriages and bear children, they are not often

---

99 In comparison with the two or three weekly flights from Beijing to Pyongyang, there are literally scores of direct, non-stop flights every day from Seoul and Busan to the key cities of Northeast China, and scores more daily flights from South Korea to Northeast China that transit through Beijing.

100   See HRNK, *Lives for Sale: Personal Accounts of Women Fleeing North Korea to China*, Washington, DC, 2009 for details.

eligible for Chinese citizenship. In some cases, the Korean wives receive a "*hukou*" certificate, which enables some residential rights such as allowing children of this union to attend school. However, many other North Korean women are picked up by the Chinese police and forcibly repatriated. There is a noticeable frequency of pregnant women among the North Koreans forcibly repatriated to the DPRK.

Protection Denied[101]

Some of the North Koreans who flee to China are "refugees" or "asylum seekers" within the precise definition of the 1951 Refugee Convention. Many more, indeed almost all, North Koreans who flee to China fall within the definition of *refugees sur place* or "refugees in place": persons who may not have fled North Korea out of a well founded fear of persecution, but who will face severe persecution, as the testimonies below indicate, if returned to North Korea against their will.

Police in China periodically sweep through areas where undocumented North Koreans work and reside, to arrest and deport them. Foreign famine-relief workers on the Chinese side of the border have observed Chinese police buses and vans transporting deportees to North Korea. But the buses and vans often have darkened or curtained windows, so an accurate count of the deportees, even when witnesses have observed the deportations, is not possible. Neither the number of forcibly repatriated North Koreans

nor trends over time can be specified in detail, but there are literally hundreds of former North Koreans now living in South Korea who were previously refouled from China or Russia to North Korea, severely persecuted, tortured and imprisoned and who, upon release, again fled to China, intent on finding asylum in South Korea. They report that there were scores or hundreds of other "border-crossers" detained with them following their forced repatriation. These policies and practices have been in place for fifteen years or more. The numbers of North Koreans *refouled* and persecuted over this fifteen-year period for having left North Korea number in the tens of thousands.[102]

To the best available knowledge, the severe persecutions and punishments detailed below continue unabated. Absent UN High Commissioner for Refugees (UNHCR) access to the North Korean border areas inside China, and absent International Committee of the Red Cross (ICRC) access to the North Korean detention facilities along the China-DPRK border, there is no dispository or conclusive evidence that the practices described below are in remission.

While it is not presently possible to cite the

---

101 See Roberta Cohen, "Legal Grounds for Protection of North Korean Refugees," *Life and Human Rights in North Korea*, Citizen's Alliance, Vol. 57, Fall 2010.

102 In the absense of Chinese or North Korean police statistics, the number of repatriations cannot be quantified more precisely; in the late 1990s and the early 2000s, it is believed to number in the thousands per year. In the later years of the first decade of the new millenium, the numbers may have dropped to the multiple hundreds per year, reflecting the decrease in the number of North Koreans seeking refuge, shelter, food or employment in China. Journalists operating along the Chinese side of the DPRK-China border believe that the numbers increased in 2011, resulting in a renewed crackdown by special North Korean units called "Storm Corps" (*Pok-pung-gun-dan*) against border crossing and trading. Many of the formerly repatriated North Koreans interviewed for this report indicate that the police detention facilities for repatriated persons were severely overcrowded, with dozens of persons packed into cells, and sometimes overflowing into the hallways and corridors.

Protection Denied

Anyone has the right to leave any country, including his own, and to return to his country.
Article 13.2 Universal Declaration of Human Rights

Everyone shall be free to leave any country, including his own.
Article 12.2 International Covenant on Civil and Political Rights

"No State Party shall expel, return ("*refouler*") or extradite a person to another State where there are substantial grounds for believing that he would be in danger of being subjected to torture. For the purposes of determining whether there are such grounds, the competent authorities shall take into account all relevant considerations including where applicable, the existence in the State concerned of a consistent pattern of gross, flagrant or mass violations of human rights."

Article 3, Convention Against Torture, Cruel, Inhuman or Degrading Treatment or Punishment (ratified by China 4 October 1988)

[T]he term "refugee" shall apply to any person who:…owing to well-founded fear of being persecuted for reasons of race, religion, nationality, membership of a particular social group or political opinion, is outside the country of his nationality and is unable or, owing to such fear, is unwilling to avail himself of the protection of that country; or who, not having a nationality and being outside the country of his former habitual residence as a result of such events, is unable or, owing to such fear, is unwilling to return to it.

Article 1, Convention relating to the Status of Refugees, 1951

… A person who was not a refugee when he left his country, but who becomes a refugee at a later date, is called a refugee "*sur place*."

… A person may become a refugee "*sur place*" as a result of his own actions, such as ….expressing his political views in his country of residence. Whether such actions are sufficient to justify a well-founded fear of persecution must be determined by a careful examination of the circumstances. Regard should be had in particular to whether such actions may have come to the notice of the authorities of the person's country of origin and how they are likely to be viewed by those authorities.

Paragraphs 94 and 96 of the UN High Commissioner for Refugees Handbook: Procedures and Standards for Registration, 2003

No contracting state shall expel or return ("*refouler*") a refugee in any manner whatsoever to the frontier of territories where his life or freedom would be threatened on account of his race, religion, nationality, membership of a particular social group or political opinion.

Article 33, Convention relating to the Status of Refugees, 1951

precise number of forcibly repatriated North Koreans, it is possible to know what happens to many of those who are repatriated. Having been exposed to the relative freedom and prosperity in China, and completely alienated by their brutal mistreatment after being handed back to the North Korean police, many of those who survive their mistreatment flee back to China upon their release from detention and recovery from detention-related illnesses and injuries. A small number of those North Koreans who have fled the DPRK a second, or even third, time have obtained asylum in South Korea, usually after a harrowing, months-long trek south through China and then further south through Southeast Asia, before flying to Seoul. Some defectors go through Mongolia or Hong Kong. The stories of some of these individuals are told on the following pages.[103]

Forced Repatriation Corridors

The Repatriation Corridors through which North Koreans interviewed for this report were apprehended by police in China and *refouled* to North Korea where they were detained and severely mistreated.

Corridors of Forced Repatriation: Pathways to Pain, Suffering and Violence Against Women

North Koreans typically go to China by walking across the frozen river or fording the shallow stretches of the Tumen River separating China from the DPRK. Denied the protection offered by international law, they are forcibly repatriated by van or bus across the bridges that connect the two countries.[104]

On the Chinese side of the repatriation corridors are detention facilities where the North Koreans are held until a large enough group is collected for repatriation by bus or van. On the Korean side of

---

103 For more information on the situation of North Koreans in China, see "A Field Survey Report of the North Korean Refugees in China," Dr. Christine Y. Chang, The Commission to Help North Korean Refugees (CNKR), December 1999, Seoul, and "The Invisible Exodus: North Koreans in the People's Republic of China," Human Rights Watch, New York, 2002. For an expansive recent survey, see Stephan Haggard and Marcus Noland, *Witness to Transformation: Refugee Insights into North Korea*, Peterson Institute of International Economics, Washington DC, 2010.

104 Interviews for this report included fourteen persons repatriated at Onsong, six at Sinuiju, six at Musan, and one each at Hoeryong and Hyesan. Reportedly, there are also repatriations at Manpo, and small numbers of repatriations at Rason, Saebyol, and Samjang, but no repatriated persons from these places were located or interviewed for this report.

the repatriation corridors there are police stations for detaining and interrogating the repatriated Koreans. They are from the two major police agencies in North Korea: one run by the *Kuk-ga-bo-wi-bu* State Security Agency police, commonly shortened to "*Bo-wi-bu,*" which administer the *kwan-li-so* prison camps described above and another interrogation/detention facility administered by *In-min-bo-an-seong* People's Safety Agency police (commonly referred to as "*An-jeon-bu*"), who run the *kyo-hwa-so* prisons described above.

According to the testimony of former *Bo-wi-bu* agents who defected to South Korea, and who were interviewed for a report by this author for the US Commission on International Religious Freedom, the *Bo-wi-bu* interrogation-detention facilities at the repatriation corridors are administered by the counter-intelligence ("anti-spy" *ban-tam-gwa*) department of *Bo-wi-bu*.[105] Their ostensible concern is that the South Korean National Intelligence Service (NIS) is running spy networks into North Korea from the China border; and it is *Bo-wi-bu*'s job to disrupt those networks. However, it is clear from the statements made by DPRK diplomats at the United Nations that North Korean concern is far wider than "counter-intelligence" as normally understood. Rather, the concern encompasses contact with or exposure to "foreign forces."[106] And this includes virtually any contact with South Koreans or Korean-Americans or exposure to any artifact of South Korean culture (radio, TV, movies, songs, videos, etc).

The testimonies of formerly repatriated North Koreans indicate that prior to 2000, persons

forcibly returned from China could be sent either to a *Bo-wi-bu* or *An-jeon-bu* detention-interrogation facility. Since 2000, forcibly repatriated persons are sent first to the *Bo-wi-bu* interrogation/detention facilities.

Whether the interrogations are conducted by the *Bo-wi-bu* State Security Agency police or the *An-jeon-bu* police, the interrogations described by former prisoners all follow a pattern clearly outlined by Former Detainee # 22, a young man originally from Kaesong. Essentially, the authorities ask: "Why did you go to China, where did you go, and what did you do in each place?"

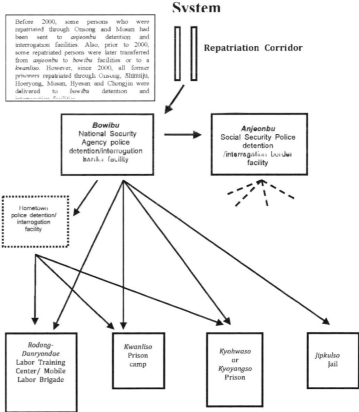

Post-Repatriation Imprisonment System

---

105 See Chapter 5, "The Policies and Practices of Repression: Testimonies of Former Security Agency Officials," *A Prison Without Walls*, US Commission on International Religious Freedom, March 2008.

106 See DPRK statement at UN on page 7 above.

And then, more ominously: "Did you meet any South Koreans?" "Did you go to a Christian church?" "Did you watch or listen to South Korean TV or radio?" and "Were you trying to go to South Korea?"

All the former detainees interviewed for this report firmly believed that an affirmative answer to any of these questions would result in execution or their being sent to a *kwan-li-so* or *kyo-hwa-so*. Therefore, they typically denied any contact with South Koreans or Christians while in China. Their denials, however, were not considered credible by their interrogators, who attempted to starve and beat admissions out of the detainees. Some of the former prisoners interviewed for this report stuck to their denials; others, broken by hunger or torture, admitted that they had met South Koreans or gone to a Christian church. One interviewee said she was in such pain that she begged her jailers to kill her to end her suffering.

At the *Bo-wi-bu* detention-interrogation station, a determination is made if the person had simply gone to China for food or employment, in which case the detainee is transferred to *An-jeon-bu*. If the case has a political component—if the person admits to having met South Koreans or watched South Korean TV or movies, or sometimes having gone to a Korean-Chinese church—the *Bo-wi-bu* police retain the detainee.

Presently, after interrogation by *Bo-wi-bu* (which can last a matter of days, or many months) the detainee is transferred to one of four places: (1) the nearby *An-jeon-bu* interrogation/detention police stations; (2) the "re-revolutionizing" zones of *kwan-li-so* Camps 15 or 18[107]; (3) one of the *kyo-hwa-so* or *kyo-yang-so* prison[108]; or, (4) one of the *ro-dong-dan-ryeon-dae* labor training centers/mobile forced-labor brigades, described further below. Sometimes detainees are sent temporarily to other interrogation/detention police stations located in their hometown for additional questioning, prior to being sent to one of the four forced-labor facilities named above.

On the basis of presently available testimony, determinative criteria that govern whether the

Schematic Repatriation Corridor

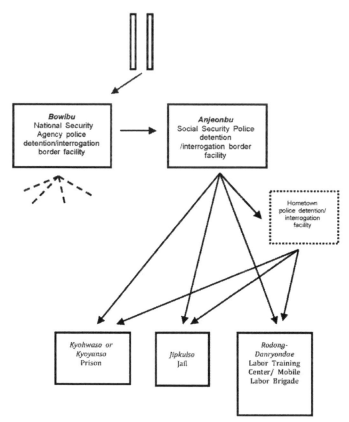

---

107 Described in Part Two as is seen on pages 25-82 above.

108 Described in Part Three on pages 83-110 above.

detainee is sent to a *kwan-li-so* or a *kyo-hwa-so* cannot be discerned. It appears to be essentially arbitrary. This is both in the legal sense of arbitrary and capricious (extra-judicial and without any "due process"), and arbitrary in the sense that the police agency interrogators seem to have considerable discretion over the prisoners' fate. The designated additional detentions appear largely a matter of happenstance.

It is possible that some repatriated detainees are sent away to the lifetime imprisonment, "total control zone" areas of *Kwan-li-so* 15 or 18, or to one of the prison-labor camps that only have lifetime "total control zones" such as Camp 22. But there is no direct testimony on this. It is also sometimes asserted that some repatriated persons are taken away for execution. But no such direct, eyewitness testimony on such executions was obtained during the research for this report. In news accounts, some publicly executed persons are denounced as "traffickers" by North Korean police officials prior to execution. It is not known if persons publicly executed for "trafficking" had been previously processed at the police stations that abut the repatriation corridors.

Detainees who are transferred from the *Bo-wi-bu* to the *An-jeon-bu* facilities are subjected to additional interrogation. Then, they are commonly transferred to police stations in their home towns. They are then transferred again to: (1) a *kyo-hwa-so* or *kyo-yang-so* prison, described in Part Three; (2) a *jip-kyul-so*, short term labor-detention facility; (3) a *ro-dong-dan-ryeon-dae* labor training centers/mobile forced-labor brigade; or, (4) on occasion to the "re-revolutionizing" section of a *kwan-li-so* political penal labor colony, described in Part Two.

Jip-kyul-so literally translates as a "gathering place." A *do-jip-kyul-so* is a provincial detention center. In reality, these are short-term hard-labor detention facilities for those serving up to six-month sentences. Several interviewees reported that the police use the *jip-kyul-so* detention centers for "small-crime" persons as well as for North Koreans forcibly repatriated from China. *Jip-kyul-so* are characterized by hard labor, such as construction work or brick-making and below-subsistence food rations, a combination that causes large numbers of deaths in detention, notwithstanding the short period of incarceration. Alternatively, prisoners receive "sick-releases," so that gravely ill prisoners will either die at home, thus reducing the number of deaths in detention, or, through the help of their families, recover at home before returning to the *jip-kyul-so* to complete their sentences.

Ro-dong-dan-ryeon-dae literally translates as "workers training corps" or "labor-training center." A descriptive translation for the *ro-dong-dan-ryeon-dae* labor training centers would be "mobile *corvee* (forced-labor) brigades." The labor-training centers for mobile labor brigades are even shorter-term *jip-kyul-so*, initially set up to accommodate the over-flow from the established detention centers caused by the large numbers of North Koreans forcibly repatriated from China. One interviewee for the first edition of *Hidden Gulag* described the labor-training centers as localized "feeder" facilities for the *jip-kyul-so*. Another interviewee for the first edition described the labor-training centers as a "not-in-the-statute-books" response to the burgeoning numbers of North Koreans traveling without authorization. These North Koreans work at enterprises other than their assigned occupations at idled state-run factories, or flee to China in response to famine in North Korea. One interviewee stated that it was becoming the practice to have separate facilities for Koreans forcibly repatriated from China because the repatriated prisoners were telling the common "light crime" criminals in the *jip-kyul-so* about the "freedom and prosperity" in China.

The labor-training centers are local, sub-district facilities where various labor or production functions are not performed on-site, but where the corvee labor brigades are housed overnight. Every morning the detainees are made to march rapidly or jog to their various and changing worksites—chanting political slogans or singing what they describe as "silly songs" praising Kim Jong-il as they march or jog along. However, it now appears that recent revisions to the DPRK legal codes have recognized the labor-training centers as part of the North Korean penal system.

Some of the repatriated persons going through this series of detention facilities have legal proceedings brought against them, although those "trials" would not meet international standards for "fair trial" or "due process." However, many of these detentions and incarcerations are entirely extra-judicial and without any legal process. On the basis of available testimony, it cannot be determined why some prisoners are given a trial while others are not. This too appears to be arbitrary, and apparently at the discretion of local police authorities.

It should not be assumed that the lifetime prison camps or the longer-term penitentiaries described in Parts Two and Three of this report are "worse" or more brutal than the short-term interrogation/detention facilities and the short-term forced-labor facilities to which the detained

repatriated North Koreans are subjected. As can be seen in the testimony, much of the worst and most systematic torture occurs in the *Bo-wi-bu* and *An-jeon-bu* interrogation facilities to which repatriated North Koreans are routinely subjected.

Nor should it be assumed that the repatriated persons deemed to have committed a political offense, such as meeting South Koreans, exposure to South Korean films, songs or TV programs, or having attended Korean-Chinese churches, are treated "worse" or more brutally than those North Koreans deemed "non-political" or "non-politicized," who went to China for food or employment. Indeed, some of the most demeaning, inhumane and brutal mistreatments are inflicted in the *An-jeon-bu* detention facilities. These are inflicted against North Korean women who have had no connection to "foreign forces" deemed hostile to the Kim Jong-il regime, such as South Koreans or Korean-Americans. North Korean women are routinely subjected to sexual humiliations. Pregnant women, including the victims of trafficking who are suspected of being impregnated by Han Chinese men, are subjected to forced abortions and infanticide.

Racially Motivated Forced Abortions and Infanticide

Indeed, along with the torture during interrogation and the high levels of deaths in detention reported by the former detainees, a particularly reprehensible phenomenon of repression is the gender-based sexual violence and racially motivated forced abortion and infanticide perpetrated against forcibly repatriated pregnant women.

According to all the refugee accounts, the North Korean police authorities make no secret of the DPRK's objective: preventing women who became pregnant in China from giving birth to "half-Chinese" babies fathered by Han Chinese, China's major ethnic group. It makes no difference if the pregnancies resulted from trafficking, or coerced or voluntary marriages between Korean women and Han Chinese men in China. In these testimonies, there seems little difference between forced-abortion and infanticide; many of the aborted fetuses are not "still born" but viable and able to survive if they had been treated as premature births.

Many of the testimonies that follow reveal how half-Chinese babies were killed.

FORCED REPATRIATION: SINUIJU CORRIDOR

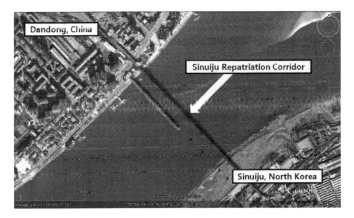

WITNESS: Ms. Choi Yong-hwa

Refouled at Sinuiju, 2002

Ms. Choi Yongh-hwa is a shy and soft-spoken woman from Hoeryong, North Hamgyong province. Before fleeing to China, Choi had lived with her father and younger brother while working in a distribution center. But as the food situation in North Korea deteriorated between 1996 and 1998, and as the country's distribution system broke down, she left that work to become a petty trader, mostly selling cuttlefish, in order to make enough money to provide food for her family. When the petty marketing did not generate enough money for food, she paid a trafficker 200 *won* to take her to China in 1998. She worked at a restaurant in Yanji, China, and then as a tour guide for visiting South Koreans in Dalian. Caught by Chinese police in Dalian, she was held for a month before being sent to Dandong, where she was turned over to North Korean police.

Interrogated by the *Bo-wi-bu* State Security Agency police in Sinuiju, Choi convincingly denied meeting South Koreans in China. She was also explicitly questioned about attending Christian churches in China. Her interrogators threatened to send her to Chongo-ri *kyo-hwa-so* in North Hamgyong province,[109] which she had heard about from a neighbor who had been sent

---

109 Described on p. 85 of this report.

there, but she ended up being sent to the *do-jip-kyul-so* provincial detention center in Sinuiju. After only ten days there, she became too ill to work, from malnutrition and exhaustion: she had been unable to sleep at night owing to infestations of maggots and lice in her sleeping quarters. Choi was released after serving two months, during which time two other detainees had died. Choi's jailers simply did not want another death in detention.

Upon release, after regaining her health, Choi crossed again into China and made her way to Dalian. She traveled west by train to Beijing, and on New Year's Day 2002, she took a train to Kunming. She was part of a group of five North Korean refugees who crossed into Myanmar (Burma) but were apprehended and turned over to the police in China, who fortunately released them after being persuaded that they were Korean-Chinese, not North Koreans. After their release, they successfully made their way through Southeast Asia. Choi obtained asylum in South Korea in March of 2002 and was interviewed for this report in Seoul in August 2002.

TESTIMONY: South Sinuiju *Do-jip-kyul-so* Provincial Detention Center (May and June 2000)

The South Sinuiju *do-jip-kyul-so* in North Pyongan province held roughly 100 detainees during Choi's detention, most of them between twenty and thirty years of age, more of them women than men. The facility was primarily for North Koreans repatriated from China who had successfully claimed no contact with South Koreans. Two cells were for men and women accused of minor crimes, and four cells held repatriated persons. Detainees performed

supervised agricultural and construction work at off-site locations. Their workday began between four-thirty and five in the morning and lasted until seven or eight at night, with half-hour breaks for breakfast, lunch, and dinner.

Meals consisted of dried corn, which the prisoners would wet, and salted radish-leaf soup. The inmates were also allowed to eat grass and other plants while working outside the detention center. Still, nourishment was insufficient. During Choi's two months in detention, two women who had been detained for three to four months died of malnutrition. Also during these two months, one female detainee was coerced into having sex with a guard.

Among the detainees were ten pregnant women, three of whom were in the eighth to ninth month of pregnancy. Choi and two other non-pregnant women were assigned to assist these three pregnant women, who were too weak to walk alone, by walking with them to a military hospital outside the detention center. The woman assisted by Choi was given a labor-inducing injection and shortly thereafter gave birth. While Choi watched in horror, the baby was suffocated with a wet towel in front of the mother, who passed out in distress. When the woman regained consciousness, both she and Choi were taken back to the detention center. The two other non-pregnant women who assisted the two other pregnant detainees told Choi that those newborns were also suffocated in front of the mothers. The explanation provided was that "no half-Han [Chinese] babies would be tolerated."

WITNESS AND TESTIMONY:

Former Detainee # 24

Refouled at Sinuiju

When interviewed for this report, Former Detainee # 24 was a sixty-six-year-old grand-mother from Chulan-district, North Hamgyong province. In 1997, her children were starving, so she fled to China with her husband, who was a former soldier, and five of her children. Two of her children were caught crossing the border, but the rest of the family lived in China for three years. Two of the children who made it with her to China were later caught and repatriated to North Korea, and her husband eventually died of natural causes. Afterward, she lived with her granddaughter in Yanji until apprehended by Chinese police while visiting Dandong.

Former Detainee # 24 was forcibly repatriated in a group of fifty North Koreans, some of whom were pregnant women, bound together by their wrists. They were taken, initially, for eighteen days to the Namin-dong *Bo-wi-bu* State Security Agency police *ku-ryu-jang* in Sinuiju. Initially, the police accused Former Detainee # 24 of being corrupted by capitalism in China. She convinced them that she had gone to China only for food, so she was sent for one month to the *do-jip-kyul-so* in South Sinuiju run by the *An-jeon-bu* People's Safety Agency police. Though she had heard that Kim Jong-il had recently said North Korean

repatriates should not be treated harshly, there were beatings.

Detainees were fed the usual steamed corn, and as it was midsummer, most prisoners were sent out to work in the rice fields. This grandmother was too old and weak for such labor, and as she herself had had seven children, she was taken in the mornings to a nearby medical building to help care for the pregnant detainees. She helped deliver seven babies, some of whom were full-term and others, injection-induced abortions. All of the babies were killed.

The first baby was born to a twenty-eight-year-old woman named Lim, who had been married to a Chinese man. The baby boy was born healthy and unusually large, owing to the mother's ability to eat well during pregnancy in China. Former Detainee # 24 assisted in hold-ing the baby's head during delivery and then cut the umbilical cord. But when she started to hold the baby and wrap him in a blanket, a guard grabbed the newborn by one leg and threw him in a large, plastic-lined box. A doctor explained that since North Korea was short on food, the country should not have to feed the children of foreign fathers. When the box was full of babies, Former Detainee # 24 later learned, it was taken outside and buried.

She next helped deliver a baby to a woman named Kim, who also gave birth to a healthy full-term boy. As Former Detainee # 24 caressed the baby, it tried to suckle her finger. The guard again came over and yelled at her to put the baby in the box. As she stood up, the guard slapped her, chipping her tooth. The third baby she delivered was premature—the size of an ear of corn—and the fourth baby was even smaller. She gently laid those babies in the box. The next day she delivered three more premature babies and also put them in the box. The babies in the box gave her nightmares.

Two days later, the premature babies died but the two full-term baby boys were still alive. Even though their skin had turned yellow and their mouths blue, they still blinked their eyes. The agent came by, and seeing that two of the babies in the box were not dead yet, stabbed them with forceps at a soft spot in their skulls. Former Detainee # 24 says she then lost her self-control and started screaming at the agent, who kicked her so hard in the leg that she fainted. Deemed unsuitable for further hospital work, she was returned to the detention center until her release several weeks later.

Upon release, Former Detainee # 24 returned to China but was again caught and this time repatriated to Hoeryong. Separated from her granddaughter, she became hysterical and started singing Christian hymns that she had learned in China, and ranting against Kim Jong-il for the ruinous conditions that forced Koreans to have to flee their native villages—while God took care of Korean people in China. Fortunately, her guards regarded her as a crazy old woman, not an enemy of the regime. Indeed, they took pity on her, even reuniting her with her granddaughter and helping the two of them to again cross the Tumen River into China. This time, she met some South Korean Christian relief workers who helped her and her granddaughter to make the trek through China to Southeast Asia. She arrived in South Korea in March 2001.

See satellite photograph of the South Sinuiju Detention Center on page 228.

For additional testimony about, and an analysis of forced abortions for women impregnated in China, see below and Part Five.

WITNESS AND TESTIMONY:

Mr. Yoo Chun-shik

Refouled at Sinuiju, early 2000

Mr. Yoo Chun-shik was repatriated to Sinuiju in early 2000. He had already been previously imprisoned in *Kyo-hwa-so* "Two-Two" at Oro, and after release he went to China for several years before being caught and repatriated. After repatriation and torture in several police facilities he was sent to a mobile labor brigade for a year of hard labor. His full testimony is on page 98 with the accounts of other former prisoners at *kyo-hwa-so* penitentiaries.

WITNESS and TESTIMONY:

Mrs. Koh Jyon-mi

Refouled at Sinuiju, early 2003

Mrs. Koh Jyon-mi's parents were originally from Jeju Island, South Korea, before migrating to Osaka, Japan. In 1963 they took their three year old daughter Jyon-mi and her older sister to North Korea in a group of 41 Korean-Japanese participants in the "repatriation" program that began in 1959. Mrs. Koh attended school in Sinuiju earning a college degree in physical education. She taught physical education and trained young athletes for participation in North Korea's mass gymnastic games. When she was 22, Mrs. Koh married a Korean-Japanese doctor from Nagasaki who graduated from the University of Tokyo before "repatriating" to North Korea in 1978. After 16 years of marriage, her husband passed away in 1998, and the family fell into hard times.

Mrs. Koh fled to China with her son and daughter in December 2000, and first settled in a rural area near Dandong City, China. Mrs. Koh's family moved to Shindo Island from there and again to Yantai, a city on the Shantung peninsula. Mrs. Koh was caught by traffickers, but managed to escape from them. She found a job cooking for 70 South Korean exchange students from Masan in South Korea who were studying at Shandong University. Her son was caught by Chinese police while traveling to Shenyang. Fearful of being separated from both her son and daughter (who remained in China), Mrs. Koh turned herself in to the Chinese police so she would be repatriated with her son.

Mrs. Koh was repatriated from Dandong, China to Sinuiju, North Korea in early 2003 and was detained for five months at the North Pyongan province *Bo-wi-bu* interrogation facility, as this was near to her sister's residence in North Korea. While detained by *Bo-wi-bu*, she was tortured so severely from beatings to the eyes, head, and mouth that she required hospitalization, where she was unconscious for ten days. While in the hospital, the *An-jeon-bu* police contacted her sister to bring her medicine and food, and to take her home when she regained consciousness. At her sister's house, Mrs. Koh learned that her son was at a local *rodong-dan-ryon-dae* mobile labor brigade.

In July 2003, Mrs. Koh and her son were sent to a rural farming village where there was no food. In August, Mrs. Koh and her son went to Sinuiju again to flee to China, where her daughter still remained. Mrs. Koh and her son made connections to enter the Japanese consulate in Beijing in March 2005. They were able to travel to Japan in late July 2005, and several months later, were joined by her daughter.

Mrs. Koh now teaches the Korean language in Osaka and lives with her children. Her son is working and her daughter is a university student.

WITNESS and TESTIMONY

Mr. Lee Yoo-keum

Refouled at Sinuiju, early 2003

Born in Sinuiju in 1984, Mr. Lee Yoo-keum went to China in December 2000 with his mother, Mrs. Koh Jyon Mi, interviewed above, and his sister. Mr. Lee and his family separated to find work. Mr. Lee went to Shenyang and worked in a noodle plant for a year. His sister worked in a restaurant washing dishes. One day, Mr. Lee heard that their mother was in Yanji. In Decem-ber 2001, Mr. Lee and his sister went to see their mother, and the family rented an apartment together.

In May 2002, Mr. Lee travelled to Beijing. However, when he reached Beijing, he was caught by the police and sent to Beijing foreigners' prison with five or six other North Koreans apprehended by the police. Mr. Lee was then sent to Dandong by train and was interrogated there for 2 days.

Upon repatriation, Mr. Lee was sent to Sinuiju *Bo-wi-bu* with about 50 people where he was held for three months. His stay was longer than other repatriates because he was from a Korean-Japanese family. Mr. Lee was interrogated at length but was not beaten because, he says, he was clever in his answers.

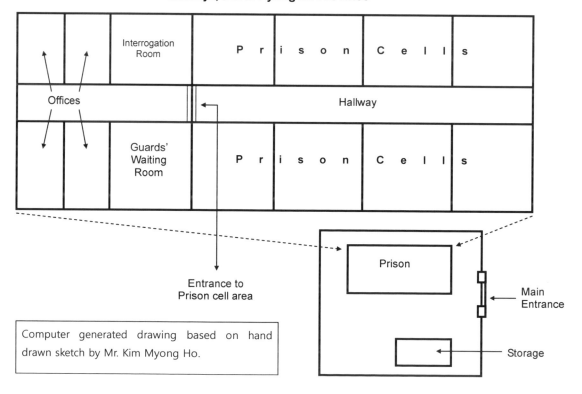

Bowibu Police *Kuryujang* Interrogation-Detention Facility
Shinuiju, North Pyong-an Province

Computer generated drawing based on hand drawn sketch by Mr. Kim Myong Ho.

He was transferred to an *An-jeon-bu* detention facility some five kilometers away from Sinuiju, where there were four cells for men and one for women. Perhaps a hundred persons passed through this detention facility while he was there. Because he had no one to come and vouch for him, he remained in detention for three months, becoming very sick and malnourished to the point of losing half his body weight. He was beaten by the *An-jeon-bu* guards, who gave no reasons or explanation for the beatings. After he collapsed from malnutrition and the beatings, the police contacted a relative to come pick him up, so he did not die in detention.

After two months recovering at his aunt's house, he was sent to a *ro-dong-dan-ryon-dae* mobile labor brigade for 6 months where he crushed rocks to be used for building housing foundations.

When Mr. Lee was released, through his aunt, he met up again with his mother. With support from his sister, who had remained in China, Mr. Lee and his mother again fled to China, with intent to seek asylum in Japan. In 2005 along with his mother, who was Korean-Japanese, he was able to travel to Japan and now resides in Osaka.

WITNESS and TESTIMONY:

Mr. Kim Myong-ho

Refouled at Sinuiju, March 2003

Mr. Kim Myong-ho was born in 1967 in Musan city, North Hamgyong province. He crossed the North Korean border and went to Shenyang, China in 2000.

He was repatriated in March 2003 to Sinuiju *Bo-wi-bu* with a group of three women and two men who were caught in Dandong. Mr. Kim spent 25 days at the Sinuiju *Bo-wi-bu* which has ten prison cells and had five prisoners incarcerated in each cell.

Mr. Kim explained that *Bo-wi-bu ku-ryu-jang* is the place where authorities filter out people with political associations or motives. However, Mr. Kim's major reason for leaving the country was for food. His interrogation was concerned with basic biographic information: how he was caught, if he watched South Korean TV, if he met Christians or went to a Korean-Chinese church. During his week of interrogation, he denied having been exposed to South Korean culture. He was hit and kicked if he did not answer the questions right away.

The worst was the sitting motionless torture, where he was hit on the fingers or knees if he talked, or even moved a little.

After twenty-five days in the *Bo-wi-bu* detention/interrogation facility he was transferred to an *An-jeon-bu*-run *ro-dong-dan-ryeon-dae* mobile work brigade where he did three months of forced labor: a mixture of logging and farming corns and beans. The prisoners were fed, he said, worse than pigs and dogs.

Repatriated persons at the labor-training center were kept separate from other prisoners who were detained for ordinary crimes.

FORCED REPATRIATION: HYESAN CORRIDOR

WITNESS and TESTIMONY:

Mrs. Lee Chun-shim

Refouled, November 2004

Mrs. Lee Chun-shim was born in Pyongyang. Having spent a decade (1982-1992) as a nurse and First Lieutenant in the North Korean People's Army, she provides expert eyewitness testimony on violence against women. In November 2004, she was caught by the Chinese police and forcibly repatriated to the North Korean *Bo-wi-bu* State Security Agency police detention facilities at Hyesan in Yangang Province.

The *Bo-wi-bu ku-ryu-jang* at Hyesan was a simple rectangular building with a corridor behind a narrow metal door. Upon arrival men and women detainees were separated as the women were compelled to undress and stand naked and

humiliated in front of their children (those ten years and younger were kept with them) and the guards who were in their twenties and thirties. Non-pregnant women were made to do the squat and jump up exercises to dislodge any money hidden in rectal or vaginal cavities. Some women were subjected to vaginal searches by hand, and those who cried out in pain or humiliation were beaten with a wooden stick. Women who admitted to swallowing money or valuables were made to drink detergent water to induce vomiting or diarrhea. These women were then isolated and given buckets to collect vomit or excrement until the swallowed valuables were recovered.

According to Mrs. Lee, a drug that in diluted form is used to treat skin wounds was injected into pregnant women's wombs, inducing labor within hours. As there had not been the normal widening of the hipbones during the advance stages of pregnancy to enlarge the birth canal, the labor pains were the same as when delivering a fully grown baby. When the women moaned or cried out in pain as they lay on wooden and cement cell floors, they were hit with wooden staves and cursed as "bitches who got Chinese sperm and brought this on themselves."

To Mrs. Lee's surprise, the fetuses were not killed in the uterus by the concentrated injections. Even three to four months premature babies were born alive, crying, and moaning. The babies were wrapped in newspaper and put in a bucket to die, after which they were buried in a yard behind the jail.

No medical care was provided following the forced abortions. No tissues or towels were provided. Nor were the women allowed to bathe or wash. They had to use their own clothes to wipe themselves. The cells in which the women gave birth were infested with lice, which even got into the women's vaginas. The women's skin festered and cracked from being scratched with dirty hands.

Mrs. Lee thought that the women subjected to these mistreatments suffered mental as well as physical harm.

Mrs. Lee's testimony was given at a conference in Tokyo in December 2008 attended by the present author.[110]

FORCED REPATRIATION: MUSAN CORRIDOR

WITNESS and TESTIMONY: Mr. Kim Tae-jin

Refouled at Musan, August 1987.

Mr. Kim Tae-jin was repatriated to Musan in August 1987. After interrogation and torture at the Musan *An-jeon-bu ku-ryu-jang*, he was transferred to the Chongjin *Bo-wi-bu ku-ryu-jang* where

---

110 Her testimony in Korean and Japanese languages can be found at the "NO FENCE" website, http://nofence.netlive.ne.jp/.

he was again interrogated and tortured. Following that, he was sent to the "re-revolutioning zone" at the No. 15 *Kwan-li-so* political penal labor colony at Yodok. His photograph and testimony appears on page 60, along with other former prisoners from Yodok.

WITNESS: Former Detainee # 1

Refouled at Musan, 1997

Former Detainee # 1 was born in 1967 in Chongjin, North Hamgyong province. He served ten years as a radio operator in the North Korean military. Upon discharge, he became a low-level courier in business transactions between North Korea and China. In 1997, he was arrested in Yanji, where he had gone to collect money owed in return for goods imported from Japan and re-exported to China without North Korean authorization. Turned over to the *Bo-wi-bu* (National Security Agency) police at Musan, he was interrogated for a day and then turned over to the *An-jeon-bu* People's Safety Agency police for a week of interrogation. He was then turned over again to the *Bo-wi-bu* at Chongjin, who placed him in a police jail in Song-pyong district in Chongjin. There, for twenty days he was shackled and forced to kneel without moving whenever he was not undergoing additional interrogation sessions. During these multiple interrogations, Former Detainee # 1 was questioned about listening to South Korean radio while in the military and accused of wanting to go to South Korea. He convincingly denied having listened to South Korean radio while in the North Korean military, even though he had. He completely denied allegations of espionage. He did not disclose information about others involved in the unauthorized re-export scheme that the officials and staff of the state enterprise had organized.

Finally, Former Detainee # 1 was sent to a *do-jip-kyul-so* provincial detention center at Nongpo. At one point, driven by hunger, he slipped away to his family home to get some food. Caught while trying to sneak back into the provincial detention center, he was beaten unconscious for having escaped. Emaciated from forced labor making bricks, his legs became numb. He was unable to walk up or down stairs and unable to carry bricks. In fact, he reports that he was so "skin and bones" that he could not even sit. Unable to change clothes or bathe, he became covered with lice. As his jailers did not want him to die in custody, Former Detainee # 1 was released in October after only two months in detention.

It took until May of the following year for Former Detainee # 1 to recover movement in his legs. At that point, accompanied by his mother, he fled to China. They gradually made their way south through China and Southeast Asia, arriving in South Korea in March 2000. This former detainee still has scars on his shoulder and hip from the chemicals in the hot, freshly fired bricks he was required to carry while in detention.

TESTIMONY: Nongpo Provincial Detention Center, Chongjin

Nongpo, now sometimes also called Eunjung, is a sub-district of Song-pyong district in Chongjin, North Hamgyong province. Nongpo held some 120 detainees during Former Detainee # 1's imprisonment: roughly seventy men and fifty women. Some inmates were single. Some were married couples, but the husbands and wives slept separately in the different men's and women's cells, where roughly twenty persons slept head-to-toe in small rooms. Conditions were highly unsanitary, with many detainees covered with lice.

Most of the female detainees were held for up to six months for having gone to China. Some of the men detainees were also held for going to China, but most of them were held for "selling" state property. Detainees were required to perform hard labor: brick-making from morning to evening, in addition to agricultural work (planting and harvesting crops). The harsh chemicals used in making bricks left the detainees with bruised and sore hands. The freshly fired bricks were heavy to lift and exhausting to carry. Rations were extremely meager: salty, watery cabbage-leaf soup and small cakes made of wheat chaff. Evenings were occupied with group self-criticism and silent, motionless self-reflection. A criticism session would not end until detainees proclaimed their own or someone else's wrongdoing. The detainees would make up wrongdoings to end the sessions.

A typical day started at five in the morning with a thirty-minute jog to an agricultural worksite for two hours of farming work followed by a half-hour breakfast. Detainees then made bricks until noon, when they were given a half-hour for lunch. Lunch was followed by repair and work preparation until one. Then came six-and-a-half more hours of brick making followed by a half hour for dinner. Dinner was followed by a self-criticism session, which lasted from eight until ten and was sometimes followed by interrogations. The work was so hard, with slow workers beaten with shovels, that the detainees wanted to be transferred from the detention-labor facility to a "real prison," meaning a *kyo-hwa-so*.

Within his two months of detention at Nongpo, Former Detainee # 1, witnessed, out of a total of 120 inmates, one public execution (a man who had sold cable in China), three deaths from malnutrition and related diseases, and one death from tetanus.

See a sketch of Nongpo Detention Center on page 134 and a satellite photograph on page 229.

WITNESS and TESTIMONY: Mrs. Bang Mi-sun

Refouled at Musan, October 1999.

Mrs. Bang was repatriated through Musan in late 1999. She was transferred from a *Bo-wi-bu* detention-interrogation facility to an *An-jeon-bu* mobile labor brigade and again to a pre-trial detention facility for six months before transfer to *Kyo-hwa-so* No. 15. Her full testimony appears on pages 93 above, along with the testimony of other former prisoners at the *kyo-hwa-so* penitentiaries.

WITNESS: Former Detainee # 26

Refouled at Musan, April 2002

A native of Chongjin City, North Hamgyong province, Former Detainee # 26 is a mother of four and a grandmother of two. In the mid-1990s, her husband died of natural causes. As the family slowly ran out of money and food in the late 1990s, she sent two daughters to China for work, but they were caught by traffickers and sold to Korean-Chinese men. Former Detainee # 26, along with her son and a grandchild, then went to China to try to rescue her daughters and reunite her family. She found her daughters in Wongchun and took them to Yanji, where they lived for a year and a half before being caught by the Chinese police in April 2002.

First repatriated to the Musan *jip-kyul-so*, this grandmother was sent to the Onsong *Bo-wi-bu ku-ryu-jang* detention center for "heavy interrogation." She believes that a whole family together in China was deemed a more politicized desertion than a single-family member in China trying to earn money to support the rest of the family back in North Korea.

She was then transferred to the Nongpo *jip-kyul-so* detention center, where after a month, a guard pushed her to the ground, breaking one of her ribs. She was sent home for forty days of "sick leave" in order for her rib to heal. However, after thirty days on leave, in June, she again crossed

133

Nongpo *Anjeonbu* Detention Center,
Chongjin, North Hamgyong Province

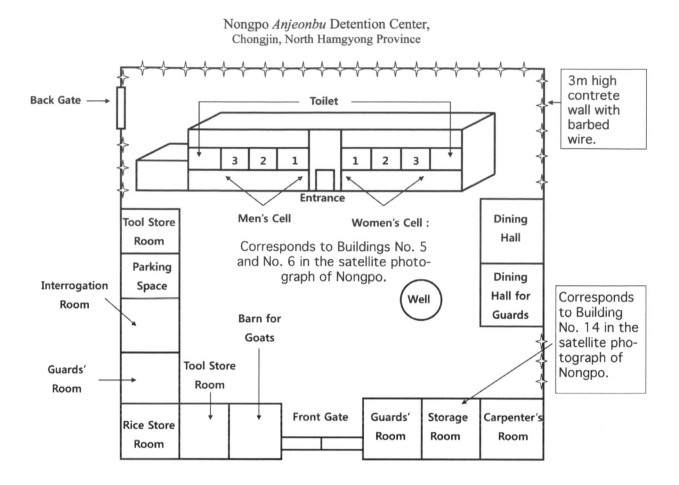

the Tumen River to look for her remaining daughter, who had not been caught in April and remained in China. Within the month, Former Detainee # 26 was caught again and this time repatriated to Hoeryong *Bo-wi-bu* jail, where she was made to sit motionless for six days. Her next destination was the Onsong Sambong-ku *Bo-wi-bu* police station, where she was heavily interrogated and threatened with being sent to Oro No. "Two-Two" penitentary. She begged and bribed the guards, who sent her instead to the *An-jeon-bu* jail for a week of solitary confinement in a dark cell (without windows or lights). After becoming ill, she was given a sick release.

After a week at home, she again fled to China in August 2001, where she remained in hiding until December. This time her luck turned when she met a Korean-American missionary in Yangji who helped her join a group of nine persons on the "underground" land-route. After traveling through Beijing and Kunming, the group made their way through Southeast Asia. In June 2002, she reached Seoul and obtained asylum.

When interviewed for this report in Seoul in November 2002, Former Detainee # 26, who had tried so hard to help her family avert starvation and keep them together, was accompanied by her young granddaughter. Former Detainee # 26's daughter, the granddaughter's mother, had been located in China and joined another group of North Korean refugees on the long overland trek to Thailand. Unfortunately, she was caught crossing the Vietnamese border and turned over to the Chinese police. At the time of this interview, her fate and whereabouts were unknown.

TESTIMONY: Nongpo Detention Center, Chongjin

According to Former Detainee # 26, in May 2000, the Nongpo *jip-kyul-so* in Chongjin[111] held roughly 75 men, 175 women, and a few orphans and teenagers. The women detainees were held in three rooms: one room for paratyphoid sufferers, one room for pregnant women, and the third room for 130 female prisoners, whose quarters were so cramped that there was not space for all of them to simultaneously lie down for sleep. Detainees were fed some 70–75 kernels of boiled corn per meal.

In May 2000, 28 women among the detainces were from three to nine months pregnant. Former Detainee # 26 saw three eight-month-old fetuses aborted and seven babies killed. Several women from Cell No. 1 (see sketch above and satellite photograph on page 229), including Former Detainee #26, were brought over to Cell No. 3 to help deliver the babies. When the babies

111 Some former prisoners referred to this detention center as Nongpo, and some referred to it as Chongjin. Nongpo is a section of Chongjin City. Some former prisoners referred to it as a provincial detention center, and some referred to it as a detention center. The author has tried to preserve each reference according to the way in which each former prisoner referred to this facility. For ease of reference, each visual image of this facility is referred to as Nongpo Detention Center.

were born, they were placed face down on the ground. Some babies died right away; others lay there breathing longer. If any babies were still alive after two days, the guards would smother them in wet vinyl. The babies lying on the ground could be seen by the women standing at the front of the other cells. The guards would say that the mothers had to see and hear the babies die because these babies were Chinese.

FORCED REPATRIATION: HOERYONG CORRIDOR

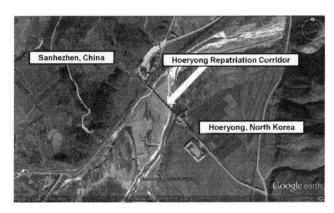

Sanhezhen, China | Hoeryong Repatriation Corridor | Hoeryong, North Korea

WITNESS and TESTIMONY:

Former Detainee # 34

Refouled at Hoeryong, 2004

Former Detainee # 34 was born in South Hamgyong province in 1966. He was trading in China when arrested in Longjiang in October

2004. Held in China for fifteen days, he was forcibly repatriated to the Hoeryong, North Hamgyong province *Bo-wi-bu* interrogation/detention facility, where he was held two and one-half months for questioning.

The Hoeryong *Bo-wi-bu* detention/interrogation facility is near to a locally famous statue of Mrs. Kim Jong-suk, Kim Il-sung's first wife. The Hoeryong *Bo-wi-bu* detention/interrogation facility had 8 cell rooms on opposite sides of a central corridor. Two rooms were for men and three for women. He doesn't know about the use of the other rooms. His cell held about thirty people, and he believes the other cells did as well. The entrances to the cell rooms were less than waist high, so that prisoners had to crawl out backwards on their hands and knees. He once crawled out head first, and was beaten for the infraction.

He was interrogated five times, and beaten twice, one time losing a tooth. But he describes the sitting motionless torture—each and every day in his cell for ten weeks—as being much more painful than the beatings. The interrogation questions were the usual ones: Did he meet South Koreans or attend churches in China? He had done so, although he initially denied it, until another prisoner told on him. He then admitted that he had, but only to get food and money.

He believes he was treated better than most fellow prisoners because he had told the State Security Agency police that he had been ten years in the army and was a member of the Korean Workers' Party. However, he complained about the unsanitary conditions: being unable to wash and having to wear the same clothes for ten weeks, and having to drink dirty, contaminated water as collective punishment, which then made the toilets extremely foul.

He was turned over to the Chongjin provincial *An-jeon-bu* People's Safety Agency police to await the local police to pick him up and escort him to Onsong, a town of more than 100,000 people on the border with China. He was again questioned and legal documents were prepared. He was taken to the prosecutor's office where charges were read against him. The charges were from the "legal code" but he did not recognize them and does not remember the specific charges except that "border crossing" was among them.

He was sentenced to one year at the Onsong *ro-dong-dan-ryeon-dae* labor-training center (mobile labor brigade) where he and his fellow prisoners collected sand and rock for construction sites, and collected excrement for use as fertilizer. He was released after four and one-half months for illness. While at Onsong mobile labor brigade in 2005, a fellow prisoner was beaten so severely that he was taken away almost dead. The prisoner never returned.

FORCED REPATRIATION: ONSONG CORRIDOR

WITNESS: Former Detainee # 27

Refouled at Onsong, 1998.

After Former Detainee # 27 was caught by Chinese police at the Vietnamese border, he was sent all the way back to the far northeast corner town of Tumen before being repatriated through Onsong in 1998. He was sent to Chongjin *Bo-wi-bu* where he was tortured and beaten before being sent to Yodok *kwan-li-so*. His story appears on page 137 with the other testimonies from the political penal labor colonies.

WITNESS: Former Detainee # 25

Refouled at Onsong, mid-1999

A young woman in her mid-thirties at the time of her interview, Former Detainee # 25 was born in Saethyol district, North Hamgyong province. In April 1998, when the food shortage in North Korea became extremely severe where she was living, she went to China to make enough money to buy corn. A year later, she was caught and repatriated to North Korea. She was sent first to the *An-jeon-bu* People's Safety Agency police *jip-kyul-so* provincial detention center for *wirl-gyong-ja*—"illegal border crossers"—at Onsong, North Hamgyong province, for five weeks in the autumn of 1999, and then taken for the month of December to the Nongpo *jip-kyul-so* detention center in Chongjin City.

When she was released from Nongpo, a local police officer escorted her back to her hometown. She was made to promise not to go to China again, but since there was no food at home, she waded across the icy Tumen River on December 31, 1999. She forded the icy stream because there were too many guards at the spots where the river was frozen. She lived in China for two years before going by bus and on foot down through China and Southeast Asia. She arrived in Seoul in June of 2002.

TESTIMONY: Onsong *Jip-kyul-so* Detention Center, North Hamgyong Province

At Onsong, during the time of Former Detainee # 25's detention, roughly 150 persons were held in two rooms. The detainees, who were assigned to make bricks, were told that they were not human beings but dogs and pigs. They were made to sing "silly songs" to honor Kim Jong-il. Detainees were asked the usual question: had they met any South Koreans or Christians while in China? Two women confessed to having converted to Christianity while in China and were taken away by police agents, who told the remaining women that the two Christian converts had been executed and that the rest of the women should consider themselves warned.[112]

When she was first taken to Onsong, Former Detainee # 25 thought she was looking at ghosts because the detainees were so skinny. She herself lost 5 kilograms (11 pounds) during

112 There is no available evidence other than the reported statements of the police officials as to whether these executions actually took place or not. While technically "hearsay," such assertions from DPRK authorities lead to the belief that North Koreans who convert to Christianity are executed for so doing.

137

Onsong *Bowibu* Holding Cells

Computer generated drawing based on hand drawn sketch by Lee Young Sook

the five weeks she was detained, being fed only half-bowls of corn soup.

Nongpo *Jip-kyul-so* Detention Center, Chongjin City

At the Nongpo *jip-kyul-so* in Chongjin, in December 1999, roughly 180 detainees were required to construct a fish farm outside the detention center. During the month that Former Detainee # 25 was there, several detainees who had been arrested in China while seeking to enter Mongo-

lia were transferred. North Korean officials presumed, perhaps not incorrectly, that they were attempting to reach South Korea rather than work for food in China. The Nongpo detainees were taken to *Kyo-hwa-so* No. 22 (commonly identified as "*Kyo-hwa-so* Two-Two"), described in Part Three. Another female prisoner, a former teacher who had also been in Mongolia, was beaten almost to death, and the next day was taken out either to die or to be transferred to "Two-Two." A four-year-old boy, who was imprisoned with his mother, died of malnutrition. According to Former Detainee # 25, almost eighty percent of the detainees at Nongpo *jip-kyul-so* were women, ten to twelve of whom were pregnant. The women were told they would not be allowed to leave the detention center still carrying "children of betrayers" in their wombs.

Former Detainee # 25 observed that the pregnant women were denied food and water and were kicked in the stomach to induce bleeding. She saw several women taken away for abortion-inducing injections before they were brought back to Nongpo. Four babies were born in a room set aside for birthing. The babies were put in a wicker basket in an adjacent storeroom, covered in vinyl cloth, and left to die.

See page 134 for a sketch of Nongpo.

Witness and Testimony: Former Detainee # 21

***Refouled* at Onsong, August 1999**

A forty-three year-old native of Kangwon province, Former Detainee # 21 formerly worked at a state-run fertilizer factory. But production slowed and then stopped completely in 1997. Without work and running out of food, she and her husband fled to China in January 1999. They were caught by the Chinese police and repatriated to North Korea in August. She was held seven months for interrogation at the *An-jeon-bu* People's Safety Agency police *ku-ryu-*

jang at Namyang-ku, Onsong district, North Hamgyong province.

At that time, the *An-jeon-bu* jail at Onsong held about 130 detainees, forty to fifty of whom were women. Former Detainee # 21's husband was put in a men's cell, and she was put in one of the women's cells. Her husband was beaten so badly that he confessed their desire to go to South Korea, after which time he died in detention from paratyphoid, a lice-borne disease that results in acute diarrhea, leading, if untreated, to dehydration and death. Her husband was left medically unattended for three days in men's Cell Block No. 8. She was beaten with sticks, and the police agents beat her head against cement walls until she screamed at them to get it over and kill her too.

According to Former Detainee # 21, beatings were common and harsh. Detainees were beaten so badly that they confessed to things they had not done. Women were beaten on the fingertips. One woman, who was very ill, near death, was made to stand up and sit down repeatedly until she collapsed and died. Among the fifteen women with Former Detainee # 21 in Cell Block No. 2, there were two repatriated pregnant women: one, six months pregnant; the other, eight months. Both were taken out for abortions. Upon return, both women said that their babies had been born alive and then were suffocated in vinyl cloth.

After seven months detention at Onsong in 1999-2000, Former Detainee # 21 was transferred to Chongjin *Bo-wi-bu jip-kyul-so* detention center in Chongjin, where she was held for another three months. Following her release from Chongjin, she again fled to China, even more determined to seek asylum in South Korea.

Witness: Former Detainee # 8

Refouled **at Onsong, May 2000**

At the time of her interview, Former Detainee # 8 was a thirty-eight-year-old woman from Musan, North Hamgyong province. She went to China in 1998 and married a Chinese citizen of ethnic Korean origin. Caught by Chinese police in May 2000, she was sent back to North Korea in June and interrogated by Onsong State Security Agency personnel. They asked her why and how many times she had left Korea and if she had met South Koreans or went to Christian churches while in China.

Satisfied that she had done none of these things, while threatening her with death if she went to China again, they sent her for two months detention at the Chongjin *jip-kyul-so*. Upon release, Former Detainee # 8 nevertheless went back to China. Believing it was unsafe to remain with her Korean-Chinese husband, she decided to try to get to South Korea. Starting her journey in late October 2001, she reached Seoul in mid-2002, after travelling to southern China and then through Southeast Asia.

TESTIMONY: Chongjin *Jip-kyul-so* Detention Center, North Hamgyong Province

Located in North Hamgyong province, this provincial detention center held roughly ninety detainees—some thirty men and some sixty women—nearly all of whom had been repatriated from China. Detainees worked from six in the morning until seven in the evening on seasonal agricultural work or collecting firewood, on a diet of dried corn and radish-leaf soup. Detainees often worked for up to three months while waiting for local police to come escort them back to their assigned places of residence.

According to Former Detainee # 8, guards did not hit women at the Chongjin *jip-kyul-so*, but men were, though "only" with fists, not clubs. However, upon entry, the women were asked if they were pregnant. If less than three to four months pregnant, the women detainees were subjected to surgical abortions. If more than four months pregnant, female detainees were given labor-inducing injections, after which, it was believed by Former Detainee # 8, the babies were killed. During Former Detainee # 8's two months of detention in mid-2000, six women were subjected to forced abortions.

Reportedly, there was no interrogation at Chongjin *jip-kyul-so*. Instead there were nightly classes on North Korean rules and regulations, accompanied by nighttime self-criticism sessions in groups of fifteen. If one member of the group of fifteen made some mistake or error during labor, or did something against the rules, the whole group would be punished.

WITNESS and TESTIMONY: Former Detainee # 9

Refouled at Onsong, June 2000

At the time of his interview, a thirty-eight-year-old native of Shinpo, South Hamgyong province, Former Detainee # 9 was desperate for work in 1998. So he went to China and spent two years in Yanji and almost a year in Harbin before being caught by the Chinese police in June 2000. Deported to Onsong, he was jailed for ten days, during which time he convincingly denied having met any South Korean Christians while in China, even though he had. He was sent to the Onsong *ro-dong-dan-ryeon-dae* labor training center mobile labor brigade while awaiting transfer to the Chongjin *jip-kyul-so* detention facility. While again being transferred by train,

he escaped from his guards. He fled to China and then made his way down through southern China to Southeast Asia before gaining asylum in South Korea in January 2002.

In July 2000, when Former Detainee #9 was detained at the Onsong labor-training camp, run by the Onsong *An-jeon-bu* People's Safety Agency police, there were roughly seventy detainees: some forty repatriates from China and some thirty petty criminals. Detainees began work at half past four in the morning, cultivating crops. In the afternoons and evenings, they did heavier labor—making bricks, sometimes until half past ten at night. At other times of the year, the detainees were sent to the mines, even though their detention was short-term, while they waited to be transferred elsewhere.

After he was transferred to the *An-jeon-bu* People's Safety Agency *do-jip-kyul-so* provincial detention facility at Chongjin, Former Detainee # 9's labor assignment in mid-2000 was additional agricultural work. There was no bathing, brushing teeth, or changing clothes. He was

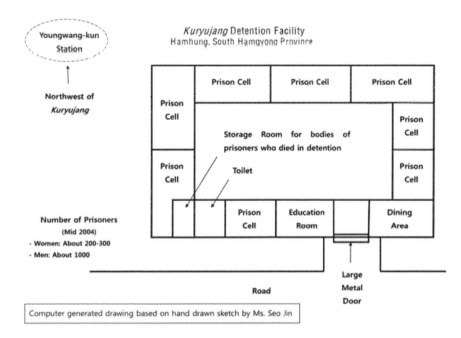

Computer generated drawing based on hand drawn sketch by Ms. Seo Jin

still wearing the same clothes he was wearing when arrested in China. Food rations were small amounts of boiled mashed corn and salty radish-leaf soup. Farm animals, he said, ate better.

The detainee population at the Chongjin detention center at that time was made up of thirty to forty men and fifty to sixty women. The guards would force the detainees to hit each other, a practice that Former Detainee # 9 believed was designed to allow the North Korean authorities to assure the Chinese that the police were not beating the prisoners. There were no deaths in detention during his brief stay at Chongjin, though he mentioned that the petty criminals there, who had been detained longer, complained that those who died at the center were not given proper burials. Former Detainee # 9's biggest complaint regarded "the inhumane treatment of pregnant women." He saw a group of ten taken away for mandatory abortions, and the women were returned to hard labor the very next day.

WITNESS: Former Prisoner # 31

Refouled at Onsong, twice in 2003.

Her story when she was sent to Chung-san *kyo-hwa-so* is told on page 92.

WITNESS: Ms. Seo Jin

Refouled at Onsong, December 2003.

She was repatriated through Onsong in December 2003. As a punishment for leaving North Korea she was sent to No. 55 *Kyo-yang-so* without trial. Her story is told on page 90.

WITNESS and TESTIMONY:

Former Detainee # 32

Refouled at Onsong three times (2001, 2002 and 2004)

Former Detainee # 32 was born in July 1962 at Deoksong-eup, Deoksong district in South Hamgyong province. She was repatriated three times from China through the Onsong corridor.

She first crossed into China in 2000 to get help from her relatives in China. She stayed in the Yanji and Wanquing areas of China. When first repatriated in 2001 to Onsong *Bo-wi-bu*, she was strip-searched by female guards and subjected to interrogation for 15 days. She was asked how she went to China, what kind of life she had in the country, and if she were involved in any Christian activities. Her male interrogators did not believe her answers so she was kicked and slapped around. At that time Onsong *Bo-wi-bu* had three very crowded prison cells that held 30 people in each. She was sent briefly to an Onsong *ro-dong-dan-ryeon-dae* labor-training center, en route to being sent to the Sunam district *jip-kyul-so* detention facility in Chongjin. But not closely guarded on the train south to Chongjin, she simply got off, and made her way back to China.

In a second forced repatriation at Onsong in July 2002, Former Detainee # 32 convinced her interrogators that it was her first repatriation to North Korea. She was held by *Bo-wi-bu* for two months. She was again heavily pressed about meeting South Koreans or attending church, and beaten to force her to confess. After two months at *Bo-wi-bu* this time she was effectively transferred to the Chongjin *jip-kyul-so* detention facility for one month. During this time, July 2002, she witnessed forced abortions. Because there was too little food to feed prisoners in the facility, her home village area police came to pick her up. She worked in a farm field with about 150 men and women. At the tiny local police station, police were preparing paper work on her case. But she got very sick, and rather than deal with her illness, they just let her go.

Once recovered, she again fled to China. She lived in the mountains and got help from Korean-Chinese Christians. Caught again, she was repatriated a third time in March 2004. She was five months pregnant but, fortunately, the *Bo-wi-bu* guards could not tell from her appearance even after they strip-searched her body for hidden money. She was fearful knowing that the guards would force an abortion if they found out she was pregnant and thought the baby was half-Chinese. Guards hit her face with fists and kicked her while she was kneeling. Since the

Bo-wi-bu facility was again over-crowded, and short of food, she was briefly sent to a labor training center mobile labor brigade for 10 days, then released.

She again fled to China, went hiding in the mountains again, and gave birth to her child. Later in 2004 she made the connections to reach South Korea.

WITNESS and TESTIMONY: Mrs. Lee Young-suk

Refouled at Onsong, April 2006

Mrs. Lee was born in 1971 at Daeheung-ri, Bochun district, Yanggang province and lived in Hyesan in North Korea.

Her husband escaped to South Korea in 2005. In March 2006, she and her four-year-old daughter set out to follow him to South Korea. But Chinese police in Inner Mongolia caught her. Mrs. Lee was taken to the Tumen Yanji Chinese detention center and held 15 days, with three other detainees. Chinese guards strip searched her, confiscated some 600 Yuan (slightly more than 100 US$) and roughed her up to obtain an admission that she was on her way to South Korea. But she would not confess to this.

143

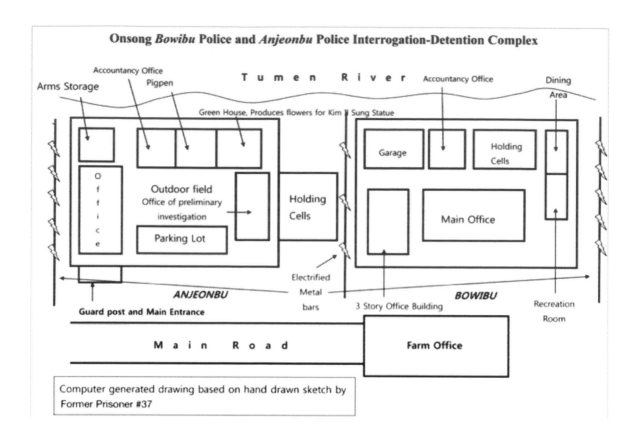

Onsong *Bowibu* Police and *Anjeonbu* Police Interrogation-Detention Complex

Computer generated drawing based on hand drawn sketch by Former Prisoner #37

Onsong *Bowibu* Holding Cells

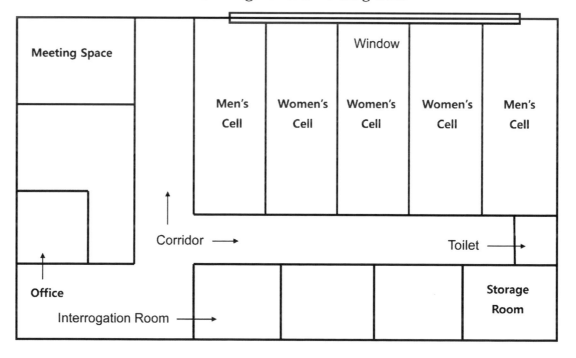

Computer generated drawing based on hand drawn sketch by Lee Young Sook

When repatriated to Onsong *Bo-wi-bu*, Mrs. Lee and all other women were made to do "stand-up, sit-down jump around" exercises in groups of five persons. Male and female prisoners were packed together inside the small police station. They were interrogated on their whereabouts in China. For 15 days she stayed in the corridor outside of the prison cell row because of her child. A supervisor (*kyo-ho-won*) saw her breast-feeding her 4-year-old daughter and gave her rice. Guards grouped people into 25 and beat them harshly with thick sticks until they confessed that they were attempting to go to South Korea. But Mrs. Lee stuck to her story and did not break. While she was at Onsong *Bo-wi-bu* there were three pregnant women who were taken away, but Mrs. Lee did not know their fate.

She provided the sketch of the Onsong *Bo-wi-bu* interrogation-detention *ku-ryu-jang* holding room within the sketch drawn by Former Prisoner # 37, whose story is told on page 84 above (Former Prisoner # 37 was also detained and harshly tortured at the Onsong police facilities for repatriated border crossers).

Mrs. Lee was sent to the *An-jeon-bu-run* Onsong *ro-dong-dan-ryeon-dae* labor training center for 17 days and then to the Chongjin *jip-kyol-so* detention facility for four days. After this, the police from her hometown of Hyesan came to pick her up and took her there. She was again interrogated by police agents but bribed her release for about 400 Chinese Yuan (roughly 60 $US). When the police came to her for more money she fled again across the river to China.

She arrived in South Korea in 2006.

WITNESS and TESTIMONY: Former Detainee # 33

Refouled at Onsong, 2004

Former Detainee # 33 was born in 1973 in Kimchaek, North Hamgyong province and raised in Hoeryong city. She worked at the post office but needed more money to support her daughter, so she went to China in 2004. Caught in Yanji only 15 days after arriving in China, Chinese authorities held her at Tumen before repatriating her to the Onsong *Bo-wi-bu*.

The Onsong *Bo-wi-bu ku-ryu-jang* detention-interrogation facility was then very crowded, holding she thought some 200 persons, about four-fifths of whom were women. She could barely lie down in her cell to sleep. Like everyone she was forced to take off all her clothes and do the sit-down-jump up exercise. Guards also followed her to the toilet to make sure she had not hidden any money. After seven days her interrogations began. These sessions took place three to four times a day, every other day.

Interrogators asked the same questions repetitively, to which Mrs. Cho did not answer and thus, was beaten severely. Guards made her kneel down with her hands tied at the front and hit her head with fists and kicked her with their shoes. Each interrogation session lasted only an hour, much shorter than most others. She thinks that her interrogation was shorter because she was caught only fifteen days after she went to China, and because she kept falling to the ground in pain from the beatings. They mainly asked her who had helped her to go to China, particularly, which border guards, but she refused to answer, which is why they beat her.

Food was in short supply, and detainees who were being held for longer periods already looked malnourished. A number of the women detainees were pregnant. Although Mrs. Cho did not see abortions herself, she witnessed guards beating pregnant women and yelling at them for their half-Chinese babies.

After 25 days, the local *Bo-an-so* (police station) police from Hoeryong, where she had been living, came for her. They took her to a local clinic and then sent her back home. She again fled to China, and arrived in South Korea in December 2007.

WITNESS and TESTIMONY: Former Detainee # 35

Refouled at Onsong, 2007

Born in 1979 in the Musan district of North Hamgyong province, Former Detainee # 35 went to China in May 1998 to find his mother and sister who had fled to China a year earlier.

But unable to locate his family, as a loyal citizen, he returned to North Korea to vote in the election for the Supreme People's Assembly. En route back home, he was caught by a security agent in Musan in August of 1998. Under interrogation at the Musan *Bo-wi-bu ku-ryu-jang* interrogation-detention facility, he was beaten with wooden poles if he failed to answer questions "correctly."

Because of overcrowding at the Musan *Bo-wi-bu* police station, he was sent to a Musan *Ro-dong-dan-ryeon-dae* mobile labor brigade for ten days in October 1998. There, he and the other prisoners were subjected to an intensely demanding labor project demolishing an iron reinforced concrete building with hammers, leaving his hands covered with blisters. Severely underfed, he suffered from constant hunger. During and after their "meal" of corn gruel, the detainees had to sing patriotic songs and shout out propaganda slogans. The worst though were the freezing cold, blanket-less nights as he was still wearing only the summer clothes he had on coming back from China. At the mobile labor brigade, he observed a pregnant woman being taunted about her "Chinese seed" for her unborn child, whom they named "Kim Cho (North Korea)-joong(China)," before forcing her to abort the half-Chinese baby. Former Detainee # 35 saw other pregnant women beaten by the guards as well.

Released from the mobile labor brigade in April 1999, he went back to China again in search of his mother and sister. Through an acquaintance from his first visit to China, he found his family and lived in China for eight years without getting caught, even taking a Chinese wife in 2002. But in 2007, he was reported to the police by another Chinese acquaintance, apprehended and repat-

Rodongdanryondae Mobile Labor Brigade
Musan–kun, North Hamgyong Province

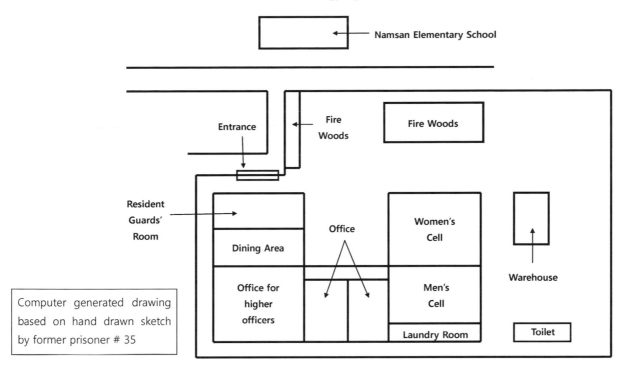

Computer generated drawing based on hand drawn sketch by former prisoner # 35

Anjeonbu Police *Kuryujang* Interrogation–Detention Facility
Musan-kun, North Hamgyong Province

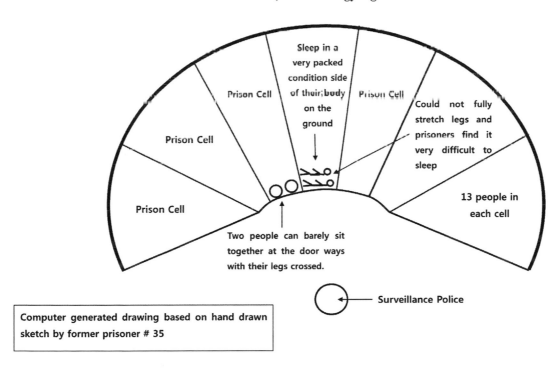

Computer generated drawing based on hand drawn sketch by former prisoner # 35

riated at Onsong and delivered to the *Bo-wi-bu ku-ryu-jang* interrogation-detention facility.

There, he was held for 21 days in a very small cell; it was so crowded that the prisoners had to sleep on their sides squeezed against each other. During interrogation, he was asked the usual questions about meeting South Koreans or Christians in China, and required to write down his life history. When he was slow to answer interrogators' questions about his written history, he was beaten on the legs.

In March 2007 he was transferred to the Onsong *An-jeon-bu* interrogation-detention facility for one day. Then he was transferred to the Onsong *ro-dong-dan-ryeon-dae* mobile labor brigade for two days, where he was slapped and punched during additional interrogations. He was again transferred to the Chongjin provincial *do-jip-kyul-so* detention facility for about 20 days where he was again beaten with sticks and chairs before being transferred to his Musan hometown *An-jeon-bu* police station. His health, by this point, was so bad he was immediately put on trial, lest he die in detention. His "trial" lasted less than an hour, during which time his "lawyer" offered no defense, and in late April 2007, Former Detainee # 35 was sentenced to two years at the Musan *ro-dong-dan-ryeon-dae* mobile labor brigade.

Through the help of family friends, he escaped after 20 days and immediately again fled to China. He rejoined his wife, regained his health, and met up with his mother. She had also been caught by Chinese police and repatriated in 2004 whereupon, she was imprisoned for a year at the Oro *kyo-yang-so* prison for women, described on page 91.

Former Detainee # 35 drew sketches of the Musan Mobile labor brigade and the Musan *An-jeon-bu* police detention-interrogation facility.

PART FIVE

SUMMARY OF TORTURE AND INFANTICIDE INFORMATION

Torture

According to almost all of the former prisoner testimony gathered for this report—from Ali Lamada's 1967 Sariwon prison testimony to the post-2000 testimonies of North Koreans forcibly repatriated from China—the practice of torture permeates the North Korean prison and detention system. Because it is so widespread and systematic, it clearly is not the work alone of sadistic elements, but reflects state policy intended to punish, degrade, intimidate and humiliate the prisoners in an effort to root out political disloyalty, connections to South Korea or belief in banned religions. At the same time, the practice of torture is intended to help amass widespread confessions that demonstrate threats to state security, thereby rationalizing or making essential constant vigilance, police presence and the use of torture. Notwithstanding, awareness that torture involves serious human rights transgressions has also led to the practice of requiring prisoners to discipline and beat other prisoners.

The following summary shows that torture is practiced in many prisons and detention facilities:

• Shin Dong-hyuk witnessed beatings of children at his primary "school" and saw his mother subjected to "kneeling motionless" punishments in the field for failing to meet work quotas. He himself was subjected to prolonged and systematic torture, including burnings and skin piercings, in an interrogation-punishment cell within *Kwan-li-so* Prison Camp No. 18. Also, he was required to sit in the front row to observe the public execution of his mother and brother, and his finger was cut off at the knuckle for an accidental error during his forced labor in a textile factory in Camp 18.

• Kim Yong reported that he was beaten at the *Bo-wi-bu* police jail at Maram and was subjected to water torture and hung by his wrists in the *Bo-wi-bu* police jail at Moonsu in 1993. Both jails are located in Pyongyang. He reports that his mother was beaten severely for being late in returning from gathering edible weeds just outside the gates of Camp No. 18.

• Kang Chol-hwan reported the existence of separate "punishment cells" within *Kwan-li-so* No. 15, Yodok, from which few prisoners returned alive.

• An Hyuk was subjected to sleep deprivation and "sitting motionless" torture for days at a time during the year-and-a-half he was detained at the Maram *Bo-wi-bu* police *ku-ryu-jang* interrogation-detention facility in the Yongsong section of Pyongyang, prior to being deported to Camp No. 15.

• Kim Tae-jin reported that he was beaten, deprived of sleep, and made to kneel motionless for many hours at the *Bo-wi-bu* police detention/interrogation facility in Chongjin in late 1998/early 1999, prior to being deported to Camp 15.

• Lee Young-kuk reported that he was subjected to motionless-kneeling and water torture and facial and shin beatings with rifle butts at a *Bo-wi-bu* interrogation/detention facility in Pyongyang in 1994, leaving permanent damage in one ear, double vision in one eye, and his shins permanently bruised and discolored.

• Former Prisoner # 27 had his front teeth knocked out from beatings administered at the Chongjin *Bo-wi-bu* police office following his repatriation at Onsong.

• Kim Eun-chol lost teeth and has permanent scars on his head, ears, and knees from beatings with wooden staves and rifle cleaning rods at the Musan *Bo-wi-bu* police detention facility.

• Jung Gwang-il lost teeth and has head scars from beatings with wooden staves. He was also subjected to prolonged food deprivation and "pigeon torture" with his arms pinned behind his back and attached to cell bars in ways that made it impossible either to stand up or sit down during his detention at the Hoeryong *Bo-wi-bu* police interrogation-detention facility.

• Former Prisoner # 28 was beaten in the face with rulers and books at a *bo-wi-bu* police interrogation facility in Pyongyang. She was also subjected to the "kneeling motionless" torture for days, causing her legs to swell painfully. This was alternated with being forced to do deep knee bends with her fingers outside the bars of the cell. When she could not continue the deep knee bends she was beaten on the fingers.

• Former Prisoner # 29 lost teeth to beatings while a teenage pupil at a school in *Kwan-li-so* Camp No. 18.

• Ahn Myong-chol, a former guard, reported that all three of the *kwan-li-so* at which he worked had isolated detention facilities in which many prisoners died from mistreatment, and that at *Kwan-li-so* No. 22 there were so many deaths by beatings from guards that the guards were told to be less violent.

• Former Prisoner # 37 was beaten at the Onsong *An-jeon-bu* police facility during his six month interrogation prior to being tried and sentenced to Chongo-ri *kyo-hwa-so* for smuggling food back and forth from China.

• Seo Jin was beaten so badly with wooden staves at the Onsong *Bo-wi-bu* interrogation center, and again at the Musan *Bo-wi-bu* interrogation center, that she could hardly walk. After transfer to the Musan *An-jeon-bu* detention facility, she was beaten by younger women guards when she objected to her third vaginal examination. And she was kicked on the legs and beaten on the back by guards at the Oro *Kyo-yang-so* penitentiary No. 55 when she did not keep up the required pace in her prison labor.

• Former Prisoner # 31 was whipped with a belt by male guards at the Onsong *Bo-wi-bu* interrogation facility, and severely beaten on her legs and back when, because of severe malnutrition, she was unable to maintain the pace of her prison labor.

• Bang Mi-sun was severely beaten on her legs with a wooden stave because she could not keep up with the work pace at the Musan *An-jeon-bu-run ro-dong-dan-ryeon-dae* mobile labor brigade owing to injuries she suffered while trafficked in China prior to her repatriation. Infection from this beating left her partially crippled. At the Musan *An-jeon-bu* pre-trial detention *ku-ryu-jang*, she and other prisoners were required to sit motionless for days, with fellow detainees forced to beat other detainees who moved.

• Yoo Chun-sik was beaten while being hung upside down at the Onsong *An-jeon-bu* run mobile labor brigade. He was kicked, beaten and subjected to the sitting-motionless torture at the Sinuiju *Bo-wi-bu* interrogation-detention facility. Additionally, he witnessed beatings of other prisoners at *Kyo-hwa-so* No. 22.

• Ji Hae-nam confirmed the existence of grossly undersized punishment cells at *Kyo-hwa-so* No. 1 where detainees could not stand up or lie down and where beatings and kicking of women prisoners were a daily occurrence in the mid-1990s. She also reported beatings during interrogation or for prison regulation infractions that she experienced in late 1999 at the Sinuiju *Bo-wi-bu* interrogation-detention facility. She was forced to kneel motionless, was hit with broomsticks and required to do stand-up/sit-down positions to the point of collapse, in her case thirty to forty minutes.

• Lee Soon-ok reported that she experienced beatings, strappings, and water torture leading to loss of consciousness, and was held outside in freezing January weather at the Chongjin pre-trial detention center in 1986. The beatings and brutalities in the early-to mid-1990s at Kaechon women's prison, *Kyo-hwa-so* No. 1, recorded in her prison memoirs are too numerous to detail here.

• Following repatriation, Koh Jeon-mi was beaten so severely on the head at the North Pyongan province *Bo-wi-bu* detention facility that she was unconscious for ten days and required hospitalization.

• Following repatriation, Lee Yoo-keum was beaten at the Sinuiju *An-jeon-bu* detention facility.

• Following repatriation, Kim Myong-ho was hit and kicked at the Sinuiju *Bo-wi-bu* interrogation-detention facility and then subjected to even more extreme sitting-motionless torture during which he was hit on the fingers or knees if he moved even slightly.

• Following repatriation, Former Detainee # 34 lost a tooth from beatings on the face at the Hoeryong *Bo-wi-bu* interrogation-detention facility, though, like other former prisoners, he describes the sitting-motionless torture as much more painful.

• Former Detainee # 32 was hit in the face and kicked while kneeling at the Onsong *Bo-wi-bu* facility in March 2004.

• Lee Young-suk witnessed other detainees being beaten with thick staves at the Onsong *Bo-wi-bu* detention facility, though she herself was not beaten as she was detained along with her young child whom she was breast feeding.

• Former Detainee # 33 was hit in the face and kicked by Onsong *Bo-wi-bu* interrogators because she refused to identify North Korean border guards who had assisted her flight to China. She witnessed beatings of pregnant women for carrying "Chinese babies."

• Former Detainee # 1 was beaten unconscious for hunger-related rule infractions in 1997 at the Nongpo *jip-kyul-so* detention center in Chongjin City. He also reported that detainees there were beaten with shovels if they did not work fast enough.

• Former Detainee # 3 reported the use of an undersized punishment box at the Danchun prison camp in which camp rule-breakers were held for fifteen days, unable to stand up or lie down. He also reported that beatings of prisoners by guards were common.

• Former Prisoner #6 reported that prisoners were beaten to death by prison work unit leaders at Danchun *Kyo-hwa-so* No. 77 in North Hamgyong province.

• Former Detainee # 8 reported that male prisoners were beaten by guards at the Chongjin *jip-kyul-so* in mid-2000.

• Former Detainee # 9 reported that detainees at the Onsong *ro-dong-dan-ryeon-dae* mobile labor brigade were compelled to beat each other.

• Kim Sung-min reported that in 1997 at the Onsong *Bo-wi-bu* detention center, his fingers were broken and he was kicked and beaten on the head and face until his ears, eyes, nose, and mouth bled.

• Ryu Young-il saw, in 1997, that out of six persons in an adjacent cell in the *bo-wi-bu* interrogation facility where he was detained in Pyongyang, two were carried out on stretchers, two could walk only with the assistance of guards, and two could walk out by themselves. Detainees who moved while they were supposed to be sitting motionless and silent for long periods were handcuffed from the upper bars of their cells with their feet off the floor. Detainees who talked when they were supposed to be sitting motionless and silent were compelled to slap and hit each other.

• Former Prisoner # 12 reported that at Hoery-ong *kyo-hwa-so* in the early to middle 1990s, minor rule-breakers were beaten by their cell-mates on the orders of the guards, and major rule-breakers were placed in a 4x4 foot punish-ment cell for a week or more.

• Lee Min-bok reported being beaten "many times" on his fingernails and the back of his hands with a metal rod during interrogation at the Hyesan detention center in 1990. He also reported that at the Hyesan *An-jeon-bu* detention facility, where he was subsequently held, prisoners were compelled to beat each other. Lee witnessed one prisoner, Kim Jae-chul, beaten to death.

• Former Detainee # 15 reported that he was beaten with chairs and sticks at both the Hoery-ong and Onsong *An-jeon-bu* detention facilities in early 2002.

• Former Detainee # 21 reported that she was beaten unconscious in mid-1999 at the *An-jeon-bu* detention/interrogation facility at Onsong, where detainees were beaten so badly that they confessed to doing things they had not done. Women were hit on their fingertips. She witnessed one very ill woman compelled to do stand-up/sit-down repetitions until she passed out and died.

• Former Detainee # 22 reported that he was beat-en with chairs at Onsong *Bo-wi- bu* police jail in late 2001 and beaten even worse at the Chongjin *An-jeon-bu* detention center in early 2002.

• Former Detainee # 24 reported that there were beatings at the *Bo-wi-bu* police jail in Sinuiju in January 2000.

• Former Detainee #25 reported that one woman, a former schoolteacher who had been caught in Mongolia and repatriated to China and North Korea, was beaten nearly to death at the Onsong *An-jeon-bu* detention center in November 1999 and then taken away either to die or, if she recovered, to be transferred to *Kyo-hwa-so* No. 22.

• Former Detainee # 26 was made to kneel motion-less at the Onsong *Bo-wi-bu* police jail in June 2000 and was made to sit motionless for six days at the Hoeryong *Bo-wi-bu* police jail in July 2001.

• Former Detainee # 28 reported that prisoners were beaten to death at the *Kyo- hwa-so* No. 12 at Chongo-ri in North Hamgyong province in 1999.[113]

Racially Motivated Forced Abortion/ Infanticide

Former prisoners interviewed for this report provided testimony about forced abortions and killings of babies at the *kwan-li-so* political penal labor colonies, where, except for a very few privileged couples, the prisoners were not allowed to have sex or children. There are also reports of killings of pregnant women who had been raped or coerced into sex by prison guards. However, this report focuses on the forced abor-tions and infanticide against and inflicted on women forcibly repatriated from China because of the racial and policy components of these atrocities. The women impregnated by Chinese men were routinely punished and their babies

---

113 For additional information on torture, see, *North Korea: Repub-lic of Torture*, Citizen's Alliance for North Korean Human Rights, Seoul, 2007.

killed, accompanied by racial slurs and refusal to accept children who were part Han Chinese.

Sinuiju, North Pyongan Province

• Choi Yong-hwa assisted in the delivery of babies, three of whom were promptly killed, at the Sinuiju *do-jip-kyul-so* (provincial detention center) in mid-2000. The explanation given was that "no half-Han [Chinese] babies would be tolerated."

• Yoo Chun-sik reported that four pregnant women at the *bo-wi-bu* National Security Agency police station in Sinuiju were subjected to forced abortions in mid-2000.

• Former Detainee # 24 helped deliver seven babies who were killed at the Bakto-ri, South Sinuiju *An-jeon-bu* police detention center in January 2000. A doctor explained that since North Korea was short on food, the country should not have to feed the children of foreign fathers.

Chongjin

• Former Detainee # 8 witnessed six forced abortions at Chongjin *do-jip-kyul-so* in mid-2000.

• Former Prisoner # 35 was informed by another prisoner that in 2002 a repatriated pregnant woman at the Chongjin *jip-kyul-so* was subjected to a forced abortion because she could not prove that the father was Korean rather than Han Chinese.

• Former Detainee # 25 witnessed four babies killed at Nongpo *An-jeon-bu* police detention

center in Chongjin in late 1999 and another six pregnant women subjected to forced abortion. The women were told they would not be allowed to leave the detention center still carrying "children of betrayers" in their wombs.

• Former Detainee # 26 witnessed three forced abortions and seven babies killed at the Nongpo *jip-kyul-so* detention center, Chongjin City, in May 2000. The guards insisted that the mothers see and hear the babies die because the babies were Chinese

Hyesan, Yanggang Province

• Following her repatriation in November 2004, Lee Chun-shim, a former nurse in the North Korean army, observed in the detention facility for repatriated persons multiple abortions through the injection of the concentrated form of the drug ravenol into the womb of the pregnant women. To her surprise, even three to four month premature fetuses were born crying and moaning, but the fetuses were wrapped in newspapers and put in a bucket until buried in a yard behind the jail. North Korean guards reportedly cursed the women as "bitches who got Chinese sperm and brought this on themselves."

Onsong, North Hamgyong Province

• Former Detainee # 21 reported two baby killings at the Onsong *An-jeon-bu* police station in late 1999.

• Former Detainee # 9 witnessed ten forced abortions at Onsong *ro-dong-dan-ryeon-da*e mobile labor brigade in mid-2000.

• Former Prisoner # 31 witnessed pregnant women losing their babies from stress during interrogations at the Onsong *Bo-wi-bu* detention facility in 2003. A few women gave birth while in the jail. Other pregnant women were taken to the hospital, but it is not known if they were forced to abort or allowed to give birth.

• Former Prisoner # 37 was informed by another detainee at the Onsong *An-jeon-bu* interrogation facility in 2003 of a pregnant woman who aborted after being kicked in her stomach by guards.

• Ms. Moon-suk witnessed the infanticide of a baby born in the Onsong *Bo-wi-bu* interrogation facility in 2003. The mother was beaten for begging for the life of her baby. Other pregnant women were cursed and slapped around for having received "foreign seed" and taken to a hospital, presumably for abortions.

• In 2004, Former Detainee # 32 carefully hid her five-month pregnancy at the Onsong *Bo-wi-bu* detention facility, as she feared a forced abortion if the police observed or learned of her pregnancy.

Musan, North Hamgyong Province

• In 1998, Former Prisoner # 35 saw guards insulting a pregnant woman at the Musan *ro-dong-dan-ryeon-dae* mobile labor brigade for receiving "Chinese seed" after which the woman was subjected to forced abortion. He saw other pregnant women slapped around by guards.

• Mrs. Bang Mi-sun observed ten pregnant women in early 2002 taken to a hospital from the Musan *An-jeon-bu* detention facility for the purpose of aborting their "half-Chinese babies." Another seven month pregnant woman adamantly refused to go to the hospital and guards compelled male prisoners to jump on her stomach until the woman aborted on the floor. The woman was then taken to the hospital where she died.

• In early 2004, Mrs. Seo Jin saw pregnant women being led away from the Musan *Bo-wi-bu* detention facility. Their destination was kept secret, but following her own release she learned that several women escaped from the hospital.

ROME STATUTE OF THE INTERNATIONAL CRIMINAL COURT

ARTICLE 7

1. For the purpose of this Statute, "crime against humanity" means any of the following acts when committed as part of a widespread or systematic attack directed against any civilian population, with knowledge of the attack:

a.   Murder;

b.   Extermination;

c.   Enslavement;

d.   Deportation or forcible transfer of population;

e.   Imprisonment or other severe deprivation of physical liberty in violation of fundamental rules of international law;

f.   Torture;

g.   Rape, sexual slavery, enforced prostitution, forced pregnancy, enforced sterilization, or any other form of sexual violence of comparable gravity;

h.   Persecution against any identifiable group or collectivity on political, racial, national, ethnic, cultural, religious, gender, … or other grounds that are universally recognized as impermissible under international law in connection with any act referred to in this paragraph or any crime within the jurisdiction of the Court;

i.   Enforced disappearance of person;

j.   The crime of apartheid;

k.   Other inhumane acts of a similar character intentionally causing great suffering or serious injury to body or to mental or physical health.

Adopted by the United Nations Diplomatic Conference of Plenipotentiaries on the Establishment of an International Criminal Court, July 17, 1998, Rome, Italy. Entered into force June 2002.

PART SIX

CONCLUSION: THE NORMATIVE AND LEGAL FRAMEWORK FOR ANALYZING HUMAN RIGHTS VIOLATIONS IN NORTH KOREA

The first edition of *Hidden Gulag*, published in 2003, evaluated human rights problems in the DPRK using the international human rights standards contained in the International Covenant on Civil and Political Rights, the International Covenant on Economic, Social and Cultural Rights, and the subsequent series of declarations and conventions dealing with particular phenomena of repression—such as torture and the persecution of particularly vulnerable groups such as women, children, and refugees. Based on these international norms and standards, that report outlined "a consistent pattern of gross violations of internationally recognized human rights" or, more simply, "gross violations."

The present, second edition, continues to use the evaluative framework of international human rights law.[114] However, just as the first edition of *Hidden Gulag* was being readied for publication, an additional normative and legal framework for evaluating especially severe "gross violations" was taking effect: the Rome Statute of the International Criminal Court. The Rome Statute contains a revised and updated definition of "crimes against humanity" that takes into fuller account contemporary phenomena of severe repression.

There has long been a considerable gap in the normative human rights framework between "gross violations" (serious contraventions of the standards set forth in the twin International Covenants) and "genocide" (as defined in international law). This normative framework failed to adequately provide for a variety of atrocities that are more severe and atrocious than "violations," but do not constitute "genocide," which is narrowly defined in the Convention on the Prevention and Punishment of the Crime of Genocide as the intentional destruction in whole or in part of a national, ethnic, racial or religious group, as such.[115]

It was recognized in the 1980s and 1990s that various atrocities and very severe violations were insufficiently delineated and proscribed in the twin Covenants when they were being negotiated in the 1950s and 1960s. Examples of insufficiently delineated phenomena of repression in existing international human rights legal instruments include, for example, "enforced disappearances" (extra-judicial abductions by state authorities, followed by *incommunicado* detention and, often, secret political killings),[116] "extra-judicial executions" (political killings and civilian massacres by State authorities without any trials or judicial proceedings), deportations and prolonged detention without trial,[117] and

---

114 See, for example, the listing of the Articles of the International Covenant on Civil and Political Rights violated in the process of arbitary detention on page 160.

115 Recognition of this normative gap was occasioned in part by the massacres in Guatemala in the mid-60s, Uganda in the 1970s and the wholesale slaughter in Cambodia under Khmer Rouge rule in the mid-to-late 1970s. These atrocities were clearly much worse than the standard "gross violations." But there was doubt and debate about whether or not such terrible and large scale massacres constituted "genocide" as defined in the 1948 Genocide Convention, with its omission of "political groups," its failure to cover "cultural genocide," and its restrictive "as such" intent provision.

116 A practice used by military dictatorships in the "dirty wars" in the southern cone of Latin America.

117 Such as the "B category" prisoners on Buru Island in Indone-

"ethnic cleansing" (deportations of ethnic or religious minorities from areas where they were previously lawfully resident).[118]

The ad hoc tribunals for Rwanda and Yugoslavia that were established by the UN Security Council in the early and mid-1990s recognized and tackled these gaps in the international human rights normative, legal, and analytical framework. Subsequent multilateral treaties such as the International Convention for the Protection of all Persons from Enforced Disappearance also tackled these gaps. And the normative gaps noted above were addressed in the 1997 negotiations to draft the Statute for the International Criminal Court (ICC). These juridical proceedings and diplomatic and legal negotiations made an invaluable adjustment to the normative framework for analyzing contemporary phenomena of repression: an inclusionary and more workable definition of "crimes against humanity."

The Nuremberg Tribunal placed crimes against humanity in the context of international armed conflict—atrocities committed against civilians in a time of war (in parallel with war crimes, which were atrocities committed against enemy combatants in time of war). The International Criminal Tribunal for the Former Yugoslavia (ICTY) retained the connection to armed conflict, but the armed conflict no longer needed to be international in character. The International Criminal Tribunal for Rwanda (ICTR) established no connection to armed conflict. At the Rome negotiations for the statutes of a permanent international criminal court, the link to armed conflict remained severed. Drawing heavily on what jurists and legal scholars refer to as customary international law and the judicial rulings and determinations of the ad hoc tribunals for Rwanda and Yugoslavia, "crimes against humanity" were defined as: murder; extermination; enslavement; deportation or forcible population transfer; imprisonment or severe deprivations of physical liberty (in violation of fundamental rules of international law); torture; rape or sexual slavery; persecution on political, racial, national, ethnic, cultural, gender or religious grounds; enforced disappearances; apartheid; and other inhumane acts of a similar character when knowingly committed as part of a widespread or systematic course of conduct against a civilian population in furtherance of state policy.

These phenomena of repression—now recognized and proscribed as atrocity crimes—are part and parcel of the systems of repression described by the former prisoners and torture victims interviewed for this report, in addition to a very large number of "gross violations" of the norms and standards set forth in the International Covenants. As noted above, this updated normative framework entered into force as the first edition of *Hidden Gulag* was being readied for publication. The present edition is able to use the updated normative framework and incorporate the judgments and proceedings of the Ad Hoc Tribunals and the standards set forth in the Rome Statute of the International Criminal Court, which, as of November 2011, has been signed by 139 UN Member States and ratified by some 117.

---

sia, to which tens of thousands were deported and detained in the late 1960s and 1970s because the Indonesian government admitted, there was no evidence of criminal acts that could be used to bring these people to trial.

118 As practiced in the Balkan conflicts in the early 1990s.

Jurisdictional issues would likely prevent the International Criminal Court from holding those most responsible for the atrocities in North Korea accountable.[119] That said, the provisions of the Rome Statute defining crimes against humanity in the contemporary era provide clear terms of reference and an invaluable framework for analyzing the consistent pattern of gross violations that are documented in this report. The fact that the Rome Statute has been recognized by three-quarters of the member states of the UN means that the norms and standards so recognized will become part of what lawyers call "customary international law" applicable to all nation states, and hence, usable as a framework for analysis for this report.

Specifically, ten of the eleven prohibited criminal actions and the introductory provision setting out the overarching requisite circumstances[120] for crimes against humanity in the Rome Statute provide a clear and precise framework for analyzing, step-by-step, the succession of gross, now criminalized, violations that take place in the *kwan-li-so* political prison-forced labor camps in the DPRK. These criminal actions are summarized below. They can be tracked throughout the stories and testimonies of the former *kwan-li-so* prisoners interviewed for this report.[121]

This analysis also applies to some of the persons imprisoned and subjected to forced labor in the *kyo-hwa-so* camps and penitentiaries who have been detained, without trial, for what are internationally recognized as essentially political, not criminal, acts.[122]

The terms and provisions of Article 7 of the Rome Statute, which defines crimes against humanity, also apply to the serial atrocities inflicted by the DPRK authorities on the North Koreans who are forcibly repatriated from China, as can be seen, step-by-step, atrocity-by-atrocity, in the testimonies of the forcibly repatriated persons summarized in this report.

Clear and Massive Crimes against Humanity: The *Kwan-li-so* Political Penal Labor Colonies

In the Democratic People's Republic of Korea, crimes against humanity are committed against persons sent to the political penal labor colonies. Evidence shows that:

1. Perceived or suspected "wrong-doers" or "wrong-thinkers," or in some instances, persons with "wrong-knowledge,"[123] and/or their family members are subjected to enforced disappearance. These persons are picked up by police officials

---

119 ICC Jurisdiction would require DPRK accession to the Rome Statute or a referral from the UN Security Council, the latter of which is subject to a veto by China or Russia.

120 What lawyers call the "*chapeau.*"

121 For more detailed applications of Article 7 of the Rome Statute to the *kwan-li-so* system of political imprisonment and forced labor in North Korea see Vaclav Havel, Kjell Bondevik and Elie Wiesel, *Failure to Protect: A Call for the UN Security Council to Act in North Korea*, DLA Piper and the Committee for Human Rights in North Korea, Washington DC, 2006; *Concentrations of Inhumanity*, Freedom House, New York, 2007; and *North Korea: A Case to Answer, A Call to Act*, Christian Solidarity Worldwide, London, 2007.

122 It should be noted that the kyo-hwa-so system in North Korea also incarcerates persons tried and convicted for violations for what are internationally recognized criminal acts, and properly specified as such in the DPRK Criminal Law and Criminal Procedures Code.

123 For example, some of the North Korean diplomats who were posted to Eastern Europe, and North Korean students who were studying in Eastern Europe at the time of the collapse of the communist regimes, were recalled to the DPRK and immediately sent to the labor camps to prevent knowledge about the collapse of the DPRK's socialist allies from spreading to the general public.

from the DPRK State Security Agency,[124] which refuses to acknowledge the deprivation of freedom and refuses to provide information on the fate or whereabouts of those persons with the intent of removing those persons from the "protection of law" for a prolonged period of time.[125]

2. The abducted persons are subjected to deportation or forcible transfer[126] from the area in which they were lawfully present[127] without grounds permitted under international law.[128]

3. The abducted and deported persons are deposited at distant, remote, penal labor colonies or encampments, where they are subjected to "imprisonment or severe deprivation of physical liberty in violation of fundamental rules of international law."[129] These abductions, deportations and the subsequent imprisonments all take place without any judicial process. There is no arrest, charge, trial, conviction or sentence, as provided in the DPRK Criminal Code and the DPRK Criminal Procedures Code. Perceived or suspected criminals are entitled to judicial proceedings conducted in accordance with *due process* and fair trial as detailed in Article 14 of the International Covenant on Civil and Political Rights (ICCPR), in international law, and in the

legal systems of most nations around the world. "Wrong-thinking" is not recognized in international law as a permissible criminal offense. The practice of forcible transfer and imprisonment of the children and/or grandchildren of perceived (though untried and unconvicted), "wrong-doers" or "wrong-thinkers" is far outside the permissible grounds of international law. These are blatant violations of Article 9(1) and (4) of the ICCPR, "…no one shall be subjected to arbitrary arrest or detention. No one shall be deprived of his liberty except on such grounds and in accordance with such procedures as are established by law… Anyone who is deprived of his liberty by arrest or detention shall be entitled to take proceedings before a court, in order that such court may decide without delay on the lawfulness of his detention and order his release if the detention is not lawful."

4. The prolonged, indefinite detention of family members is a violation of Article 26 of the ICCPR, "…the law shall prohibit any discrimination and guarantee to all persons equal and effective protection against discrimination on any ground such as race, colour, sex, language, religion, political or other opinion, national or social origin, property, birth or other status." The imprisonment of family members amounts to what the ICC Statute terms as "persecution." Most family members of suspected wrong-doers or wrong-thinkers are detained for the rest of their lives in sections of the prison camps termed "total control zones." The small numbers who are released from sections of the prison camps termed "revolutionizing process zones" are subjected to discrimination even after their release.[130] This also is "persecution" within

---

124 The North Korean term for the political police, *Kuk ga-bo-wi-bu*, is also sometimes translated as the National Security Agency.

125 This is precisely the definition of "enforced disappearance" in Articles 7.1(i) and 7.2(i) of the Statute of the International Criminal Court.

126 ICC Statute, Article 7.1(d).

127 Almost all such persons would have been previously assigned to their former residential areas by state authorities.

128 ICC Statute, Article 7.2(d).

129 ICC Statute, Article 7.1(e). A group of attorneys have enumerated the "fundamental rules of international law" that are violated in "the severe deprivation of physical liberty" within the DPRK political penal labor colonies. See box below.

130 Thus, many former North Korean political prisoners, possessed of a well-founded fear of persecution should they remain

---

Fundamental Rules of International Law

Articles of the International Covenant on Civil and Political Rights violated in North Korea's political penal labor colonies:

Article 6 (right to life);
Article 7 (right not be subjected to torture or to cruel, inhuman, or degrading treatment);
Article 8 (right not to be held in slavery or servitude);
Article 9 (right not be held in arbitrary detention):
Article 10 (right for all persons deprived of liberty to be treated with humanity);
Article 12 (right to free movement);
Article 16 (right to recognition as a person before the law);
Article 17 (right not to be subjected to arbitrary interference with privacy, family, home or correspondence);
Article 18 (right to freedom of thought, conscience and religion);
Article 19 (right to hold opinion without interference);
Article 21 (right to peaceable assembly);
Article 22 (right to freedom of association);
Article 26 (rights to equal protection and non-discrimination, including on grounds of political or other opinion, birth, or other status.)

Failure to Protect, op cit., page 91.

---

the meaning of the ICC Statute. The camp system in its entirety can be characterized as a massive and elaborate system of persecution on political grounds.[131]

5. Once cut off from any contact with the country or world outside of the prison camp, includ- ing former family and friends, the imprisoned persons are subjected, usually for a lifetime, to arduous forced labor under extremely severe circumstances. This begins with the provision of below subsistence level food rations. These prac- tices contravene Article 10(1) of the Internation- al Covenant on Civil and Political Rights, "All persons deprived of their liberty shall be treated with humanity and with respect for the inherent dignity of the human person." The conditions of detention in the labor camps contravene, to an astonishing extent, the UN Standard Minimum

---

in their country of origin (in the language of the 1951 Refugee Convention) flee North Korea in search of refuge abroad after their release from detention. There are hundreds of former North Korean political prisoners now residing in South Korea, sixty of whom were interviewed for this report.

131 ICC Statute, Article 7.1(h) and 7.2(g).

Rules for the Treatment of Prisoners. The forced labor in the prison camps violates Article 8 (3.1.) of the ICCPR, "No one shall be required to perform forced or compulsory labor."[132] As noted, while some forms of prison labor are permitted under international law, exacting such extreme forms of forced labor under such severe conditions has been judged by the Ad Hoc International Criminal Tribunals to constitute enslavement.[133] Food ration policies in the labor camps violate Article 11 of the International Covenant on Economic, Social and Cultural Rights (CESCR). Deprivation of liberty does not negate the right to "adequate food" and "freedom from hunger." Indeed, states have even more direct responsibility (and State Parties to the ICESCR have the legal obligation) to provide "adequate food" to those residing involuntarily in state institutions where such persons are denied the ability to obtain or provide food for themselves and their families.

6. The political penal camp system itself is entirely outside the DPRK legal framework or DPRK laws. North Korean laws and courts do not cover or reach into the prison camps, which are thus "extra-judicial." The prisoners have been "removed from the protection of the law" for the duration of the imprisonment, which for most prisoners is a lifetime. Actions that should be subject to the law[134] and legal proceedings even when a person is deprived of his or her physical liberty, such as the execution of prisoners, are carried out extra-judicially. These extra-judicial executions, many of which are carried out publicly, constitute murder,[135] a crime against humanity. The executions in the camps, which have been witnessed by virtually all former prisoners interviewed for this report, violate Article 6(1) of the ICCPR, "Every human being has the inherent right to life…No one shall be arbitrarily deprived of his life." The executions in the camps violate Article 6(2) which further stipulates that "for countries which have not abolished the death penalty…this penalty can only be carried out pursuant to a final judgment rendered by a competent court."

7. Prisoners are regularly subjected to beatings and sometimes more systematic torture for infractions of prison camp regulations and during interrogations. "Torture, cruel, inhuman or degrading treatment or punishment" is prohibited by Article 7 of the International Covenant on Civil and Political Rights. Torture and the cruel, inhuman or degrading punishments experienced or witnessed by virtually all former prisoners in the DPRK forced-labor camps are crimes against humanity.[136]

8. On numerous occasions, prisoners compelled to observe executions (which are carried out publicly to demonstrate to other prisoners the severe consequences of escape attempts and/or non-compliance with camp regulations) were also compelled to pass close by and defile the hanging

---

132 Article 8 of the ICCPR further stipulates that when hard labor is punishment for a crime, it must be pursuant to the lawful order of a competent court.

133 See, for example, *Kunarac, Kovac and Vokovic*, Appeals Chambers, International Criminal Tribunal for the Former Yugoslavia (ICTY), June 12, 2002, para. 119 "In determining whether or not enslavement has been established, the indicia of enslavement… include: control of someone's movement, control of physical environment, psychological control, measures taken to prevent or deter escape, force, threat of force or coercion, duration, assertion of exclusivity, subjugation to cruel treatment and abuse, control of sexuality, and forced labor."

134 ICC Statute 7.2(i).

135 ICC Statute 7.1(a).

136 ICC Statute 7.1(f) and 7.2(e).

or slumped-over corpse of the just-executed prisoner. This practice constitutes an "other inhumane act... causing great suffering and injury to... mental health."[137] The severe working conditions imposed on deliberately underfed prisoners, particularly in the mining and lumber processing sectors of the labor camps (which lead to a large number of industrial accidents and deaths) could also be deemed "other inhumane acts."

9. Prison camp officials and guards are regularly able to exact sexual relations with female prisoners under circumstances that have been judged to constitute rape or sexual violence[138] as defined by judges at the Ad Hoc Tribunals, namely, "any act of a sexual nature which is committed on a person under circumstances which are coercive.... [noting further that] coercive circumstances need not be evidenced by a show of physical force. Threats, intimidation, extortion and other forms of duress which prey on fear or desperation may constitute coercion, and coercion may be inherent in certain circumstances."[139]

10. Extermination,[140] as defined by the ICC Statute, "includes the intentional infliction of conditions of life, inter alia the deprivation of access to food and medicine, calculated to bring about the destruction of a part of the population."[141] The high rates of deaths in detention from combinations of malnutrition, starvation, exhaustion (from forced labor) and disease would likely constitute the crime against humanity of extermination in the views of legal scholars and judges[142] to constitute the crime against humanity of extermination.

The high rate of deaths-in-detention is accompanied by a prohibition on procreation by prisoners. With rare exception, young men and women sent to, or growing up in the prison camps, are not allowed to marry or have children.[143] Such pregnancies as inevitably occur are terminated by involuntary abortion and severe punishment for the woman, including execution. It is the clear and stated intention of the political prison camp system to terminate up to three generations of the families of these perceived or imagined opponents of the Kim family dynasty. The prevention of births or the deliberate termination of the family lineage of the scores of thousands of prisoners in the gulag camps would also likely qualify as the crime against humanity of extermination.[144]

11. With the exception of the crime of apartheid,[145] virtually all of the particular criminal acts included within the various iterations of crimes against humanity in modern international law are committed in North Korea. However, while most of these acts are criminal under most domestic laws, penal codes and legal systems of most UN Member States, it is only when these acts are conducted under specified conditions that they become "crimes against humanity." Those conditions

---

137 ICC Statute 7.1(k).

138 ICC Statute 7.1(g).

139 Akayesu, (Trial Chamber, International Criminal Tribunal for Rwanda (ICTR), September 2, 1998, paras. 686-688). ICC Statute 7.1(b).

140 ICC Statute 7.2(b).

141 ICC Statute 7.2(b).

142 See *Failure to Protect*, op cit., pp. 91-93.

143 See pages 48-51 for one such exception.

144 It should be noted that the "intent" (*mens rea*) requirements for extermination are much more manageable than the highly restrictive intent requirements for genocide.

145 ICC Statute, Article 7.1(j): systematic, institutionalized racial oppression (ICC Statute, Article 7.2(h))

apply when these acts are "committed as part of a widespread or systematic attack directed against any civilian population, with knowledge of the attack."

The specific use of the word "attack" reflects the historical association of crimes against humanity with war crimes: war crimes being specified atrocities committed against enemy soldiers or combatants, crimes against humanity being committed against civilians. Hence, the retention of the word "attack."[146]

However, "attack" is carefully defined as "a course of conduct involving the multiple commission of acts [as specifically described above] against any civilian population, pursuant to or in furtherance of State or organizational policy...."[147] And the judges at the UN-established International Tribunals have made further clarifications: "An attack may also be non-violent in nature, like imposing a system of apartheid…, or **extending pressure on the population to act in a particular manner** (emphasis added)."[148]

This is obviously one of the intended consequences of the *kwan-li-so* gulag system in North Korea both for the victim populations in the camps, and for the general population which is well aware of the "people who are sent to the mountains," a euphemism for people who disappear into the prison camps.

12. Prisoners in the *kwan-li-so* camps are subjected to widespread and systematic abuse. "Widespread or systematic" has been defined by judges at the Ad Hoc International Criminal Tribunals as "massive, frequent, large scale actions, carried out collectively with considerable seriousness against a multiplicity of victims"[149] and as a reference to the "scale of the acts perpetrated and the number of victims."[150] According to the judges of the International Tribunal for Rwanda, "The concept of 'systematic' may be defined as thoroughly organized, and following a regular pattern on the basis of a common policy involving substantial public or private resources."[151]

Further, the judges have noted that the conditions—*widespread or systematic*—are intended to "exclude isolated or random inhumane acts committed for purely personal reasons."[152] It is not required that the inhumane acts be both widespread and systematic. However, any system such as the *kwan-li-so* political prison camp system in North Korea that involves hundreds of thousands of victims, exists over a period of at least forty years, and necessitates thousands of military and police personnel to operate, administer, and control, is obviously both widespread *and* systematic.

13. Lastly, the Statute of the International Criminal Court specifies that to be a crime against humanity the proscribed inhumane acts have to be conducted "with knowledge of the attack."[153] This formulation is the "mental element," "intent" or "guilty mind" (*mens rea*) requirement for crimes against humanity. The purpose of

---

146 ICC Statute, Article 7.1.

147 ICC Statute, Article 7.2(a).

148 *Akayesu*, (Trial Chamber, ICTR, September 2, 1998, para. 581).

149 Ibid, para. 580.

150 *Blaskic*, (Trial Chamber, ICTY, March 3, 2000, para. 206).

151 *Akayesu* (Trial Chamber, ICTR, September 2, 1998, para. 580).

152 *Kayishema and Ruzindana* (Trial Chamber, ICTR, May 21, 1999, para. 122-123, n.28).

153 ICC Statute, Article 7.1.

this provision is to exclude inhumane acts that have occurred accidentally, inadvertently or for personal reasons. In short, it means that the perpetrators had to have known what they were doing and did it on purpose. Obviously, again, the construction and continued operation of a large-scale prison forced-labor camp system is deliberate and purposeful.

These separate and distinct phenomena of repression, now defined in international law as crimes against humanity, are clearly apparent in the testimony and brief biographies of the former prisoners interviewed for this report.

Serial Atrocities Inflicted on Forcibly Repatriated Koreans

Just as the severe human rights violations perpetrated against hundreds of thousands of North Koreans deported to the political penal labor colonies constitute clear and massive crimes against humanity, there is also a strong case that the series of severe punishments inflicted on North Koreans forcibly repatriated from China exceeds the characterization of "a consistent pattern of gross violations of internationally recognized human rights" and meets the threshold requirements for characterization as crimes against humanity.

As noted above, reflecting 'crimes against humanity's' historic usage as atrocities committed against civilians in time of war, the revised and updated approach retains the wording of such crimes as "a *widespread or systematic* attack conducted against a civilian population..."[154] While "attack" is defined as a "course of conduct involving the multiple commission of acts against any civilian population, pursuant to or in furtherance of State or organizational policy,"[155] "attack" seems exactly the right word for what the North Korean police agencies do to the DPRK citizens who are repatriated from China, revealed in the testimonies of the formerly repatriated persons.

The threshold requirement for a crime against humanity is that the course of conduct pursued in furtherance of state policy be either systematic or widespread. In the case of the *kwan-li-so* slave labor camps, the practice of processing hundreds of thousands of prisoners over the course of the half-century of the camps' operation is both *systematic and widespread*. The repatriated North Koreans, severely mistreated in the ways detailed in this report, number in the thousands. There are literally hundreds of forcibly repatriated North Koreans who fled the DPRK a second time and now reside in South Korea. And there are hundreds more who again fled to China and who have been interviewed there. These numbers may or may not merit the designation *widespread*.

But the phenomena of repression against the North Koreans forcibly repatriated from China are, on the basis of the available evidence, systematic. While the system of detention-interrogation-torture-and forced labor to which the repatriated persons are subjected, as described in this report,

---

154 ICC Statute, 7.1.

155 ICC Statute, 7.2(a).

is certainly "arbitrary," it is also a well-delineated, well-honed, and carefully coordinated system that operates in the same way in multiple locations along the China-DPRK border. It has been going on for fifteen to twenty years and continues at present. The two North Korean police forces, the *Bo-wi-bu* State Security Agency and the *An-jeon-bu* People's Safety Agency, operate the system together in coordinated ways. And the punishment system operates across a multiplicity of state-operated detention, interrogation and forced labor facilities in dozens of cities and localities in the northern portions of North Korea.

The economic logic of the DPRK state policy is questionable.[156] But the political logic of the North Korean system is straightforward. Leaving North Korea requires written permission from DPRK and/or Korean Workers' Party authorities. And state policy is to severely punish those who have left the country without state or Party authorization, as part of its strenuous efforts to control and limit its citizens' knowledge of the world outside "the Kim Il-sung nation," and prevent them from participating in the booming capitalist cash economy on the Chinese side of the China-DPRK border. Practices include:

1. Repatriated Koreans are detained by DPRK police authorities for having exercised their right to leave their country of origin, a right recognized in Article 13(1) of the Universal Declaration of Human Rights. The imprisonment of repatriated persons—violates Article 12(2) of the International

Covenant on Civil and Political Rights.[157] The UN implementation review committee for this covenant has notified the DPRK of the incompatibility between its policy and practice and the international legal standards North Korea formally accepted. Detention can, for a few people, last only several days. But for many, as is seen in the testimony in this report, imprisonment for having exercised the "right to leave" stretches out into months or years across a variety of harsh penal and brutal forced-labor institutions and facilities. This "severe deprivation of physical liberty" is a direct "violation of fundamental rules of international law."[158]

Most of the detention and related imprisonment takes place without any trial or judicial process. The rare trials that occur fall far short of what international law posits as "fair trial" or "due process."[159]

2. Nearly all repatriated persons interviewed for this report tell of prolonged and repeated kicking and beatings, usually with wooden staves or clubs, or the metal rods used for cleaning rifle barrels (sometimes even prior to the beginning of interrogation to soften-up the prisoners) and other systematic tortures, most commonly the "sitting-still-for-hours" or "kneeling-motionless-for-hours" (sometimes with a circulation-cutting bar between the legs), which the former detain-

---

156 Most countries welcome and some may even rely on the hard currency remittances earned by their citizens who work in neighboring countries, even if those laborers are working abroad without documentation or legal status.

157 Normally, it is the legal obligation of ratifying States Parties to bring their domestic law into conformity with the provisions of the convention acceded to by the State Party.

158 ICC Statute, 7.1(e); Article 9.1 of the International Covenant on Civil and Political Rights.

159 Articles 9.1-4 and 14.3(1)-(7) of the International Covenant on Civil and Political Rights.

ees describe as much more painful than the beatings. These punishments constitute torture, cruel and inhuman treatment and punishment as defined and prohibited in Article 7.1(f) of the Rome Statute and Article 7 of the International Covenant on Civil and Political Rights.

3. The punishments against North Koreans who met South Koreans, watched South Korean movies or television programs, or attended churches while in China would likely constitute a violation of Article 7.1(h) prohibiting "persecution against any identifiable group or collectivity on *political, racial, national, ethnic, cultural, religious...* or other grounds that are universally recognized as impermissible under international law...."

4. Bearing in mind that a large majority of North Koreans repatriated from China are women, several aspects of the violence against women to which they are routinely subjected constitute a number of different crimes against humanity. Virtually all forcibly repatriated women report that they were required to strip naked and go through what they describe as the "sit-down-stand-up-jump-around" routine (comparable to "squat-thrusts" warm-up exercises for athletes) to dislodge any money earned while in China that might have been hidden in rectal or vaginal cavities.

On the face of it, the attempted confiscation itself seems economically illogical and wantonly cruel to the individuals involved. It is clear from their testimony that the women forced to bend over and jump around naked regard this as "inhuman or degrading treat-

ment or punishment,"[160] as is the practice of requiring them to defecate under observation or with their hands in the air so that any ingested valuables cannot be retrieved.[161]

5. The racially motivated infanticide against babies born in custody who are believed to have been fathered by Han Chinese men is a brutal form of ethnic cleansing and constitutes the crime of murder.[162] (As noted in the testimony of former nurses compelled to act as mid-wives in the detention facilities, even many of the forcibly aborted fetuses are "born alive.") In the words of one legal expert, "One particular category of official murder which is singled out for special condemnation by international law is that carried out on racial grounds."[163]

6. The racially motivated forced abortions carried out on repatriated women who are believed to be carrying "half-Chinese" fetuses would likely qualify as "persecution against any identifiable group or collectivity on political, racial, national, ethnic, cultural, religious, gender... or other grounds that are universally recognized as impermissible under international law..."[164] The racially motivated

---

160 Article 10 of the ICCPR states that "All persons deprived of their liberty shall be treated with humanity and with respect for the inherent dignity of the human person."

161 The full title of the torture convention is "The Convention Against Torture, and Other Forms of Cruel, Inhuman or Degrading Treatment or Punishment," and the full provision of Article 7 of the International Covenant on Civil and Political Rights is "No one shall be subjected to torture or to cruel, inhuman or degrading treatment or punishment..."

162 ICC Statute, 7.1(a).

163 Nigel Rodley and Matt Pollard, *The Treatment of Prisoners under International Law*, (Third Edition), Oxford University Press, 2009, p. 251.

164 ICC Statute, 7.1(h).

abortions forced on these North Korean women would also qualify as a violation of Article 7.1(k) of the Rome Statute prohibiting "Other inhumane acts ... intentionally causing great suffering or serious injury to body or to mental or physical health."

7. Seventeen persons interviewed for this report provided testimony on upwards of sixty instances of forced abortion or infanticide between 1998 and 2004 occurring at five different locations along the China-DPRK border in three different kinds of detention facilities (*ku-ryu-jang* police interrogation units, *jip-kyul-so* provincial and sub-provincial detention facilities and *ro-dong-dan-ryeon-dae* labor training centers) operated by two different police forces (both the *An-jeon-bu* regular police and the *Bo-wi-bu* political police).

A recent survey by the Seoul-based NGO, Database Center for North Korea Human Rights (NKDB) of some 460 former North Korean women who fled to China and made their way to South Korea in 2010 and 2011 found that eighteen women had themselves been subjected to forced abortion, and forty women had been eyewitnesses to forced abortions performed on other women, most recently in a Chongjin *jip-kyul-so* police holding facility in 2010. Another 135 women had heard accounts of forced abortion. The NKDB survey shows high levels of forced abortion continuing through 2007, with decreasing levels in 2008, 2009 and 2010. These arose, not from a discernable change in policy, but, rather, from the decrease in the number of North Korean women fleeing to and living in China, and the concomitant diminution in the number of forced repatriations. In addition to the forced abortion

testimony, the NKDB Central Database has information on forty-five cases of reported infanticide, continuing through 2008.[165]

If these testimonies on forced abortion and infanticide are insufficient in number and size to constitute a "widespread" course of conduct against a civilian population in pursuit of state policy, it would seem likely to qualify as "systematic" in terms of the "organized nature of the pattern, that is, the non-accidental repetition of similar criminal conduct and the improbability of their random occurrence... [taking] into account the existence of a political objective.., or an ideology, in the broad sense that contemplates the destruction, persecution or weakening of a community,... the use of public or private resources, the participation of high-level political or military authorities"[166] or as "acts committed...as part of a public policy against a segment of the population, acts committed with the consent of the government...and exceptionally serious crimes of international concern."[167]

165 Lee Ja-Eun, "The Current Human Rights Situation of North Korean Women," paper presented at the Johns-Hopkins School of Advanced International Studies (SAIS), Washington DC, November 15, 2011, pp. 8-9.

166 William Schabas, *The UN International Criminal Tribunals*, Cambridge University Press, 2006, pp. 192-193.

167 M. Cherif Bassiouni, *The Statute of the International Criminal Court: A Documentary History*, Transnational Publisher, Ardsley NY, 1998, p. 398.

PART SEVEN

RECOMMENDATIONS

The measures that North Korea could take and the measures that other UN member states should take to encourage North Korea to end the human rights violations documented in this report are outlined in the following recommendations.

The following recommendations are made with that hope or expectation in mind. Many recommendations can and should be implemented on an immediate basis whereas others are part of a longer-term process. Many of the recommendations are based on the international standard to end imprisonment or other severe deprivation of liberty in violation of the fundamental rules of international law.

I. To the Democratic People's Republic of Korea

Following the death of Kim Jong-il in December 2011, North Korea entered a leadership transition as Kim Jong-un succeeded his father. In due course, North Korea's new leadership constellation might facilitate an altered policy orientation, particularly if the DPRK seeks to achieve the growth and prosperity common to other states in East Asia.

Additionally, North Korea may choose to seek greater integration with the international community and improved relations with neighboring states bilaterally or multilaterally, possibly via a "peace regime" for the Korean peninsula, or possibly through a peace and security mechanism for Northeast Asia in conjunction with progress toward a coordinated effort to resolve the security concerns of all states in the region. In almost all other areas of the world, conflict resolution and the construction of new regional orders for peace, mutual security and cooperation have involved humanitarian and human rights issues and considerations. This certainly should also be the case in Northeast Asia.

Regarding the *Kwan-li-so* Political Penal Labor Colonies

1. Allow the International Committee of the Red Cross (ICRC) access to the *kwan-li-so* "managed places" that are, in fact, detention facilities as defined by international standards.[168]

2. Stop further *incommunicado* deportations to the *kwan-li-so* "managed places." North Korean citizens suspected of violating North Korean laws should be subject to prosecutions carried out in accordance with both international standards and the DPRK Criminal Code and Criminal Procedures Code, and if convicted, sent to a penal facility as specified in DPRK criminal law and procedure.

3. Immediately release those persons held within the *hyuk-myung-kwa-koo-yeok* "re-revolutionizing

---

168 As many of the following recommendations are addressed directly to the DPRK, the literal English translation of *kwan-li-so* ("managed places") is frequently used herein. Similarly, according to former prisoners interviewed for this report, the formal term used by *kwan-li-so* officials for those held in the "managed places" is not "prisoner" but *e-ju-min* "migrants" or *ju-min* "residents." The English language term "resident" is sometimes used in these recommendations, particularly for the series of measures that would restore to these "residents" the liberties to which they are so severely deprived.

zones" within the labor camps, who are eligible for eventual release. Those persons should be freed immediately according to what the North Koreans term *gwang-bok-jung-chi* ("generous politics") releases or amnesties such as are implemented within the present management system. (Unlike the lifetime deportees in the *wan-jeon-tong-je-koo-yeok* "total control zones" of the *kwan-li-so* "managed places," most of the residents of the "re-revolutionizing zones" retain their ties and connections to North Korean society from which they were summarily deported, and can be re-integrated into North Korean society with relative ease.)[169]

4. Release children and family members deported to the *kwan-li-so* because of *yeon-jwa-je* "guilt by association."[170]

5. Release all other persons deported to and deposited in the *kwan-li-so* "managed places" who have not been convicted of a violation of a specific provision of the DPRK Criminal Code in a North Korean court in the course of a judicial process conducted in accordance with the DPRK Criminal Procedures Code and international standards by which North Korea is bound. Take the measures necessary to enable camp residents to return to their previous place of lawful residence.

6. Prior to the release of persons arbitrarily

detained within the *kwan-li-so* (which will take some time, given the tens of thousands of persons involved), begin a process of restoring the liberties to which the residents in the camps have been so severely deprived. This process should begin with allowing the detained residents to have greater access to the food crops grown within the sprawling encampments. Provide foods sufficient to relieve what former prisoners describe as constant, unrelenting hunger and end the high incidence of deaths in detention from combinations of prolonged and severe malnutrition and disease within the labor camps. Recognizing that "persons deprived of their liberty" are regarded by the United Nations as a "vulnerable group," request that the World Food Program provide residents of the *kwan-li-so* "managed places" with humanitarian food aid, as has been requested for other vulnerable groups within North Korea.

7. End virtual slave labor within the *kwan-li-so* "managed places." Agricultural, mining and industrial laborers, production record keepers, and service workers (such as the women deportees assigned to clean the offices of camp officials and guards) within the *kwan-li-so* should earn the same wages and/or remuneration in goods and services provided to workers in comparable occupations outside of the labor camps—whether the compensation is provided in wages or in food and clothing dispensed by the state-run Public Distribution System (PDS) should the PDS be reconstituted. If markets—the provision of goods and services in exchange for denominations of currency—are being allowed to function in the general society, they should be allowed to function within the encampments as well, on the same terms as markets outside the *kwan-li-so* "managed places."

---

169 See p. 27-28 for descriptions of "re-revolutionizing zones" and the existing release procedures.

170 In his most recent report to the General Assembly, the Special Rapporteur for human rights in the DPRK recommended starting releases with certain categories of prisoners, such as the elderly, those having medical conditions, long-serving prisoners, women who have children and persons imprisoned due to guilt by association. See "Report to the General Assembly," UN Doc. A/66/322, 24 August 2011, para 62.

Ending forced labor should also include reforming prohibitive work hours and unsafe working conditions, taking measures to prevent the large number of industrial and work related deaths and accidents, and requesting that the International Labour Organization (ILO) visit the "managed places"[171] to ensure that working conditions are brought into line with international standards.

8. End the extra-judicial nature of the *kwan-li-so* "managed places" by extending the jurisdiction of the DPRK constitution, Criminal Code, Criminal Procedures Code, and court system to the labor camps and the residents within the *kwan-li-so* "managed places." This measure would extend the "protection of law" provided to North Korean citizens as a whole to the residents of the encampments.

9. Observe and enforce within the areas of the encampments the standards against torture and assault provided for in the updated DPRK legal codes and specified in the international conventions that the DPRK has ratified. This includes preventing prisoners (rather than encouraging them) from assaulting other prisoners for purported failure to maintain daily per capita production quotas.

10. To end the present *incommunicado* nature of residence within the *kwan-li-so* "managed places," the residents therein should be allowed the same correspondence rights and privileges by mail and telephone that most persons deprived of their physical liberty are entitled in most detention facilities in most countries around the world. Residents of the *kwan-li-so* should be entitled to receive packages by mail (with food, medicines and clothing) from friends, families, and co-workers outside the encampments. They also should be allowed visits by their families and friends.

11. Allow residents within the *kwan-li-so* encampments access to the radio, television, newspapers, magazines, books and motion pictures to which citizens of North Korea are allowed access[172] and to which many persons deprived of their physical liberty are entitled in detention facilities in other countries around the world.

12. Until such time when all children are released from the *kwan-li-so*, provide them with education through the middle and high school levels. Use the same learning curricula for primary schools within the *kwan-li-so* that are used outside the encampments.[173] Make the schools within the encampments places of learning rather than organizational focal points for child labor projects.

---

171 Prior to the economic collapse in the 1990s, North Korea made very little use of money as a medium of exchange or store of value. Citizens were assigned to houses and jobs and provided with food and clothing via the state-run Public Distribution System (PDS), the quantity and quality determined in part by occupation and in part by *songbun* socio-political status rankings. During the famine, when the PDS lacked food to distribute to the populace, various barter arrangements emerged followed by markets without government planning or approval. The regime has repeatedly taken measures to restrict or close the markets, and confiscate currency in the hands of the populace. However, these measures have not succeeded, and the use of money and markets has continued.

172 As the country with the single most restrictive approach to freedoms of expression and opinion, the DPRK does not allow the general North Korean population access to any newspapers, magazines, books, radio or TV programs that are not produced or authorized by the Party, the government bureaucracy, or the army. The recommendation above is that the residents of the camps should be allowed the same limited access to newspapers, magazines, radio and TV programs as the rest of the North Korean population.

173 For example, former child prisoners who attended primary schools within the camps report they were only taught simple mathematical addition and subtraction, but not multiplication or division. See p. 48.

13. As long as the present labor camp system remains in operation, fully restore the right to marry persons within the encampments. Allow men and women to select husbands and wives of their own choosing, to marry with legal recognition, and to have children and live together as families.

14. Finally, to fully restore the liberties that are so severely lacking for camp residents, the residents of the encampments should be allowed the same, albeit limited, internal travel within the DPRK as North Korean citizens are otherwise allowed.

It is important to note that there is an existing model within North Korea for the above series of recommendations in the *hae-je-min* (cleared people) arrangement at Camp No. 18 at Bukchang, South Pyongan province, described on pages 213 to 218 of this report, where former prisoners who have been "cleared" continue to remain at the camp. (Most of those who remain were subjected to *incommunicado* detention for multiple decades and have lost connections with their former residences and places of work [the latter connection is needed for access to the Public Distribution System]. Rather than face unemployment and itinerant homelessness, these former prisoners chose to remain in the camps but with the [albeit limited] rights and freedoms of communication and travel available to the general public).[174]

---

174 See the story of Mrs. Kim Hye-sook, page 70 above, for a prisoner released after almost three decades of *incommunicado* detention and who was subsequently unable to find a local North Korean authority who would provide her with a residence, job and registration with the PDS, and who then, to survive, resorted to cross border trading with China for which she was arrested by the local police.

Regarding the *Kyo-hwa-so, Jip-kyul-so,* and *Ro-dong-dan-ryeon-dae* Penitentiaries, Prisons and "Labor Training" Facilities

15. Release all persons in detention who have not been charged and tried according to provisions of the DPRK criminal codes, and convicted in a DPRK court of law operating under international standards for due process and fair trial.

16. Bring all prisons and places of detention in line with the provisions of the UN Standard Minimum Rules for the Treatment of Prisoners and the UN Body of Principles for the Protection of All Persons under any Form of Detention or Imprisonment. (See the Appendix for these Rules and Principles.)

17. Invite the International Labour Organization (ILO) to observe the operation of the mobile labor brigades known as "labor training centers."

Regarding the Treatment of Persons Repatriated from China

18. Allow access by the ICRC to the *ku-ryu-jang* detention-interrogation facilities along the DPRK-China border area.

19. As recommended by the UN Human Rights Committee, end requirements for an exit visa in order for citizens to travel abroad, a provision the UN Committee held to be incompatible with Article 12 of the International Covenant on Civil and Political Rights. De-criminalize the right to leave, and release all persons currently being detained for having crossed the border with China in search of food, employment, seeing relatives or seeking asylum.

20. Cease persecuting, prosecuting, and punishing North Koreans repatriated by police authorities of neighboring countries. North Koreans should not be punished by their government for exercising their right to leave the DPRK.

21. Observe the provisions of the DPRK Criminal Code and Criminal Procedures Code on arrests, trials, and treatment of detained persons—particularly prohibiting the use of torture or confessions obtained by the police under torture or forced starvation in order to justify the detention and imprisonment of North Koreans who crossed the DPRK-China border. The disregard by both North Korean police agencies of the DPRK's own Criminal Code and Criminal Procedures Code should be ended.

22. Ratify the Convention on the Elimination of All Forms of Racial Discrimination, and immediately cease performing involuntary abortions on pregnant repatriated women who are suspected of having ethnic Chinese spouses, and immediately end the practice of suffocating new-born infants or fetuses suspected of ethnic Chinese fathers.

Regarding International Standards and Procedures

23. Implement the recommendations made to the DPRK by the UN Human Rights Committee, the UN Committee on Economic, Social and Cultural Rights, the Committee on the Rights of the Child and the Committee on the Elimination of Discrimination Against Women.

24. Implement the key recommendations made by other UN Member States during the Universal Periodic Review at the UN Human Rights Council in 2009. Report to the Council on the measures taken to implement the recommendations that the DPRK has acted upon.

25. Ratify the Convention against Torture and other forms of Cruel, Inhuman and Degrading Treatment and Punishment, and implement those standards, and all standards against torture and related practices in the International Covenants and DPRK domestic legislation in all places of detention within the DPRK.

26. Initiate a dialogue with the UN High Commissioner for Human Rights, and the relevant thematic UN rapporteurs and working groups, including the Special Rapporteur on the situation of human rights in the DPRK. Renew a human rights dialogue with the member states of the European Union that have diplomatic representation in Pyongyang. Invite the U.S. Special Envoy for North Korean Human Rights Issues to Pyongyang for regular discussions of humanitarian and human rights issues.

II. Recommendations To the People's Republic of China

1. In accordance with recommendations made to China by the UN Committee on the Elimination of Discrimination against Women and the UN Committee on the Rights of the Child, review the situation of North Korean women and asylum seekers to ensure that they do not become victims of trafficking and marriage enslavement because of their status as illegal

aliens. Ensure that no unaccompanied child from North Korea is returned to a country where there are substantial grounds to believe that there is a real risk of irreparable harm to the child.

2. Cease the forcible repatriation of North Koreans found inside China to the DPRK until it is verified that North Korea has ceased its abuse and imprisonment of repatriated North Koreans. Immediately stop repatriating pregnant women under all circumstances.

3. Allow the UN High Commissioner for Refugees (UNHCR) access to North Koreans in China; enable the UNHCR to extend its concern and protection to those North Koreans who possess a well founded fear of persecution if returned to their country of origin. The UNHCR has already made known that it considers North Koreans in Northeast China to be "persons of concern." Until international protection policies are in place, China should comply with the Refugee Convention, which it signed, regarding North Koreans in northeast China. These persons can be adequately tended to by UNHCR and by humanitarian NGOs until the food situation in North Korea stabilizes and its human rights situation has substantially improved, including government recognition of the right of North Koreans to leave their country.

4. Allow North Korean women who have "married" Chinese men and have had children in China to obtain documentation (*hukous*) necessary for residence, and allow the children of such unions to have access to schools and hospitals.

III. Recommendations To UN Member States

1. Continue to support, and vote for the resolutions on the human rights situation in North Korea at the UN Human Rights Council and General Assembly. Include within the General Assembly or Council resolution a request for the Secretary-General or High Commissioner for Human Rights to appoint a commission of inquiry or group of experts to make a prima facie determination if the human rights violations cited in previous General Assembly resolutions, detailed in the reports of the Special Rapporteur on the situation of human rights in the DPRK, and in the reports of reputable non-governmental organizations constitute crimes against humanity or other grave breaches of international humanitarian, criminal, and human rights law.[175]

---

175 "Commissions of inquiry," "groups of experts," "expert panels," "fact-finding teams," and "boards of inquiry" have been launched by the UN Secretary General, the High Commissioner for Human Rights, or the President of the Human Rights Council, usually at the request of the Security Council, the General Assembly or the Human Rights Council, to investigate possible breaches of international humanitarian, criminal or human rights law in, for example, East Timor, Rwanda, Burundi, Darfur, Lebanon, Togo, the Jenin Refugee Camp, Guinea, Cambodia, the former Yugoslavia, Gaza, Sri Lanka, and the Democratic Republic of Congo. When, in 2005, the Government of Uzbekistan refused to cooperate with a UN investigation of the massacres at Andijan, the High Commissioner for Human Rights sent a team of investigators to gather information from eyewitnesses who had fled to neighboring Kyrgyzstan. Commissions of inquiry have also been established for Cote d'Ivoire, Libya and Syria.

NB: the mandate of the Special Rapporteur on Human Rights in the DPRK is to assess the overall situation of human rights in North Korea. The variety of UN mechanisms listed above usually have the more specific mandate to ascertain, *prima facie*, if there have been breaches or violations of international humanitarian, criminal or human rights law. The panels are usually composed of several legal experts from three to five, regionally balanced, UN Member States who work for several months or sometimes more, and report their findings, often via the Secretary General, back to the Security Council, General Assembly or Human Rights Council for further action.

A commission of inquiry is especially important in the case of North Korea because the International Criminal Court cannot extend its application to crimes against humanity in North Korea. The DPRK does not recognize the jurisdiction of the Court and it is unlikely that the Security Council will refer the case of North Korea to the Court (China in particular can be expected to veto a referral). The Prosecutor of the ICC advised a group of survivors from North Korea's prison camps, detention facilities and torture centers (including some of the interviewees for this report) to consider raising these serious violations with "appropriate national or international authorities."[176] A move by the General Assembly or the Human Rights Council to set up a commission of inquiry or panel of experts would be an important step forward.

Recognition by the international community that crimes against humanity are being perpetrated on a massive scale in North Korea would make it more difficult for North Korean authorities to deny that the prison camps exist and to defy international standards regarding its criminal mistreatment of a substantial portion of its population.

2. Encourage the DPRK to allow the ICRC access to all places of detention within North Korea, including the *kwan-li-so* "managed places."

3. Encourage the World Food Program to find ways to provide humanitarian food aid to those persons residing within the *kwan-li-so* and *kyo-hwa-so* prison facilities, given that the UN system, particularly the Office of the High Commissioner for Human Rights, recognizes "persons deprived of their liberty" to be among what the UN designates as a "vulnerable group."

4. Strengthen the annual resolutions in the General Assembly and Human Rights Council by endorsing the applicability of the "Responsibility to Protect" doctrine to the situation in North Korea.[177] In 2005, 193 heads of state adopted the World Summit Outcome document, which endorsed a collective responsibility to protect persons when their own governments fail to do so and they are subjected to crimes against humanity, genocide, war crimes or ethnic cleansing. There is a strong case that North Korea's human rights violations constitute crimes against humanity and should be part of deliberations in the Security Council. North Korea's recurring security threats—along with its human rights issues, endemic food insecurity and refugee outflows—should be examined and discussed in a more integrated and comprehensive framework internationally, preferably via Chapter VI proceedings at the UN Security Council.[178]

---

176 This recommendation was in response to a request from former political prisoners in North Korea, including some of those interviewed for this report. The Prosecutor's Office responded that in the absence of DPRK's recognition of the ICC or a referral from the UN Security Council, the "serious allegations will be beyond the reach of this institution to address." However, the ICC Prosecutor advised the petitioners to consider raising these matters with "appropriate national or international authorities." (5 November 2010 Office of the Prosecutor, International Criminal Court, Reference OTP-CR-946/09.)

177 See Paragraph 139, World Summit Outcome Document, 16 September 2005: "The international community, through the United Nations, also has the responsibility to use appropriate diplomatic, humanitarian and other peaceful means in accordance with Chapter VI and VII of the Charter, to help protect populations from genocide, war crimes, ethnic cleansing and crimes against humanity....We stress the need for the General Assembly to continue consideration of the responsibility to protect populations from genocide, war crimes, ethnic cleansing and crimes against humanity and its implications, bearing in mind the principles of the Charter and international law." See also Kjell Magne Bondevik and Kristen Abrams, "Democratic Peoples Republic of Korea," in Jared Genser and Irwin Cotler, The Responsibility to Protect, Oxford University Press, 2011.

178 Unlike Chapter VII proceedings, which can authorize the use

IV. To UN Member States Enjoying Diplomatic Relations with the DPRK

1. Reiterate to DPRK officials that North Korea must address the human rights concerns expressed by the international community, including the matters discussed in this report, if their countries are to improve relations with the DPRK.

2. Seek discussions with the DPRK on a series of practical measures, such as those outlined above that can restore liberties to those presently imprisoned in the camps.

V. To the United States, the Republic of Korea, and Japan

1. Take human rights issues, including the problems cited in this report, into consideration in any process leading to improved relations and the normalization of diplomatic relations with the DPRK. In the event that the Six Party Talks resume, include relevant human rights concerns in the various working groups, particularly the working groups on economic cooperation and a security system or framework for Northeast Asia, and in subsidiary, four party discussions to convert the Korean War armistice into a peace agreement.

2. Continue to provide asylum, residence and/or citizenship to North Koreans who present themselves to consulates, embassies or officials in third countries, as well as North Koreans who arrive in the US, the Republic of Korea, and Japan by boat, plane, or other means of transportation.

3. Offer a voluntary orderly departure program and third country resettlement program for those released from the prisons and labor camps who cannot remain in North Korea without facing persecution stemming from their previous confinement in the camps. It should be noted that, as described in the text of this report,[179] all of the persons previously released from the "re-revolutionizing" sections of the labor camps are required to take an oath never to disclose any information about the "managed places" to other citizens within the DPRK. It also should be noted that a number of the persons previously released from the "re-revolutionizing" sections of the labor camps subsequently sought asylum outside of North Korea because of a well founded fear of persecution should they remain in their country of origin. An offer should thus be made to the DPRK of a voluntary orderly departure program and third country resettlement program for former prisoners. Such a program, comparable to the one organized in the early 1980s to end the Vietnamese "boat people" crisis, would avoid burdening neighboring countries with a potential influx of asylum seekers transiting across multiple borders in search of refuge or re-settlement. Countries with sizable Korean communities should inform the DPRK of their willingness to cooperate with respect to third country resettlement.

---

of armed force, Chapter VI deliberations prescribe the seeking of solutions "by negotiation, enquiry, mediation, conciliation, arbitration, judicial settlement, resort to regional agencies or arrangements, or other peaceful means of their own choice."

---

179 See p. 53.

APPENDIX

UN STANDARD MINIMUM RULES FOR THE TREATMENT OF PRISONERS

Adopted by the First United Nations Congress on the Prevention of Crime and the Treatment of Offenders, held at Geneva in 1955, and approved by the Economic and Social Council by its resolutions 663 C (XXIV) of 31 July 1957 and 2076 (LXII) of 13 May 1977

PRELIMINARY OBSERVATIONS

1. The following rules are not intended to describe in detail a model system of penal institutions. They seek only, on the basis of the general consensus of contemporary thought and the essential elements of the most adequate systems of today, to set out what is generally accepted as being good principle and practice in the treatment of prisoners and the management of institutions.

2. In view of the great variety of legal, social, economic and geographical conditions of the world, it is evident that not all of the rules are capable of application in all places and at all times. They should, however, serve to stimulate a constant endeavour to overcome practical difficulties in the way of their application, in the knowledge that they represent, as a whole, the minimum conditions which are accepted as suitable by the United Nations.

3. On the other hand, the rules cover a field in which thought is constantly developing. They are not intended to preclude experiment and practices, provided these are in harmony with the principles and seek to further the purposes which derive from the text of the rules as a whole. It will always be justifiable for the central prison administration to authorize departures from the rules in this spirit.

4. (1) Part I of the rules covers the general management of institutions, and is applicable to all categories of prisoners, criminal or civil, untried or convicted, including prisoners subject to "security measures" or corrective measures ordered by the judge.

(2) Part II contains rules applicable only to the special categories dealt with in each section. Nevertheless, the rules under section A, applicable to prisoners under sentence, shall be equally applicable to categories of prisoners dealt with in sections B, C and D, provided they do not conflict with the rules governing those categories and are for their benefit.

5. (1) The rules do not seek to regulate the management of institutions set aside for young persons such as Borstal institutions or correctional schools, but in general part I would be equally applicable in such institutions.

(2) The category of young prisoners should include at least all young persons who come within the jurisdiction of juvenile courts. As a rule, such young persons should not be sentenced to imprisonment.

Part I: Rules of General Application
Basic Principle

6. (1) The following rules shall be applied impartially. There shall be no discrimination on grounds of race, colour, sex, language, religion, political or other opinion, national or social origin, property, birth or other status.

(2) On the other hand, it is necessary to respect the religious beliefs and moral precepts of the group to which a prisoner belongs.

Register

7. (1) In every place where persons are imprisoned there shall be kept a bound registration book with numbered pages in which shall be entered in respect of each prisoner received:
(a) Information concerning his identity;
(b) The reasons for his commitment and the authority therefor;
(c) The day and hour of his admission and release.
(2) No person shall be received in an institution without a valid commitment order of which the details shall have been previously entered in the register.

Separation of Categories

8. The different categories of prisoners shall be kept in separate institutions or parts of institutions taking account of their sex, age, criminal record, the legal reason for their detention and the necessities of their treatment. Thus,
(a) Men and women shall so far as possible be detained in separate institutions; in an institution which receives both men and women the whole of the premises allocated to women shall be entirely separate;
(b) Untried prisoners shall be kept separate from convicted prisoners;
(c) Persons imprisoned for debt and other civil prisoners shall be kept separate from persons imprisoned by reason of a criminal offence;
(d) Young prisoners shall be kept separate from adults.

Accommodation

9. (1) Where sleeping accommodation is in individual cells or rooms, each prisoner shall occupy by night a cell or room by himself. If for special reasons, such as temporary overcrowding, it becomes necessary for the central prison administration to make an exception to this rule, it is not desirable to have two prisoners in a cell or room.
(2) Where dormitories are used, they shall be occupied by prisoners carefully selected as being suitable to associate with one another in those conditions. There shall be regular supervision by night, in keeping with the nature of the institution.

10. All accommodation provided for the use of prisoners and in particular all sleeping accommodation shall meet all requirements of health, due regard being paid to climatic conditions and particularly to cubic content of air, minimum floor space, lighting, heating and ventilation.

11. In all places where prisoners are required to live or work,
(a) The windows shall be large enough to enable the prisoners to read or work by natural light, and shall be so constructed that they can allow the entrance of fresh air whether or not there is artificial ventilation;
(b) Artificial light shall be provided sufficient for the prisoners to read or work without injury to eyesight.

12. The sanitary installations shall be adequate to enable every prisoner to comply with the needs of nature when necessary and in a clean and decent manner.

13. Adequate bathing and shower installations shall be provided so that every prisoner may be enabled and required to have a bath or shower, at a temperature suitable to the climate, as frequently as necessary for general hygiene according to season and geographical region, but at least once a week in a temperate climate.

14. All parts of an institution regularly used by prisoners shall be properly maintained and kept scrupulously clean at all times.

Personal Hygiene

15. Prisoners shall be required to keep their persons clean, and to this end they shall be provided with water and with such toilet articles as are necessary for health and cleanliness.

16. In order that prisoners may maintain a good appearance compatible with their self-respect, facilities shall be provided for the proper care of the hair and beard, and men shall be enabled to shave regularly.

Clothing and Bedding

17. (1) Every prisoner who is not allowed to wear his own clothing shall be provided with an outfit of clothing suitable for the climate and adequate to keep him in good health. Such clothing shall in no manner be degrading or humiliating.

(2) All clothing shall be clean and kept in proper condition. Underclothing shall be changed and washed as often as necessary for the maintenance of hygiene.

(3) In exceptional circumstances, whenever a prisoner is removed outside the institution for an authorized purpose, he shall be allowed to wear his own clothing or other inconspicuous clothing.

18. If prisoners are allowed to wear their own clothing, arrangements shall be made on their admission to the institution to ensure that it shall be clean and fit for use.

19. Every prisoner shall, in accordance with local or national standards, be provided with a separate bed, and with separate and sufficient bedding which shall be clean when issued, kept in good order and changed often enough to ensure its cleanliness.

Food

20. (1) Every prisoner shall be provided by the administration at the usual hours with food of nutritional value adequate for health and strength, of wholesome quality and well prepared and served.

(2) Drinking water shall be available to every prisoner whenever he needs it.

Exercise and Sport

21. (1) Every prisoner who is not employed in outdoor work shall have at least one hour of suitable exercise in the open air daily if the weather permits.

(2) Young prisoners, and others of suitable age and physique, shall receive physical and recreational training during the period of exercise. To this end space, installations and equipment should be provided.

Medical Services

22. (1) At every institution there shall be available the services of at least one qualified medical officer who should have some knowledge of psychiatry. The medical services should be organized in close relationship to the general health administration of the community or nation. They shall include a psychiatric service for the diagnosis and, in proper cases, the treatment of states of mental abnormality.

(2) Sick prisoners who require specialist treatment shall be transferred to specialized institutions or to civil hospitals. Where hospital facilities are provided in an institution, their equipment, furnishings and pharmaceutical supplies shall be proper for the medical care and treatment of sick prisoners, and there shall be a staff of suitable trained officers.

(3) The services of a qualified dental officer shall be available to every prisoner.

23. (1) In women's institutions there shall be special accommodation for all necessary pre-natal and post-natal care and treatment. Arrangements shall be made wherever practicable for children to be born in a hospital outside the institution. If a child is born in prison, this fact shall not be mentioned in the birth certificate.

(2) Where nursing infants are allowed to remain in the institution with their mothers, provision shall be made for a nursery staffed by qualified persons, where the infants shall be placed when they are not in the care of their mothers.

24. The medical officer shall see and examine every prisoner as soon as possible after his admission and thereafter as necessary, with a view particularly to the discovery of physical or mental illness and the taking of all necessary measures; the segregation of prisoners suspected of infectious or contagious conditions; the noting of physical or mental defects which might hamper rehabilitation, and the determination of the physical capacity of every prisoner for work.

25. (1) The medical officer shall have the care of the physical and mental health of the prisoners and should daily see all sick prisoners, all who complain of illness, and any prisoner to whom his attention is specially directed.

(2) The medical officer shall report to the director whenever he considers that a prisoner's physical or mental health has been or will be injuriously affected by continued imprisonment or by any condition of imprisonment.

26. (1) The medical officer shall regularly inspect and advise the director upon:

(a) The quantity, quality, preparation and service of food;

(b) The hygiene and cleanliness of the institu-tion and the prisoners;

(c) The sanitation, heating, lighting and ventilation of the institution;

(d) The suitability and cleanliness of the prisoners' clothing and bedding;

(e) The observance of the rules concerning physical education and sports, in cases where there is no technical personnel in charge of these activities.

(2) The director shall take into consideration the reports and advice that the medical officer submits according to rules 25 (2) and 26 and, in case he concurs with the recommendations made, shall take immediate steps to give effect to those recommendations; if they are not within his competence or if he does not concur with them, he shall immediately submit his own report and the advice of the medical officer to higher authority.

Discipline and Punishment

27. Discipline and order shall be maintained with firmness, but with no more restriction than is necessary for safe custody and well-ordered community life.

28. (1) No prisoner shall be employed, in the service of the institution, in any disciplinary capacity.

(2) This rule shall not, however, impede the proper functioning of systems based on self-government, under which specified social, educational or sports activities or responsibilities are entrusted, under supervision, to prisoners who are formed into groups for the purposes of treatment.

29. The following shall always be determined by the law or by the regulation of the competent administrative authority:

(a) Conduct constituting a disciplinary offence;

(b) The types and duration of punishment which may be inflicted;

179

(c) The authority competent to impose such punishment.

30. (1) No prisoner shall be punished except in accordance with the terms of such law or regulation, and never twice for the same offence.

(2) No prisoner shall be punished unless he has been informed of the offence alleged against him and given a proper opportunity of presenting his defence. The competent authority shall conduct a thorough examination of the case.

(3) Where necessary and practicable the prisoner shall be allowed to make his defence through an interpreter.

31. Corporal punishment, punishment by placing in a dark cell, and all cruel, inhuman or degrading punishments shall be completely prohibited as punishments for disciplinary offences.

32. (1) Punishment by close confinement or reduction of diet shall never be inflicted unless the medical officer has examined the prisoner and certified in writing that he is fit to sustain it.

(2) The same shall apply to any other punishment that may be prejudicial to the physical or mental health of a prisoner. In no case may such punishment be contrary to or depart from the principle stated in rule 31.

(3) The medical officer shall visit daily prisoners undergoing such punishments and shall advise the director if he considers the termination or alteration of the punishment necessary on grounds of physical or mental health.

Instruments of Restraint

33. Instruments of restraint, such as handcuffs, chains, irons and strait-jackets, shall never be applied as a punishment. Furthermore, chains or irons shall not be used as restraints. Other instruments of restraint shall not be used except in the following circumstances:

(a) As a precaution against escape during a transfer, provided that they shall be removed when the prisoner appears before a judicial or administrative authority;

(b) On medical grounds by direction of the medical officer;

(c) By order of the director, if other methods of control fail, in order to prevent a prisoner from injuring himself or others or from damaging property; in such instances the director shall at once consult the medical officer and report to the higher administrative authority.

34. The patterns and manner of use of instruments of restraint shall be decided by the central prison administration. Such instruments must not be applied for any longer time than is strictly necessary.

Information to and Complaints by Prisoners

35. (1) Every prisoner on admission shall be provided with written information about the regulations governing the treatment of prisoners of his category, the disciplinary requirements of the institution, the authorized methods of seeking information and making complaints, and all such other matters as are necessary to enable him to understand both his rights and his obligations and to adapt himself to the life of the institution.

(2) If a prisoner is illiterate, the aforesaid information shall be conveyed to him orally.

36. (1) Every prisoner shall have the opportunity each week day of making requests or complaints to the director of the institution or the officer authorized to represent him.

(2) It shall be possible to make requests or complaints to the inspector of prisons during his inspection. The prisoner shall have the opportunity to talk to the inspector or to any other

inspecting officer without the director or other members of the staff being present.

(3) Every prisoner shall be allowed to make a request or complaint, without censorship as to substance but in proper form, to the central prison administration, the judicial authority or other proper authorities through approved channels.

(4) Unless it is evidently frivolous or groundless, every request or complaint shall be promptly dealt with and replied to without undue delay.

Contact with the Outside World

37. Prisoners shall be allowed under necessary supervision to communicate with their family and reputable friends at regular intervals, both by correspondence and by receiving visits.

38. (1) Prisoners who are foreign nationals shall be allowed reasonable facilities to communicate with the diplomatic and consular representatives of the State to which they belong.

(2) Prisoners who are nationals of States without diplomatic or consular representation in the country and refugees or stateless persons shall be allowed similar facilities to communicate with the diplomatic representative of the State which takes charge of their interests or any national or international authority whose task it is to protect such persons.

39. Prisoners shall be kept informed regularly of the more important items of news by the reading of newspapers, periodicals or special institutional publications, by hearing wireless transmissions, by lectures or by any similar means as authorized or controlled by the administration.

Books

40. Every institution shall have a library for the use of all categories of prisoners, adequately stocked with both recreational and instructional books, and prisoners shall be encouraged to make full use of it.

Religion

41. (1) If the institution contains a sufficient number of prisoners of the same religion, a qualified representative of that religion shall be appointed or approved. If the number of prisoners justifies it and conditions permit, the arrangement should be on a full-time basis.

(2) A qualified representative appointed or approved under paragraph (1) shall be allowed to hold regular services and to pay pastoral visits in private to prisoners of his religion at proper times.

(3) Access to a qualified representative of any religion shall not be refused to any prisoner. On the other hand, if any prisoner should object to a visit of any religious representative, his attitude shall be fully respected.

42. So far as practicable, every prisoner shall be allowed to satisfy the needs of his religious life by attending the services provided in the institution and having in his possession the books of religious observance and instruction of his denomination.

Retention of Prisoners' Property

43. (1) All money, valuables, clothing and other effects belonging to a prisoner which under the regulations of the institution he is not allowed to retain shall on his admission to the institution be placed in safe custody. An inventory thereof shall be signed by the prisoner. Steps shall be taken to keep them in good condition.

(2) On the release of the prisoner all such articles and money shall be returned to him except in so far as he has been authorized to spend money or

send any such property out of the institution, or it has been found necessary on hygienic grounds to destroy any article of clothing. The prisoner shall sign a receipt for the articles and money returned to him.

(3) Any money or effects received for a prisoner from outside shall be treated in the same way.

(4) If a prisoner brings in any drugs or medicine, the medical officer shall decide what use shall be made of them.

Notification of Death, Illness, Transfer, etc.

44. (1) Upon the death or serious illness of, or serious injury to a prisoner, or his removal to an institution for the treatment of mental affections, the director shall at once inform the spouse, if the prisoner is married, or the nearest relative and shall in any event inform any other person previously designated by the prisoner.

(2) A prisoner shall be informed at once of the death or serious illness of any near relative. In case of the critical illness of a near relative, the prisoner should be authorized, whenever circumstances allow, to go to his bedside either under escort or alone.

(3) Every prisoner shall have the right to inform at once his family of his imprisonment or his transfer to another institution.

Removal of Prisoners

45. (1) When the prisoners are being removed to or from an institution, they shall be exposed to public view as little as possible, and proper safeguards shall be adopted to protect them from insult, curiosity and publicity in any form.

(2) The transport of prisoners in conveyances with inadequate ventilation or light, or in any way which would subject them to unnecessary physical hardship, shall be prohibited.

(3) The transport of prisoners shall be carried out at the expense of the administration and equal conditions shall obtain for all of them.

Institutional Personnel

46. (1) The prison administration shall provide for the careful selection of every grade of the personnel, since it is on their integrity, humanity, professional capacity and personal suitability for the work that the proper administration of the institutions depends.

(2) The prison administration shall constantly seek to awaken and maintain in the minds both of the personnel and of the public the conviction that this work is a social service of great importance, and to this end all appropriate means of informing the public should be used.

(3) To secure the foregoing ends, personnel shall be appointed on a full-time basis as professional prison officers and have civil service status with security of tenure subject only to good conduct, efficiency and physical fitness. Salaries shall be adequate to attract and retain suitable men and women; employment benefits and conditions of service shall be favourable in view of the exacting nature of the work.

47. (1) The personnel shall possess an adequate standard of education and intelligence.

(2) Before entering on duty, the personnel shall be given a course of training in their general and specific duties and be required to pass theoretical and practical tests.

(3) After entering on duty and during their career, the personnel shall maintain and improve their knowledge and professional capacity by attending courses of in-service training to be organized at suitable intervals.

48. All members of the personnel shall at all times so conduct themselves and perform their

duties as to influence the prisoners for good by their example and to command their respect.

49. (1) So far as possible, the personnel shall include a sufficient number of specialists such as psychiatrists, psychologists, social workers, teachers and trade instructors.

(2) The services of social workers, teachers and trade instructors shall be secured on a permanent basis, without thereby excluding part-time or voluntary workers.

50. (1) The director of an institution should be adequately qualified for his task by character, administrative ability, suitable training and experience.

(2) He shall devote his entire time to his official duties and shall not be appointed on a part-time basis.

(3) He shall reside on the premises of the institution or in its immediate vicinity.

(4) When two or more institutions are under the authority of one director, he shall visit each of them at frequent intervals. A responsible resident official shall be in charge of each of these institutions.

51. (1) The director, his deputy, and the majority of the other personnel of the institution shall be able to speak the language of the greatest number of prisoners, or a language understood by the greatest number of them.

(2) Whenever necessary, the services of an interpreter shall be used.

52. (1) In institutions which are large enough to require the services of one or more full-time medical officers, at least one of them shall reside on the premises of the institution or in its immediate vicinity.

(2) In other institutions the medical officer shall visit daily and shall reside near enough to be able to attend without delay in cases of urgency.

53. (1) In an institution for both men and women, the part of the institution set aside for women shall be under the authority of a responsible woman officer who shall have the custody of the keys of all that part of the institution.

(2) No male member of the staff shall enter the part of the institution set aside for women unless accompanied by a woman officer.

(3) Women prisoners shall be attended and supervised only by women officers. This does not, however, preclude male members of the staff, particularly doctors and teachers, from carrying out their professional duties in institutions or parts of institutions set aside for women.

54. (1) Officers of the institutions shall not, in their relations with the prisoners, use force except in self-defence or in cases of attempted escape, or active or passive physical resistance to an order based on law or regulations. Officers who have recourse to force must use no more than is strictly necessary and must report the incident immediately to the director of the institution.

(2) Prison officers shall be given special physical training to enable them to restrain aggressive prisoners.

(3) Except in special circumstances, staff performing duties which bring them into direct contact with prisoners should not be armed. Furthermore, staff should in no circumstances be provided with arms unless they have been trained in their use.

Inspection

55. There shall be a regular inspection of penal institutions and services by qualified and experienced inspectors appointed by a competent authority. Their task shall be in particular to ensure that these institutions are administered in accordance with existing laws and regulations and with a view to bringing about the objectives of penal and correctional services.

Part II: Rules Applicable to Special Categories

A. Prisoners under Sentence
Guiding principles

56. The guiding principles hereafter are intended to show the spirit in which penal institutions should be administered and the purposes at which they should aim, in accordance with the declaration made under Preliminary Observation 1 of the present text.

57. Imprisonment and other measures which result in cutting off an offender from the outside world are afflictive by the very fact of taking from the person the right of self-determination by depriving him of his liberty. Therefore the prison system shall not, except as incidental to justifiable segregation or the maintenance of discipline, aggravate the suffering inherent in such a situation.

58. The purpose and justification of a sentence of imprisonment or a similar measure deprivative of liberty is ultimately to protect society against crime. This end can only be achieved if the period of imprisonment is used to ensure, so far as possible, that upon his return to society the offender is not only willing but able to lead a law-abiding and self-supporting life.

59. To this end, the institution should utilize all the remedial, educational, moral, spiritual and other forces and forms of assistance which are appropriate and available, and should seek to apply them according to the individual treatment needs of the prisoners.

60. (1) The regime of the institution should seek to minimize any differences between prison life and life at liberty which tend to lessen the responsibility of the prisoners or the respect due to their dignity as human beings.

(2) Before the completion of the sentence, it is desirable that the necessary steps be taken to ensure for the prisoner a gradual return to life in society. This aim may be achieved, depending on the case, by a pre-release regime organized in the same institution or in another appropriate institution, or by release on trial under some kind of supervision which must not be entrusted to the police but should be combined with effective social aid.

61. The treatment of prisoners should emphasize not their exclusion from the community, but their continuing part in it. Community agencies should, therefore, be enlisted wherever possible to assist the staff of the institution in the task of social rehabilitation of the prisoners. There should be in connection with every institution social workers charged with the duty of maintaining and improving all desirable relations of a prisoner with his family and with valuable social agencies. Steps should be taken to safeguard, to the maximum extent compatible with the law and the sentence, the rights relating to civil interests, social security rights and other social benefits of prisoners.

62. The medical services of the institution shall seek to detect and shall treat any physical or mental illnesses or defects which may hamper a prisoner's rehabilitation. All necessary medical, surgical and psychiatric services shall be provided to that end.

63. (1) The fulfilment of these principles requires individualization of treatment and for this purpose a flexible system of classifying prisoners in groups; it is therefore desirable that such groups should be distributed in separate institutions suitable for the treatment of each group.

(2) These institutions need not provide the same degree of security for every group. It is desirable to provide varying degrees of security according to the needs of different groups. Open institu-

tions, by the very fact that they provide no physical security against escape but rely on the self-discipline of the inmates, provide the conditions most favourable to rehabilitation for carefully selected prisoners.

(3) It is desirable that the number of prisoners in closed institutions should not be so large that the individualization of treatment is hindered. In some countries it is considered that the population of such institutions should not exceed five hundred. In open institutions the population should be as small as possible.

(4) On the other hand, it is undesirable to maintain prisons which are so small that proper facilities cannot be provided.

64. The duty of society does not end with a prisoner's release. There should, therefore, be governmental or private agencies capable of lending the released prisoner efficient after-care directed towards the lessening of prejudice against him and towards his social rehabilitation.

Treatment

65. The treatment of persons sentenced to imprisonment or a similar measure shall have as its purpose, so far as the length of the sentence permits, to establish in them the will to lead law-abiding and self-supporting lives after their release and to fit them to do so. The treatment shall be such as will encourage their self-respect and develop their sense of responsibility.

66. (1) To these ends, all appropriate means shall be used, including religious care in the countries where this is possible, education, vocational guidance and training, social casework, employment counselling, physical development and strengthening of moral character, in accordance with the individual needs of each prisoner, taking account of his social and criminal history,

his physical and mental capacities and aptitudes, his personal temperament, the length of his sentence and his prospects after release.

(2) For every prisoner with a sentence of suitable length, the director shall receive, as soon as possible after his admission, full reports on all the matters referred to in the foregoing paragraph. Such reports shall always include a report by a medical officer, wherever possible qualified in psychiatry, on the physical and mental condition of the prisoner.

(3) The reports and other relevant documents shall be placed in an individual file. This file shall be kept up to date and classified in such a way that it can be consulted by the responsible personnel whenever the need arises.

Classification and individualization

67. The purposes of classification shall be:

(a) To separate from others those prisoners who, by reason of their criminal records or bad characters, are likely to exercise a bad influence;

(b) To divide the prisoners into classes in order to facilitate their treatment with a view to their social rehabilitation.

68. So far as possible separate institutions or separate sections of an institution shall be used for the treatment of the different classes of prisoners.

69. As soon as possible after admission and after a study of the personality of each prisoner with a sentence of suitable length, a programme of treatment shall be prepared for him in the light of the knowledge obtained about his individual needs, his capacities and dispositions.

Privileges

70. Systems of privileges appropriate for the different classes of prisoners and the different methods of treatment shall be established at every institution, in order to encourage good conduct, develop a sense of responsibility and secure the interest and co-operation of the prisoners in their treatment.

Work

71. (1) Prison labour must not be of an afflictive nature.

(2) All prisoners under sentence shall be required to work, subject to their physical and mental fitness as determined by the medical officer.

(3) Sufficient work of a useful nature shall be provided to keep prisoners actively employed for a normal working day.

(4) So far as possible the work provided shall be such as will maintain or increase the prisoners, ability to earn an honest living after release.

(5) Vocational training in useful trades shall be provided for prisoners able to profit thereby and especially for young prisoners.

(6) Within the limits compatible with proper vocational selection and with the requirements of institutional administration and discipline, the prisoners shall be able to choose the type of work they wish to perform.

72. (1) The organization and methods of work in the institutions shall resemble as closely as possible those of similar work outside institutions, so as to prepare prisoners for the conditions of normal occupational life.

(2) The interests of the prisoners and of their vocational training, however, must not be subordinated to the purpose of making a financial profit from an industry in the institution.

73. (1) Preferably institutional industries and farms should be operated directly by the administration and not by private contractors.

(2) Where prisoners are employed in work not controlled by the administration, they shall always be under the supervision of the institution's personnel. Unless the work is for other departments of the government the full normal wages for such work shall be paid to the administration by the persons to whom the labour is supplied, account being taken of the output of the prisoners.

74. (1) The precautions laid down to protect the safety and health of free workmen shall be equally observed in institutions.

(2) Provision shall be made to indemnify prisoners against industrial injury, including occupational disease, on terms not less favourable than those extended by law to free workmen.

75. (1) The maximum daily and weekly working hours of the prisoners shall be fixed by law or by administrative regulation, taking into account local rules or custom in regard to the employment of free workmen.

(2) The hours so fixed shall leave one rest day a week and sufficient time for education and other activities required as part of the treatment and rehabilitation of the prisoners.

76. (1) There shall be a system of equitable remuneration of the work of prisoners.

(2) Under the system prisoners shall be allowed to spend at least a part of their earnings on approved articles for their own use and to send a part of their earnings to their family.

(3) The system should also provide that a part of the earnings should be set aside by the administration so as to constitute a savings fund to be handed over to the prisoner on his release.

Education and recreation

77. (1) Provision shall be made for the further education of all prisoners capable of profiting thereby, including religious instruction in the countries where this is possible. The education of illiterates and young prisoners shall be compulsory and special attention shall be paid to it by the administration.

(2) So far as practicable, the education of prisoners shall be integrated with the educational system of the country so that after their release they may continue their education without difficulty.

78. Recreational and cultural activities shall be provided in all institutions for the benefit of the mental and physical health of prisoners.

Social Relations and after-care

79. Special attention shall be paid to the maintenance and improvement of such relations between a prisoner and his family as are desirable in the best interests of both.

80. From the beginning of a prisoner's sentence consideration shall be given to his future after release and he shall be encouraged and assisted to maintain or establish such relations with persons or agencies outside the institution as may promote the best interests of his family and his own social rehabilitation.

81. (1) Services and agencies, governmental or otherwise, which assist released prisoners to re-establish themselves in society shall ensure, so far as is possible and necessary, that released prisoners be provided with appropriate documents and identification papers, have suitable s and work to go to, are suitably and adequately clothed having regard to the climate and season, and have sufficient means to reach their destination and maintain themselves in the period

immediately following their release.

(2) The approved representatives of such agencies shall have all necessary access to the institution and to prisoners and shall be taken into consultation as to the future of a prisoner from the beginning of his sentence.

(3) It is desirable that the activities of such agencies shall be centralized or co-ordinated as far as possible in order to secure the best use of their efforts.

B. Insane and Mentally Abnormal Prisoners

82. (1) Persons who are found to be insane shall not be detained in prisons and arrangements shall be made to remove them to mental institutions as soon as possible.

(2) Prisoners who suffer from other mental diseases or abnormalities shall be observed and treated in specialized institutions under medical management.

(3) During their stay in a prison, such prisoners shall be placed under the special supervision of a medical officer.

(4) The medical or psychiatric service of the penal institutions shall provide for the psychiatric treatment of all other prisoners who are in need of such treatment.

83. It is desirable that steps should be taken, by arrangement with the appropriate agencies, to ensure if necessary the continuation of psychiatric treatment after release and the provision of social-psychiatric after-care.

C. Prisoners Under Arrest or Awaiting Trial

84. (1) Persons arrested or imprisoned by reason of a criminal charge against them, who are detained either in police custody or in prison custody (jail) but have not yet been tried and sentenced, will be referred to as "untried prison-

ers" hereinafter in these rules.

(2) Unconvicted prisoners are presumed to be innocent and shall be treated as such.

(3) Without prejudice to legal rules for the protection of individual liberty or prescribing the procedure to be observed in respect of untried prisoners, these prisoners shall benefit by a special regime which is described in the following rules in its essential requirements only.

85. (1) Untried prisoners shall be kept separate from convicted prisoners.

(2) Young untried prisoners shall be kept separate from adults and shall in principle be detained in separate institutions.

86. Untried prisoners shall sleep singly in separate rooms, with the reservation of different local custom in respect of the climate.

87. Within the limits compatible with the good order of the institution, untried prisoners may, if they so desire, have their food procured at their own expense from the outside, either through the administration or through their family or friends. Otherwise, the administration shall provide their food.

88. (1) An untried prisoner shall be allowed to wear his own clothing if it is clean and suitable.

(2) If he wears prison dress, it shall be different from that supplied to convicted prisoners.

89. An untried prisoner shall always be offered opportunity to work, but shall not be required to work. If he chooses to work, he shall be paid for it.

90. An untried prisoner shall be allowed to procure at his own expense or at the expense of a third party such books, newspapers, writing materials and other means of occupation as are compatible with the interests of the administration of justice and the security and good order of the institution.

91. An untried prisoner shall be allowed to be visited and treated by his own doctor or dentist if there is reasonable ground for his application and he is able to pay any expenses incurred.

92. An untried prisoner shall be allowed to inform immediately his family of his detention and shall be given all reasonable facilities for communicating with his family and friends, and for receiving visits from them, subject only to restrictions and supervision as are necessary in the interests of the administration of justice and of the security and good order of the institution.

93. For the purposes of his defence, an untried prisoner shall be allowed to apply for free legal aid where such aid is available, and to receive visits from his legal adviser with a view to his defence and to prepare and hand to him confidential instructions. For these purposes, he shall if he so desires be supplied with writing material. Interviews between the prisoner and his legal adviser may be within sight but not within the hearing of a police or institution official.

D. Civil Prisoners

94. In countries where the law permits imprisonment for debt, or by order of a court under any other non-criminal process, persons so imprisoned shall not be subjected to any greater restriction or severity than is necessary to ensure safe custody and good order. Their treatment shall be not less favourable than that of untried prisoners, with the reservation, however, that they may possibly be required to work.

E. Persons Arrested or Detained Without Charge

95. Without prejudice to the provisions of article 9 of the International Covenant on Civil and Political Rights, persons arrested or imprisoned without charge shall be accorded the same

protection as that accorded under part I and part II, section C. Relevant provisions of part II, section A, shall likewise be applicable where their application may be conducive to the benefit of this special group of persons in custody, provided that no measures shall be taken implying that re-education or rehabilitation is in any way appropriate to persons not convicted of any criminal offence.

UN BODY OF PRINCIPLES FOR THE PROTECTION OF ALL PERSONS UNDER ANY FORM OF DETENTION OR IMPRISONMENT

A/RES/43/173 76th plenary meeting 9 December 1988 43/173. Body of Principles for the Protection of All Persons under Any Form of Detention or Imprisonment

The General Assembly,
Recalling its resolution 35/177 of 15 December 1980, in which it referred the task of elaborating the draft Body of Principles for the Protection of All Persons under Any Form of Detention or Imprisonment to the Sixth Committee and decided to establish an open-ended working group for that purpose,
Taking note of the report of the Working Group on the Draft Body of Principles for the Protection of All Persons under Any Form of Detention or Imprisonment, which met during the forty-third session of the General Assembly and completed the elaboration of the draft Body of Principles,
Considering that the Working Group decided to submit the text of the draft Body of Principles to the Sixth Committee for its consideration and adoption,
Convinced that the adoption of the draft Body of Principles would make an important contribution to the protection of human rights,
Considering the need to ensure the wide dissemination of the text of the Body of Principles,

1. Approves the Body of Principles for the Protection of All Persons under Any Form of Detention or Imprisonment, the text of which is annexed to the present resolution;

2. Expresses its appreciation to the Working Group on the Draft Body of Principles for the Protection of All Persons under Any Form of Detention or Imprisonment for its important contribution to the elaboration of the Body of Principles;

3. Requests the Secretary-General to inform the States Members of the United Nations or members of specialized agencies of the adoption of the Body of Principles;

4. Urges that every effort be made so that the Body of Principles becomes generally known and respected.

ANNEX

Body of Principles for the Protection of All Persons under Any Form of Detention or Imprisonment Scope of the Body of Principles

These principles apply for the protection of all persons under any form of detention or imprisonment.

Use of Terms

For the purposes of the Body of Principles:

(a) "Arrest" means the act of apprehending a person for the alleged commission of an offence or by the action of an authority;

(b) "Detained person" means any person deprived of personal liberty except as a result of conviction for an offence;

(c) "Imprisoned person" means any person deprived of personal liberty as a result of conviction for an offence;

(d) "Detention" means the condition of detained persons as defined above;

(e) "Imprisonment" means the condition of imprisoned persons as defined above;

(f) The words "a judicial or other authority" mean a judicial or other authority under the law whose status and tenure should afford the strongest possible guarantees of competence, impartiality and independence.

Principle 1

All persons under any form of detention or imprisonment shall be treated in a humane manner and with respect for the inherent dignity of the human person.

Principle 2

Arrest, detention or imprisonment shall only be carried out strictly in accordance with the provisions of the law and by competent officials or persons authorized for that purpose.

Principle 3

There shall be no restriction upon or derogation from any of the human rights of persons under any form of detention or imprisonment recognized or existing in any State pursuant to law, conventions, regulations or custom on the pretext that this Body of Principles does not recognize such rights or that it recognizes them to a lesser extent.

Principle 4

Any form of detention or imprisonment and all measures affecting the human rights of a person under any form of detention or imprisonment shall be ordered by, or be subject to the effective control of, a judicial or other authority.

Principle 5

1. These principles shall be applied to all persons within the territory of any given State, without distinction of any kind, such as race,

colour, sex, language, religion or religious belief, political or other opinion, national, ethnic or social origin, property, birth or other status.

2. Measures applied under the law and designed solely to protect the rights and special status of women, especially pregnant women and nursing mothers, children and juveniles, aged, sick or handicapped persons shall not be deemed to be discriminatory. The need for, and the application of, such measures shall always be subject to review by a judicial or other authority.

Principle 6

No person under any form of detention or imprisonment shall be subjected to torture or to cruel, inhuman or degrading treatment or punishment.* No circumstance whatever may be invoked as a justification for torture or other cruel, inhuman or degrading treatment or punishment.

   * The term "cruel, inhuman or degrading treatment or punishment" should be interpreted so as to extend the widest possible protection against abuses, whether physical or mental, including the holding of a detained or imprisoned person in conditions which deprive him, temporarily or permanently, of the use of any of his natural senses, such as sight or hearing, or of his awareness of place and the passing of time.

Principle 7

1. States should prohibit by law any act contrary to the rights and duties contained in these principles, make any such act subject to appropriate sanctions and conduct impartial investigations upon complaints.

2. Officials who have reason to believe that a violation of this Body of Principles has occurred or is about to occur shall report the matter to their superior authorities and, where necessary, to other appropriate authorities or organs vested with reviewing or remedial powers.

3. Any other person who has ground to believe that a violation of this Body of Principles has occurred or is about to occur shall have the right to report the matter to the superiors of the officials involved as well as to other appropriate authorities or organs vested with reviewing or remedial powers.

Principle 8

Persons in detention shall be subject to treatment appropriate to their unconvicted status. Accordingly, they shall, whenever possible, be kept separate from imprisoned persons.

Principle 9

The authorities which arrest a person, keep him under detention or investigate the case shall exercise only the powers granted to them under the law and the exercise of these powers shall be subject to recourse to a judicial or other authority.

Principle 10

Anyone who is arrested shall be informed at the time of his arrest of the reason for his arrest and shall be promptly informed of any charges against him.

Principle 11

1. A person shall not be kept in detention without being given an effective opportunity to be heard promptly by a judicial or other authority. A detained person shall have the right to defend himself or to be assisted by counsel as prescribed by law.

2. A detained person and his counsel, if any, shall receive prompt and full communication of any order of detention, together with the reasons therefore.

3. A judicial or other authority shall be empowered to review as appropriate the continuance of detention.

Principle 12

1. There shall be duly recorded:

(a) The reasons for the arrest;

(b) The time of the arrest and the taking of the arrested person to a place of custody as well as that of his first appearance before a judicial or other authority;

(c) The identity of the law enforcement officials concerned;

(d) Precise information concerning the place of custody.

2. Such records shall be communicated to the detained person, or his counsel, if any, in the form prescribed by law.

Principle 13

Any person shall, at the moment of arrest and at the commencement of detention or imprisonment, or promptly thereafter, be provided by the authority responsible for his arrest, detention or imprisonment, respectively, with information on and an explanation of his rights and how to avail himself of such rights.

Principle 14

A person who does not adequately understand or speak the language used by the authorities responsible for his arrest, detention or imprisonment is entitled to receive promptly in a language which he understands the information referred to in principle 10, principle 11, paragraph 2, principle 12, paragraph 1, and principle 13 and to have the assistance, free of charge, if necessary, of an interpreter in connection with legal proceedings subsequent to his arrest.

Principle 15

Notwithstanding the exceptions contained in principle 16, paragraph 4, and principle 18, paragraph 3, communication of the detained or imprisoned person with the outside world, and in particular his family or counsel, shall not be denied for more than a matter of days.

Principle 16

1. Promptly after arrest and after each transfer from one place of detention or imprisonment to another, a detained or imprisoned person shall be entitled to notify or to require the competent authority to notify members of his family or other appropriate persons of his choice of his arrest, detention or imprisonment or of the transfer and of the place where he is kept in custody.

2. If a detained or imprisoned person is a foreigner, he shall also be promptly informed of his right to communicate by appropriate means with a consular post or the diplomatic mission of the State of which he is a national or which is otherwise entitled to receive such communication in accordance with international law or with the representative of the competent international organization, if he is a refugee or is otherwise under the protection of an intergovernmental organization.

3. If a detained or imprisoned person is a juvenile or is incapable of understanding his entitlement, the competent authority shall on its own initiative undertake the notification referred to in the present principle. Special attention shall be given to notifying parents or guardians.

4. Any notification referred to in the present principle shall be made or permitted to be made without delay. The competent authority may however delay a notification for a reasonable period where exceptional needs of the investigation so require.

Principle 17

1. A detained person shall be entitled to have the assistance of a legal counsel. He shall be informed of his right by the competent authority promptly after arrest and shall be provided with reasonable facilities for exercising it.

2. If a detained person does not have a legal counsel of his own choice, he shall be entitled to have a legal counsel assigned to him by a judicial or other authority in all cases where the interests of justice so require and without payment by him if he does not have sufficient means to pay.

Principle 18

1. A detained or imprisoned person shall be entitled to communicate and consult with his legal counsel.

2. A detained or imprisoned person shall be allowed adequate time and facilities for consultations with his legal counsel.

3. The right of a detained or imprisoned person to be visited by and to consult and communicate, without delay or censorship and in full confidentiality, with his legal counsel may not be suspended or restricted save in exceptional circumstances, to be specified by law or lawful-regulations, when it is considered indispensable by a judicial or other authority in order to maintain security and good order.

4. Interviews between a detained or imprisoned person and his legal counsel may be within sight, but not within the hearing, of a law enforcement official.

5. Communications between a detained or imprisoned person and his legal counsel mentioned in the present principle shall be inadmissible as evidence against the detained or imprisoned person unless they are connected with a continuing or contemplated crime.

Principle 19

A detained or imprisoned person shall have the right to be visited by and to correspond with, in particular, members of his family and shall be given adequate opportunity to communicate with the outside world, subject to reasonable conditions and restrictions as specified by law or lawful regulations.

Principle 20

If a detained or imprisoned person so requests, he shall if possible be kept in a place of detention or imprisonment reasonably near his usual place of residence.

Principle 21

1. It shall be prohibited to take undue advantage of the situation of a detained or imprisoned person for the purpose of compelling him to confess, to incriminate himself otherwise or to testify against any other person.

2. No detained person while being interrogated shall be subject to violence, threats or methods of interrogation which impair his capacity of decision or his judgement.

Principle 22

No detained or imprisoned person shall, even with his consent, be subjected to any medical or scientific experimentation which may be detrimental to his health.

Principle 23

1. The duration of any interrogation of a detained or imprisoned person and of the intervals between interrogations as well as the identity of the officials who conducted the interrogations and other persons present shall be recorded and certified in such form as may be prescribed by law.

2. A detained or imprisoned person, or his coun-

sel when provided by law, shall have access to the information described in paragraph 1 of the present principle.

Principle 24

A proper medical examination shall be offered to a detained or imprisoned person as promptly as possible after his admission to the place of detention or imprisonment, and thereafter medical care and treatment shall be provided whenever necessary. This care and treatment shall be provided free of charge.

Principle 25

A detained or imprisoned person or his counsel shall, subject only to reasonable conditions to ensure security and good order in the place of detention or imprisonment, have the right to request or petition a judicial or other authority for a second medical examination or opinion.

Principle 26

The fact that a detained or imprisoned person underwent a medical examination, the name of the physician and the results of such an examination shall be duly recorded. Access to such records shall be ensured. Modalities therefor shall be in accordance with relevant rules of domestic law.

Principle 27

Non-compliance with these principles in obtaining evidence shall be taken into account in determining the admissibility of such evidence against a detained or imprisoned person.

Principle 28

A detained or imprisoned person shall have the right to obtain within the limits of available resources, if from public sources, reasonable quantities of educational, cultural and informational material, subject to reasonable conditions to ensure security and good order in the place of detention or imprisonment.

Principle 29

1. In order to supervise the strict observance of relevant laws and regulations, places of detention shall be visited regularly by qualified and experienced persons appointed by, and responsible to, a competent authority distinct from the authority directly in charge of the administration of the place of detention or imprisonment.

2. A detained or imprisoned person shall have the right to communicate freely and in full confidentiality with the persons who visit the places of detention or imprisonment in accordance with paragraph 1 of the present principle, subject to reasonable conditions to ensure security and good order in such places.

Principle 30

1. The types of conduct of the detained or imprisoned person that constitute disciplinary offences during detention or imprisonment, the description and duration of disciplinary punishment that may be inflicted and the authorities competent to impose such punishment shall be specified by law or lawful regulations and duly published.

2. A detained or imprisoned person shall have the right to be heard before disciplinary action is taken. He shall have the right to bring such action to higher authorities for review.

Principle 31

The appropriate authorities shall endeavour to ensure, according to domestic law, assistance when needed to dependent and, in particular, minor members of the families of detained or imprisoned persons and shall devote a particular measure of care to the appropriate custody of children left without supervision.

Principle 32

1. A detained person or his counsel shall be entitled at any time to take proceedings according to domestic law before a judicial or other authority to challenge the lawfulness of his detention in order to obtain his release without delay, if it is unlawful.

2. The proceedings referred to in paragraph 1 of the present principle shall be simple and expeditious and at no cost for detained persons without adequate means. The detaining authority shall produce without unreasonable delay the detained person before the reviewing authority.

Principle 33

1. A detained or imprisoned person or his counsel shall have the right to make a request or complaint regarding his treatment, in particular in case of torture or other cruel, inhuman or degrading treatment, to the authorities responsible for the administration of the place of detention and to higher authorities and, when necessary, to appropriate authorities vested with reviewing or remedial powers.

2. In those cases where neither the detained or imprisoned person nor his counsel has the possibility to exercise his rights under paragraph 1 of the present principle, a member of the family of the detained or imprisoned person or any other person who has knowledge of the case may exercise such rights.

3. Confidentiality concerning the request or complaint shall be maintained if so requested by the complainant.

4. Every request or complaint shall be promptly dealt with and replied to without undue delay.

If the request or complaint is rejected or, in case of inordinate delay, the complainant shall be entitled to bring it before a judicial or other authority. Neither the detained or imprisoned person nor any complainant under paragraph 1 of the present principle shall suffer prejudice for making a request or complaint.

Principle 34

Whenever the death or disappearance of a detained or imprisoned person occurs during his detention or imprisonment, an inquiry into the cause of death or disappearance shall be held by a judicial or other authority, either on its own motion or at the instance of a member of the family of such a person or any person who has knowledge of the case. When circumstances so warrant, such an inquiry shall be held on the same procedural basis whenever the death or disappearance occurs shortly after the termination of the detention or imprisonment. The findings of such inquiry or a report thereon shall be made available upon request, unless doing so would jeopardize an ongoing criminal investigation.

Principle 35

1. Damage incurred because of acts or omissions by a public official contrary to the rights contained in these principles shall be compensated according to the applicable rules on liability provided by domestic law.

2. Information required to be recorded under these principles shall be available in accordance with procedures provided by domestic law for use in claiming compensation under the present principle.

Principle 36

1. A detained person suspected of or charged with a criminal offence shall be presumed inno-

cent and shall be treated as such until proved guilty according to law in a public trial at which he has had all the guarantees necessary for his defence.
2. The arrest or detention of such a person pending investigation and trial shall be carried out only for the purposes of the administration of justice on grounds and under conditions and procedures specified by law. The imposition of restrictions upon such a person which are not strictly required for the purpose of the detention or to prevent hindrance to the process of investigation or the administration of justice, or for the maintenance of security and good order in the place of detention shall be forbidden.

Principle 37

A person detained on a criminal charge shall be brought before a judicial or other authority provided by law promptly after his arrest. Such authority shall decide without delay upon the lawfulness and necessity of detention. No person may be kept under detention pending investigation or trial except upon the written order of such an authority. A detained person shall, when brought before such an authority, have the right to make a statement on the treatment received by him while in custody.

Principle 38

A person detained on a criminal charge shall be entitled to trial within a reasonable time or to release pending trial.

Principle 39

Except in special cases provided for by law, a person detained on a criminal charge shall be entitled, unless a judicial or other authority decides otherwise in the interest of the administration of justice, to release pending trial subject to the conditions that may be imposed in accord-

ance with the law. Such authority shall keep the necessity of detention under review.

General Clause

Nothing in this Body of Principles shall be construed as restricting or derogating from any right defined in the International Covenant on Civil and Political Rights.

SATELLITE PHOTOGRAPHS

Camp 15:

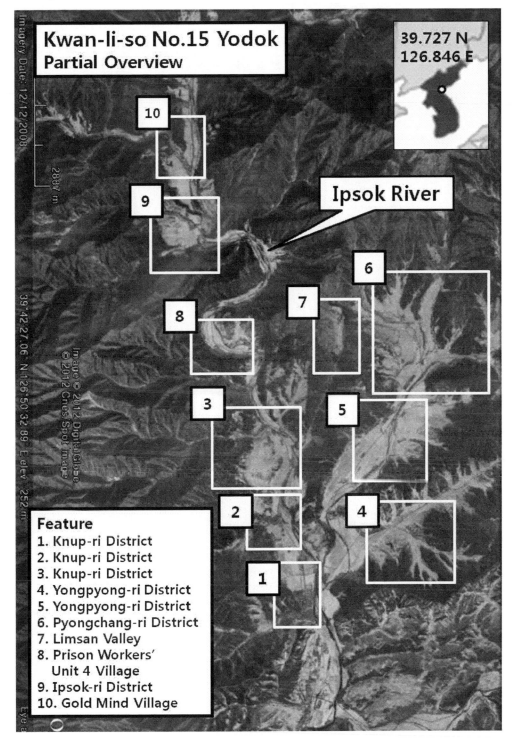

Kwan-li-so No.15 Yodok
Partial Overview

39.727 N
126.846 E

Ipsok River

Feature
1. Knup-ri District
2. Knup-ri District
3. Knup-ri District
4. Yongpyong-ri District
5. Yongpyong-ri District
6. Pyongchang-ri District
7. Limsan Valley
8. Prison Workers'
   Unit 4 Village
9. Ipsok-ri District
10. Gold Mind Village

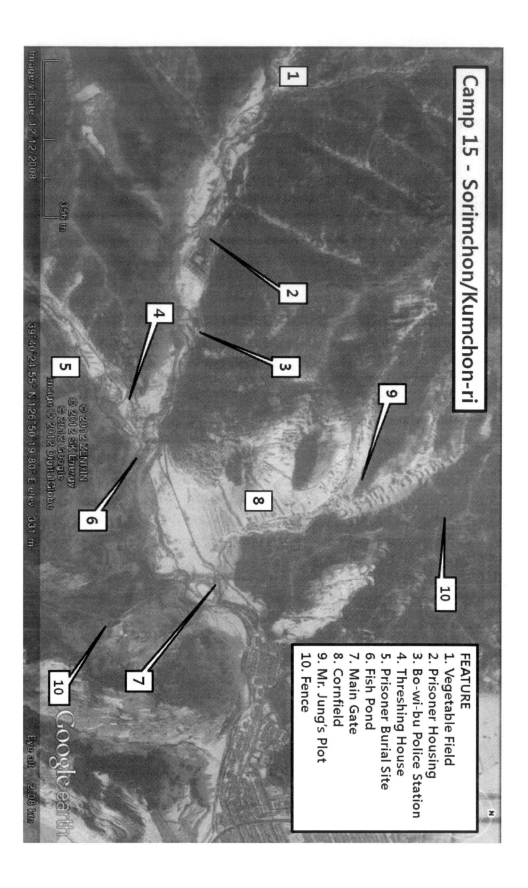

Camp 15 - Sorimchon/Kumchon-ri

FEATURE
1. Vegetable Field
2. Prisoner Housing
3. Bo-wi-bu Police Station
4. Threshing House
5. Prisoner Burial Site
6. Fish Pond
7. Main Gate
8. Cornfield
9. Mr. Jung's Plot
10. Fence

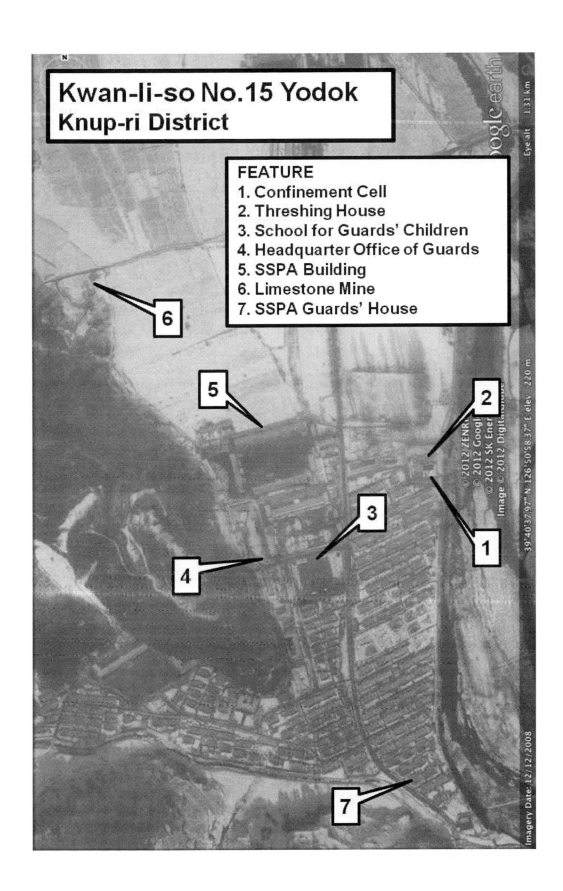

Kwan-li-so No.15 Yodok
Knup-ri District

FEATURE
1. Confinement Cell
2. Threshing House
3. School for Guards' Children
4. Headquarter Office of Guards
5. SSPA Building
6. Limestone Mine
7. SSPA Guards' House

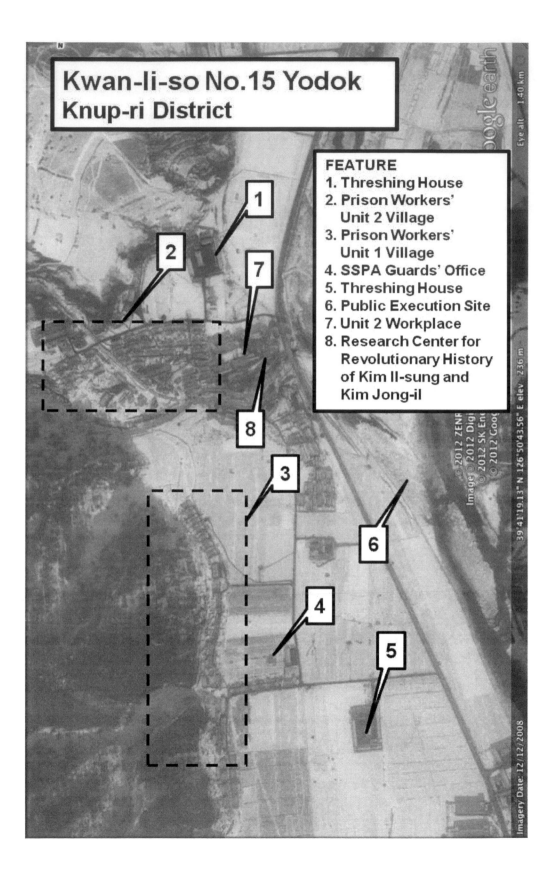

Kwan-li-so No.15 Yodok
Knup-ri District

FEATURE
1. Threshing House
2. Prison Workers'
   Unit 2 Village
3. Prison Workers'
   Unit 1 Village
4. SSPA Guards' Office
5. Threshing House
6. Public Execution Site
7. Unit 2 Workplace
8. Research Center for
   Revolutionary History
   of Kim Il-sung and
   Kim Jong-il

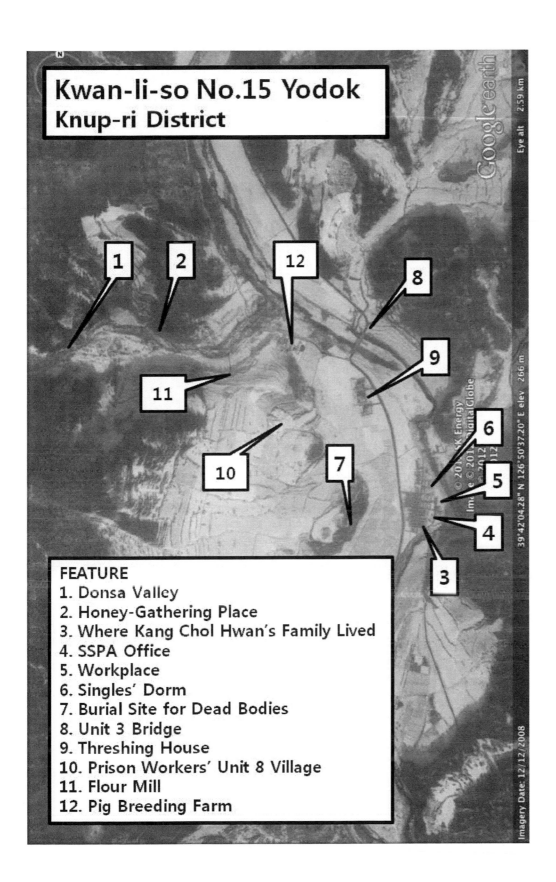

Kwan-li-so No.15 Yodok
Knup-ri District

FEATURE
1. Donsa Valley
2. Honey-Gathering Place
3. Where Kang Chol Hwan's Family Lived
4. SSPA Office
5. Workplace
6. Singles' Dorm
7. Burial Site for Dead Bodies
8. Unit 3 Bridge
9. Threshing House
10. Prison Workers' Unit 8 Village
11. Flour Mill
12. Pig Breeding Farm

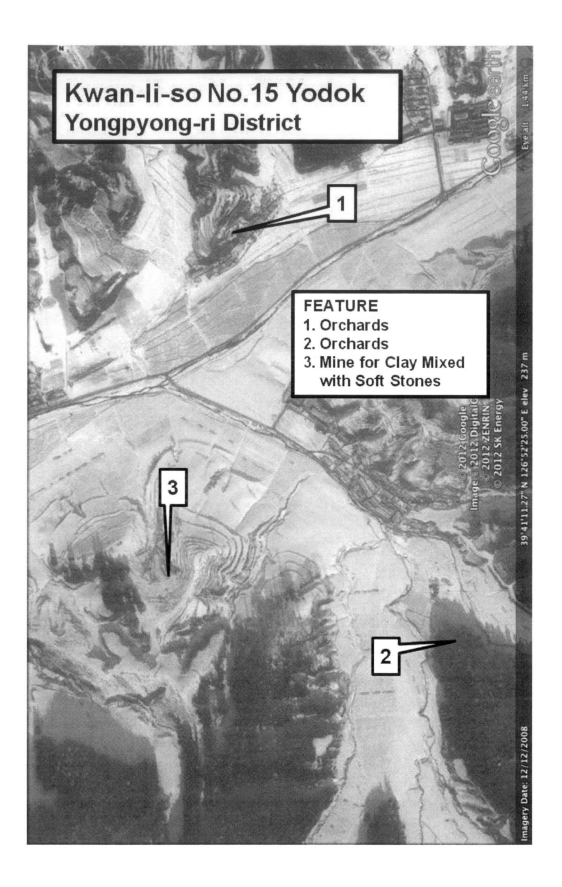

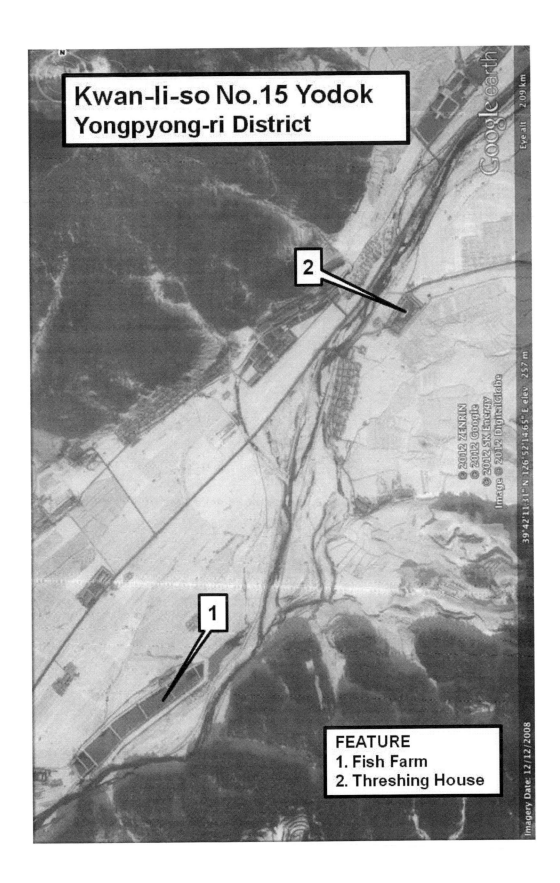

Kwan-li-so No.15 Yodok
Yongpyong-ri District

FEATURE
1. Fish Farm
2. Threshing House

Kwan-li-so No. 15 Yodok
Pyongchang-ri District

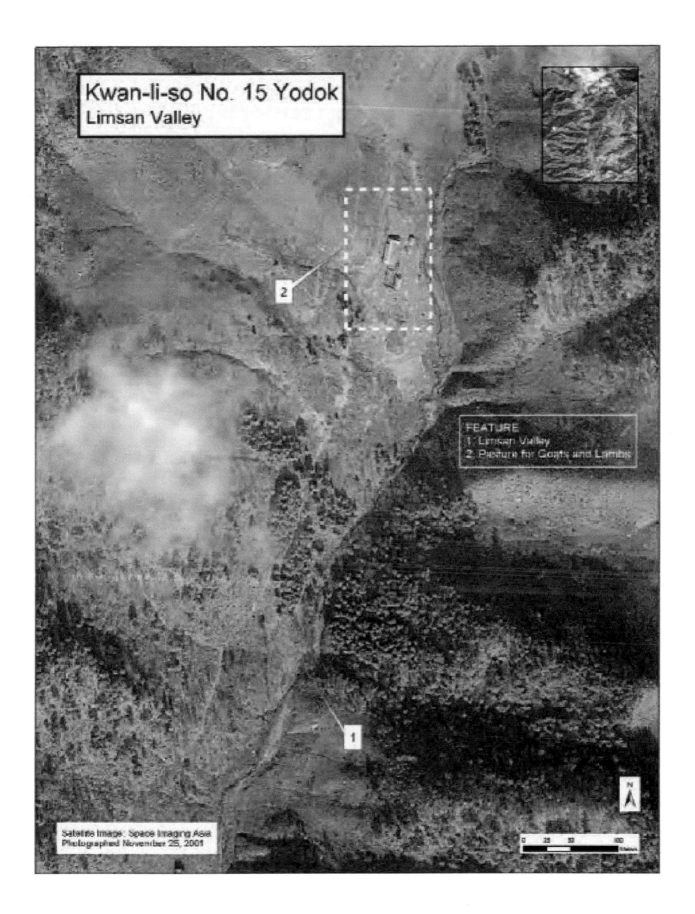

Kwan-li-so No. 15 Yodok
Limsan Valley

FEATURE
1. Limsan Valley
2. Pasture for Goats and Lambs

Satellite Image: Space Imaging Asia
Photographed November 25, 2001

Kwan-li-so No. 15 Yodok
Prison Workers' Unit 4 Village

Prison Workers' Unit 4 Village

Satellite Image: Space Imaging Asia
Photographed November 25, 2001

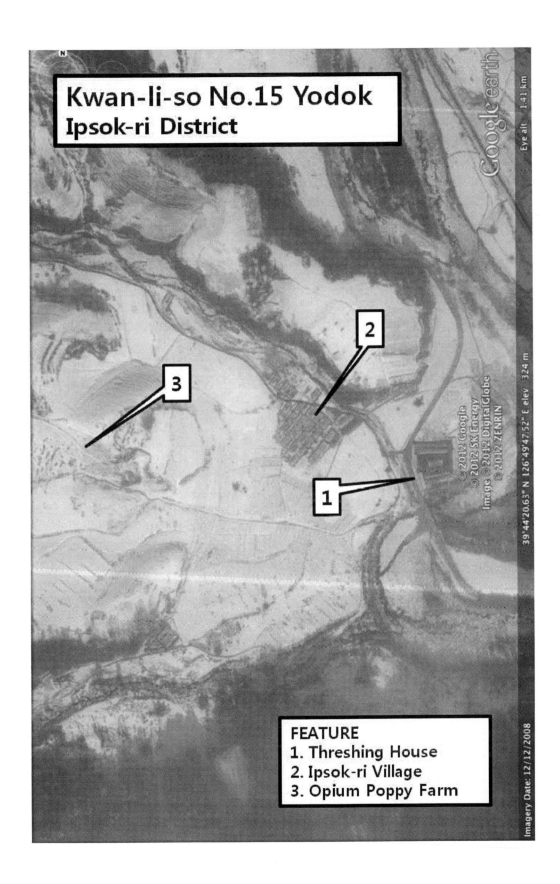

Kwan-li-so No.15 Yodok
Ipsok-ri District

FEATURE
1. Threshing House
2. Ipsok-ri Village
3. Opium Poppy Farm

Camp 14:

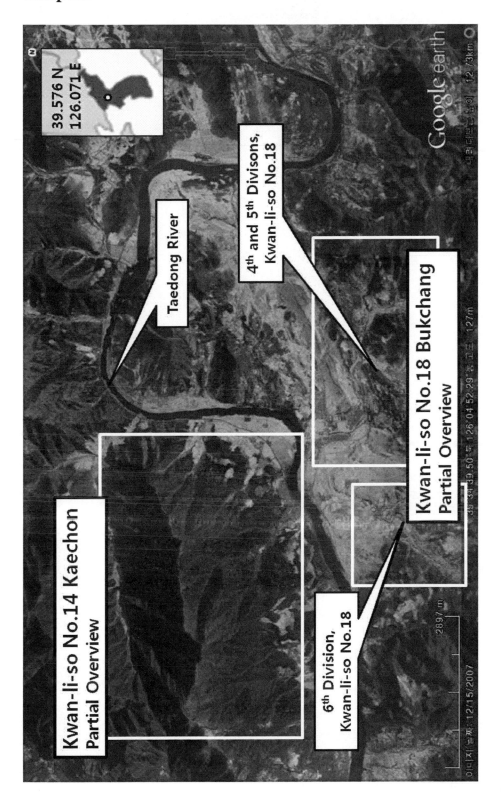

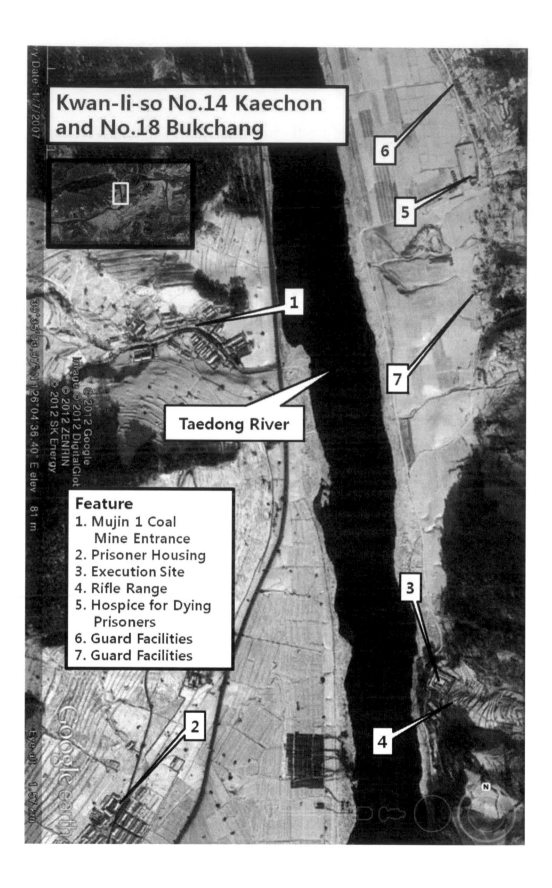

Kwan-li-so No.14 Kaechon and No.18 Bukchang

Taedong River

Feature
1. Mujin 1 Coal Mine Entrance
2. Prisoner Housing
3. Execution Site
4. Rifle Range
5. Hospice for Dying Prisoners
6. Guard Facilities
7. Guard Facilities

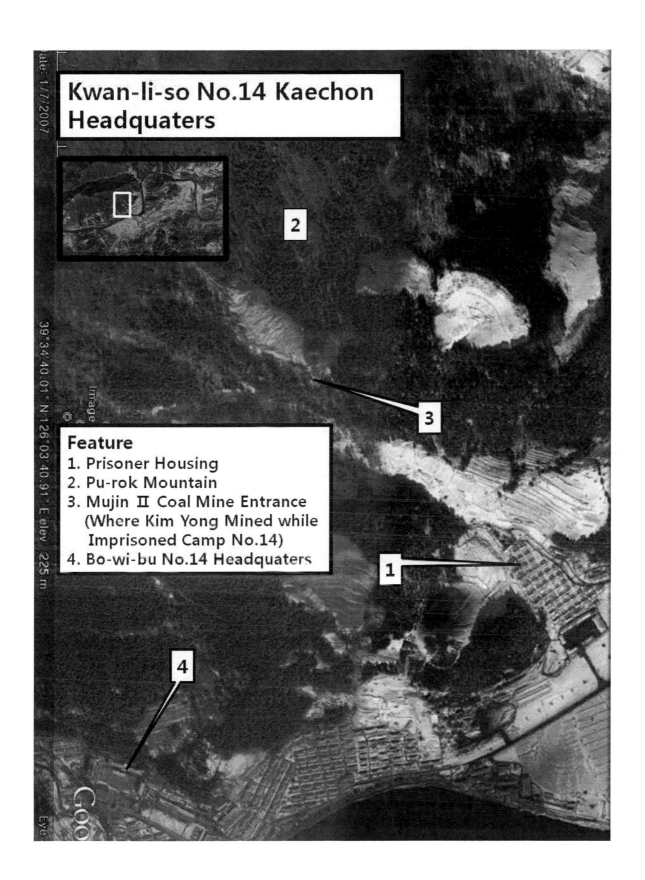

Kwan-li-so No.14 Kaechon Headquaters

Feature
1. Prisoner Housing
2. Pu-rok Mountain
3. Mujin II Coal Mine Entrance (Where Kim Yong Mined while Imprisoned Camp No.14)
4. Bo-wi-bu No.14 Headquaters

Kwan-li-so No.14 Kaechon
Prisoner Housing

Prisoner Housing

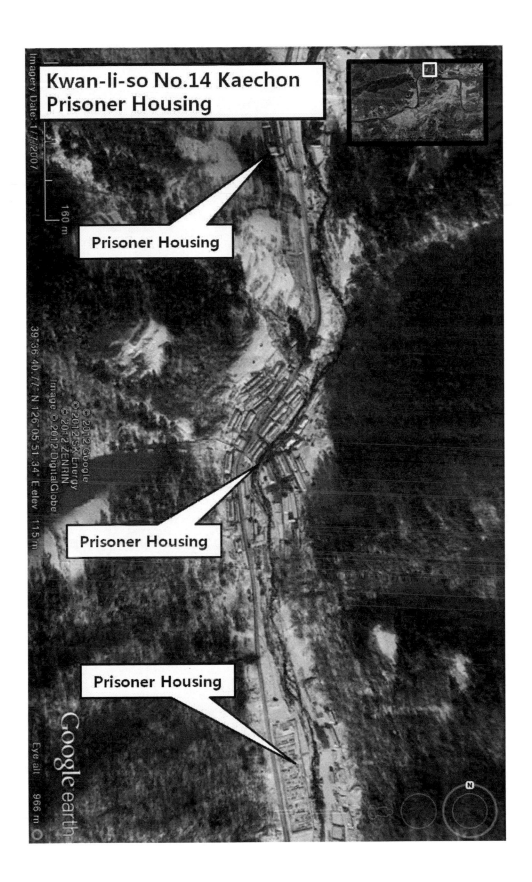

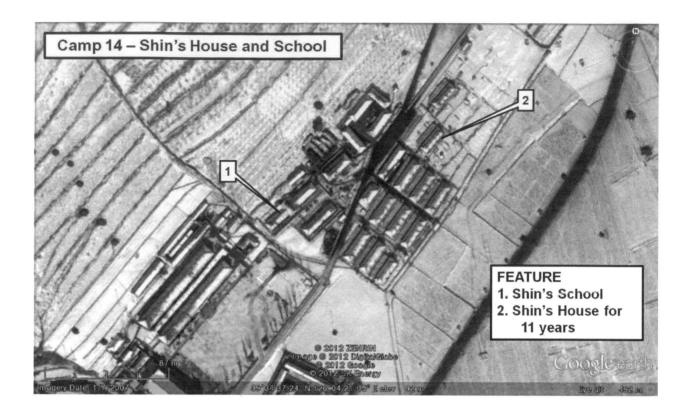

Camp 14 – Shin's House and School

FEATURE
1. Shin's School
2. Shin's House for
   11 years

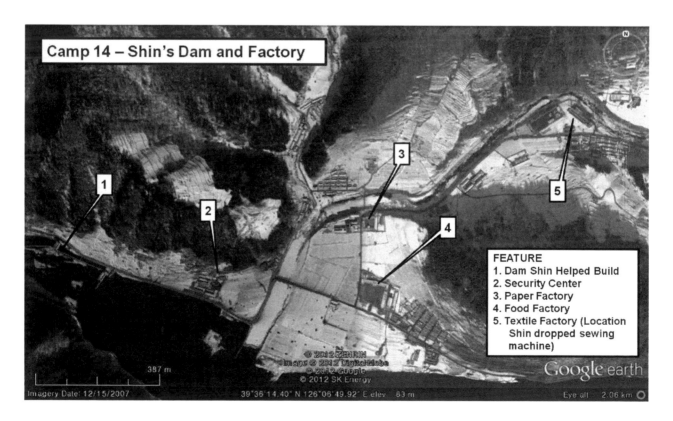

Camp 14 – Shin's Dam and Factory

FEATURE
1. Dam Shin Helped Build
2. Security Center
3. Paper Factory
4. Food Factory
5. Textile Factory (Location
   Shin dropped sewing
   machine)

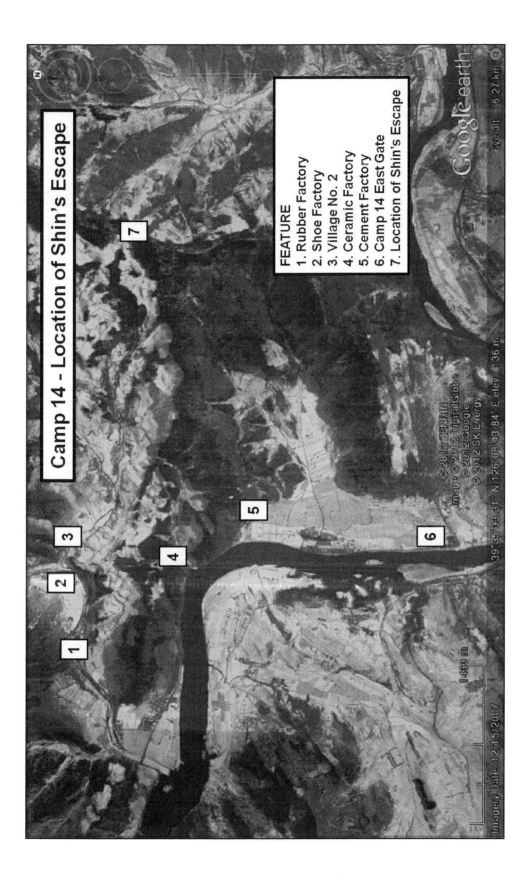

Camp 14 - Location of Shin's Escape

FEATURE
1. Rubber Factory
2. Shoe Factory
3. Village No. 2
4. Ceramic Factory
5. Cement Factory
6. Camp 14 East Gate
7. Location of Shin's Escape

Kwan-li-so No. 18 Bukchang:

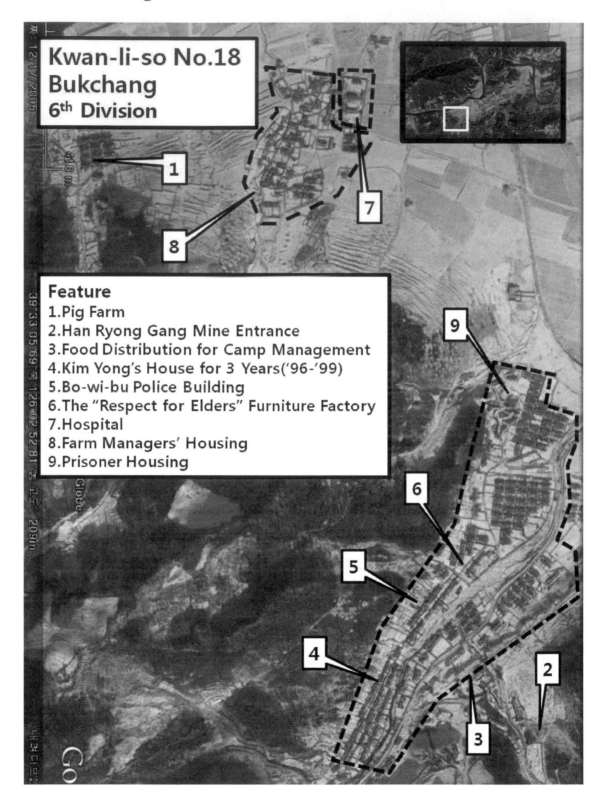

Kwan-li-so No.18
Bukchang
6th Division

Feature
1. Pig Farm
2. Han Ryong Gang Mine Entrance
3. Food Distribution for Camp Management
4. Kim Yong's House for 3 Years('96-'99)
5. Bo-wi-bu Police Building
6. The "Respect for Elders" Furniture Factory
7. Hospital
8. Farm Managers' Housing
9. Prisoner Housing

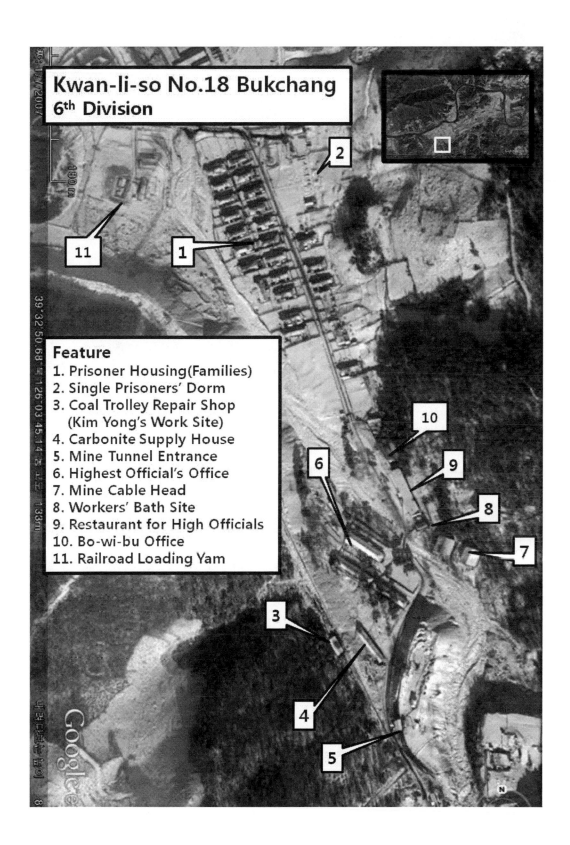

Kwan-li-so No.18 Bukchang
6th Division

Feature
1. Prisoner Housing(Families)
2. Single Prisoners' Dorm
3. Coal Trolley Repair Shop
   (Kim Yong's Work Site)
4. Carbonite Supply House
5. Mine Tunnel Entrance
6. Highest Official's Office
7. Mine Cable Head
8. Workers' Bath Site
9. Restaurant for High Officials
10. Bo-wi-bu Office
11. Railroad Loading Yam

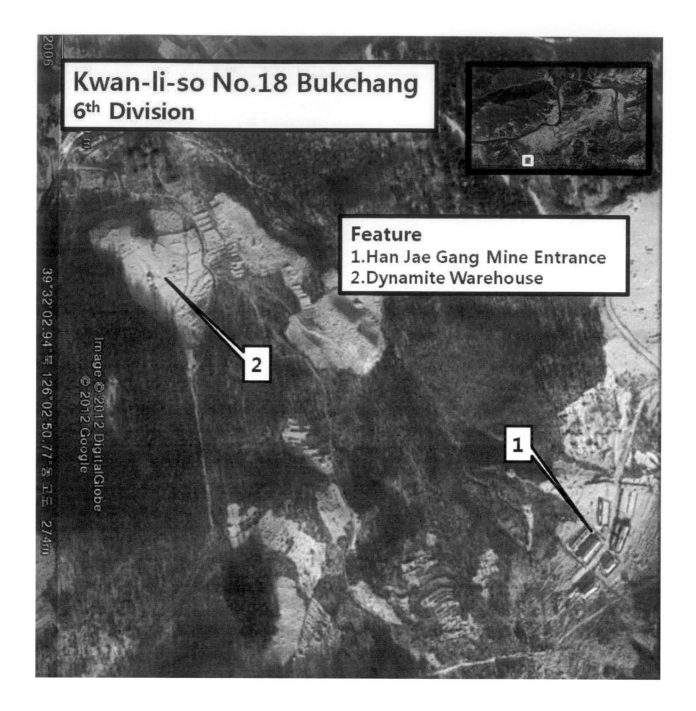

Kwan-li-so No.18 Bukchang
6th Division

Feature
1. Han Jae Gang Mine Entrance
2. Dynamite Warehouse

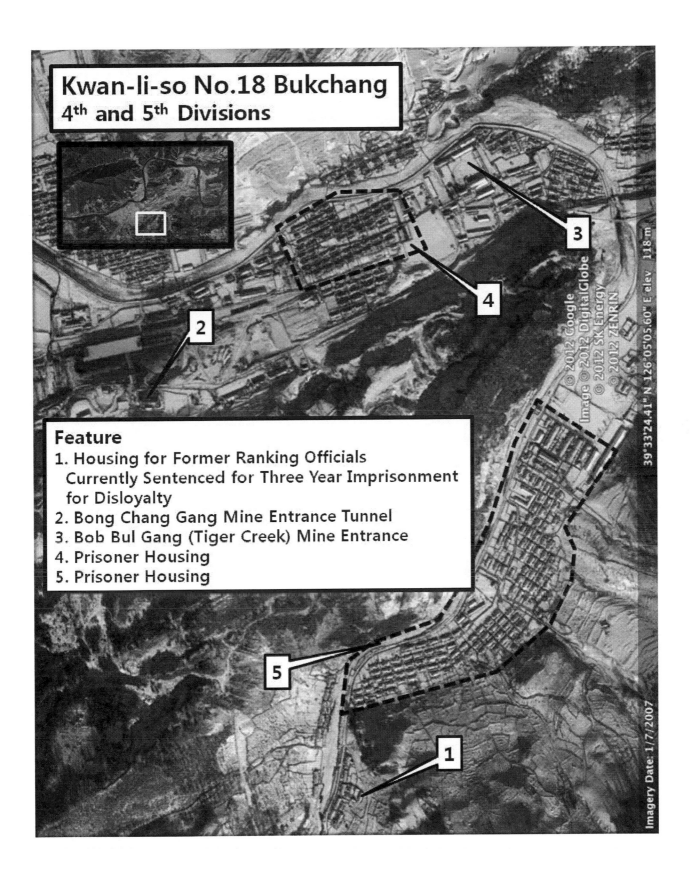

Kwan-li-so No.18 Bukchang
4th and 5th Divisions

Feature
1. Housing for Former Ranking Officials Currently Sentenced for Three Year Imprisonment for Disloyalty
2. Bong Chang Gang Mine Entrance Tunnel
3. Bob Bul Gang (Tiger Creek) Mine Entrance
4. Prisoner Housing
5. Prisoner Housing

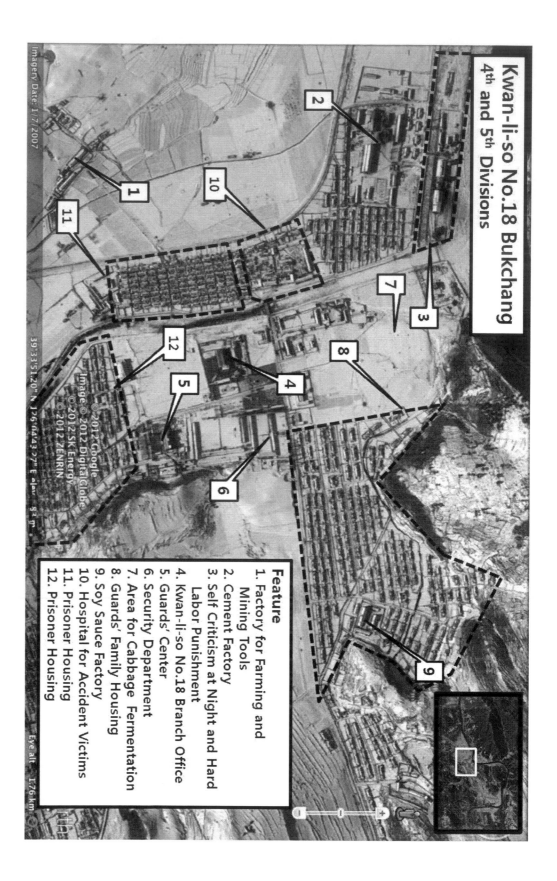

Kwan-li-so No.18 Bukchang
4th and 5th Divisions

Feature
1. Factory for Farming and
   Mining Tools
2. Cement Factory
3. Self Criticism at Night and Hard
   Labor Punishment
4. Kwan-li-so No.18 Branch Office
5. Guards' Center
6. Security Department
7. Area for Cabbage Fermentation
8. Guards' Family Housing
9. Soy Sauce Factory
10. Hospital for Accident Victims
11. Prisoner Housing
12. Prisoner Housing

Imagery Date: 1/7/2007

Image © 2012 Google
© 2012 DigitalGlobe
© 2012 SK Energy
© 2012 ZENRIN

39°33′51.20″ N 126°04′43.77″ E elev 93 m

Eye alt   1.76 km

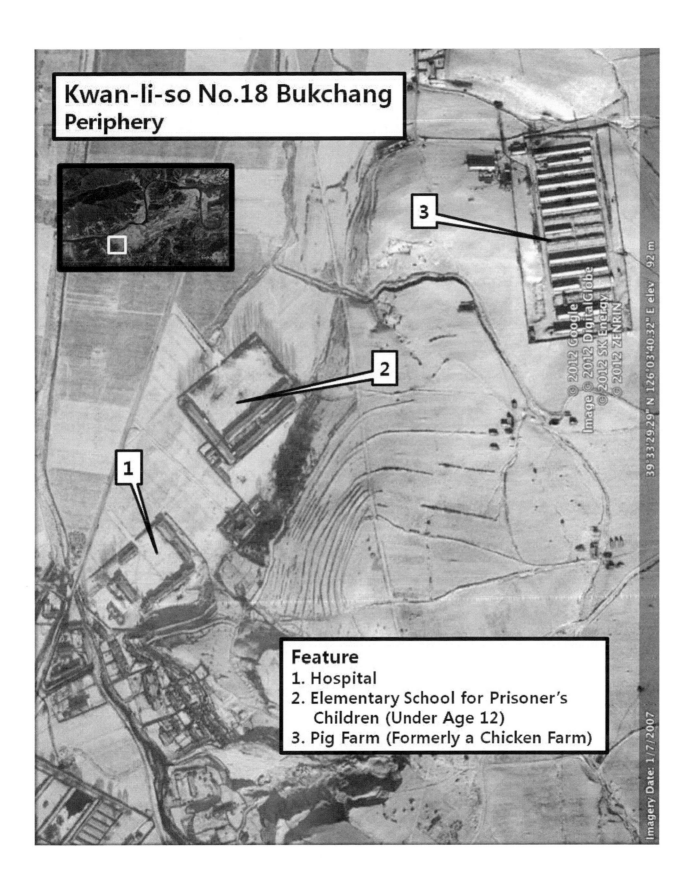

Kwan-li-so No.18 Bukchang
Periphery

39°33'29.29" N 126°03'40.32" E elev 92 m

Image © 2012 Google
© 2012 DigitalGlobe
© 2012 SK Energy
© 2012 ZENRIN

Imagery Date: 1/7/2007

Feature
1. Hospital
2. Elementary School for Prisoner's
   Children (Under Age 12)
3. Pig Farm (Formerly a Chicken Farm)

Kwan-li-so No. 22:

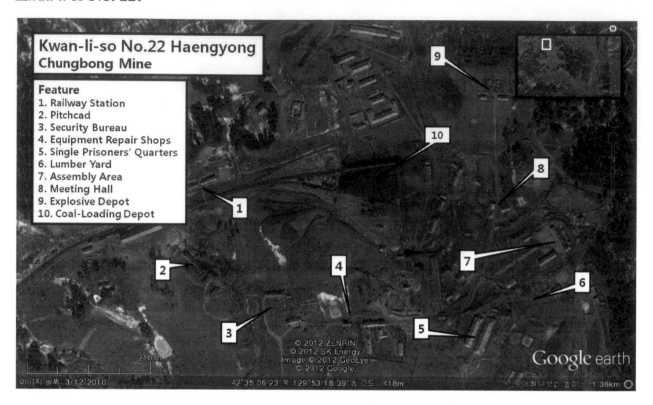

Kwan-li-so No.22 Haengyong
Chungbong Mine

Feature
1. Railway Station
2. Pitchcad
3. Security Bureau
4. Equipment Repair Shops
5. Single Prisoners' Quarters
6. Lumber Yard
7. Assembly Area
8. Meeting Hall
9. Explosive Depot
10. Coal-Loading Depot

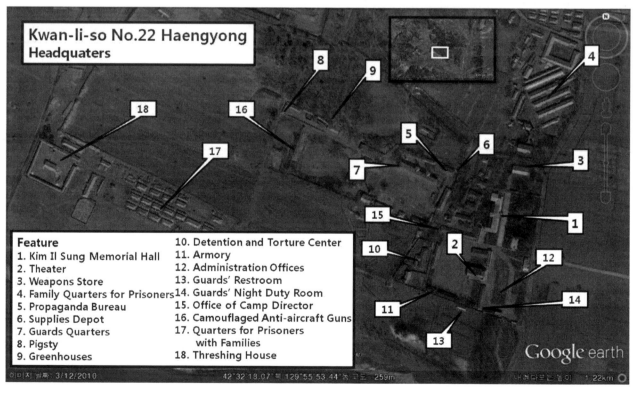

Kwan-li-so No.22 Haengyong
Headquaters

Feature
1. Kim Il Sung Memorial Hall
2. Theater
3. Weapons Store
4. Family Quarters for Prisoners
5. Propaganda Bureau
6. Supplies Depot
7. Guards Quarters
8. Pigsty
9. Greenhouses
10. Detention and Torture Center
11. Armory
12. Administration Offices
13. Guards' Restroom
14. Guards' Night Duty Room
15. Office of Camp Director
16. Camouflaged Anti-aircraft Guns
17. Quarters for Prisoners
    with Families
18. Threshing House

Kwan-li-so No. 25 Chongjin:

Committee for Human Rights in North Korea

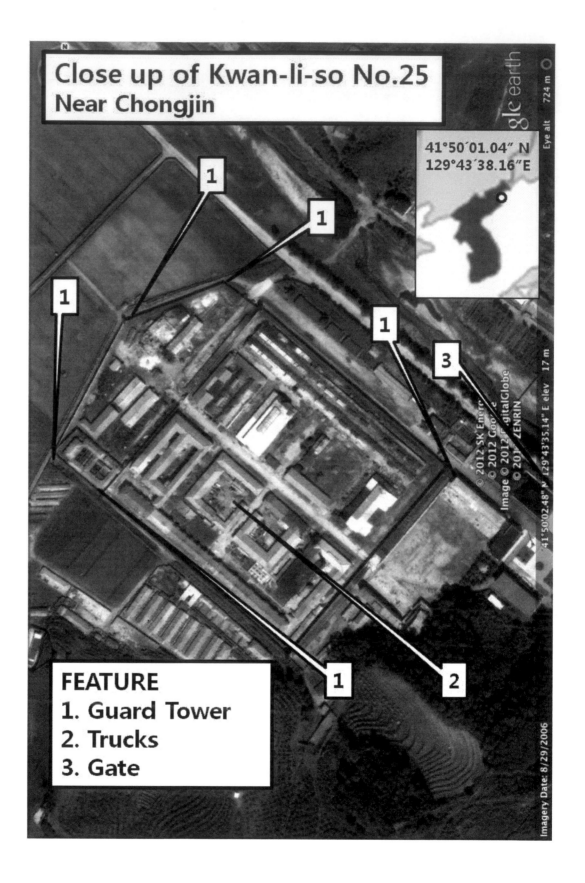

Close up of Kwan-li-so No.25
Near Chongjin

41°50´01.04″ N
129°43´38.16″E

FEATURE
1. Guard Tower
2. Trucks
3. Gate

Kyo-hwa-so No. 1

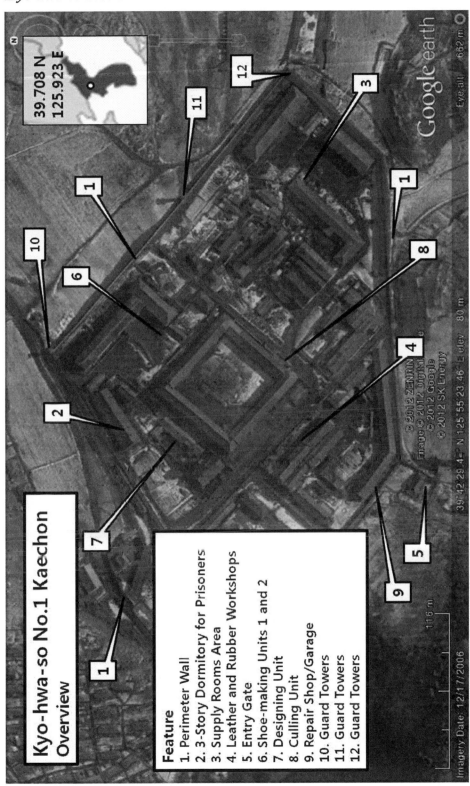

Kyo-hwa-so No.1 Kaechon
Overview

Feature
1. Perimeter Wall
2. 3-Story Dormitory for Prisoners
3. Supply Rooms Area
4. Leather and Rubber Workshops
5. Entry Gate
6. Shoe-making Units 1 and 2
7. Designing Unit
8. Culling Unit
9. Repair Shop/Garage
10. Guard Towers
11. Guard Towers
12. Guard Towers

39.708 N
125.923 E

Imagery Date: 12/17/2006

Kyo-hwa-so No. 4 Kangdong:

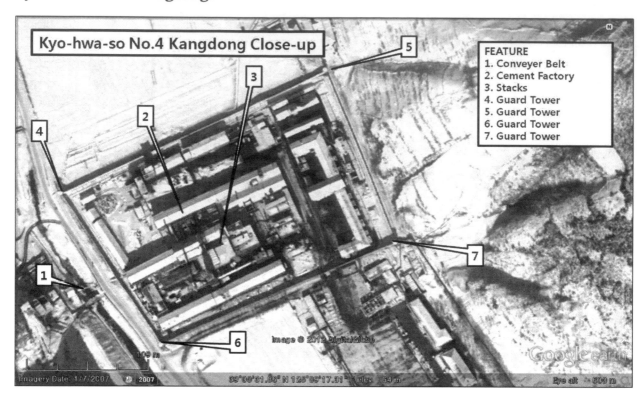

Kyo-hwa-so No.4 Kangdong Close-up

FEATURE
1. Conveyer Belt
2. Cement Factory
3. Stacks
4. Guard Tower
5. Guard Tower
6. Guard Tower
7. Guard Tower

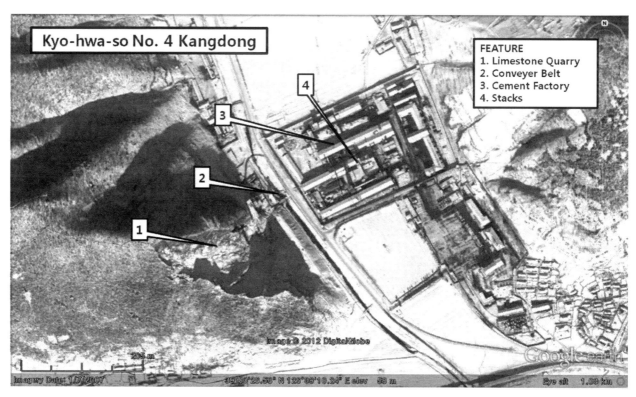

Kyo-hwa-so No. 4 Kangdong

FEATURE
1. Limestone Quarry
2. Conveyer Belt
3. Cement Factory
4. Stacks

Kyo-hwa-so No. 12 Chongo-ri:

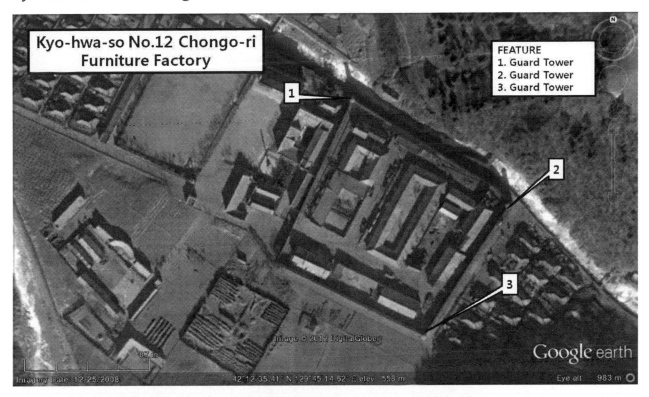

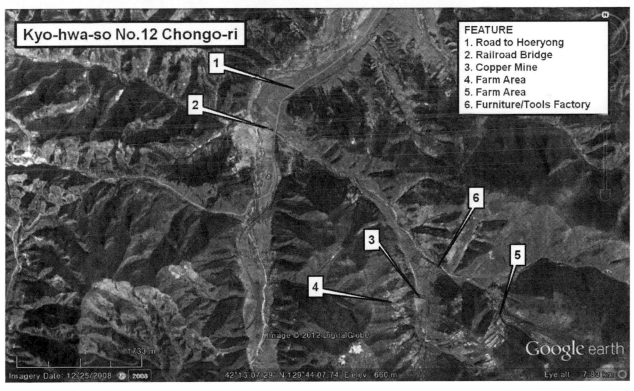

South Sinuiju Detention Center:

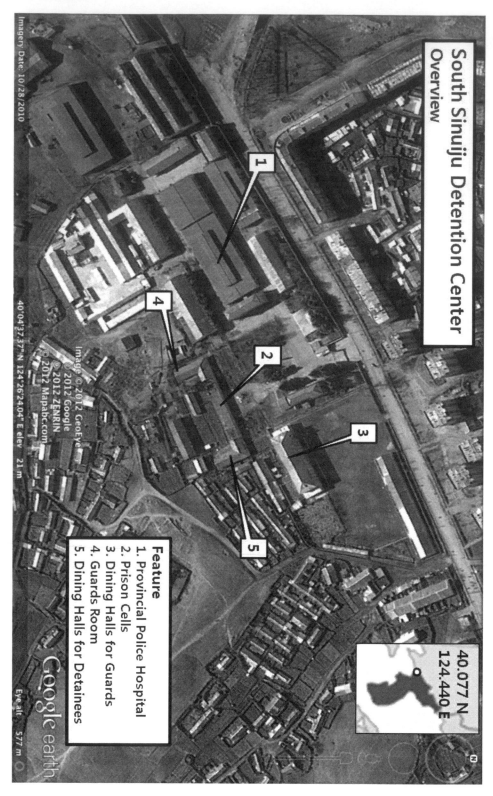

South Sinuiju Detention Center
Overview

Feature
1. Provincial Police Hospital
2. Prison Cells
3. Dining Halls for Guards
4. Guards Room
5. Dining Halls for Detainees

40.077 N
124.440 E

Imagery Date: 10/28/2010

40°04'37.37" N 124°26'24.04" E elev 21 m   Eye alt 577 m

Nongpo Detention Center:

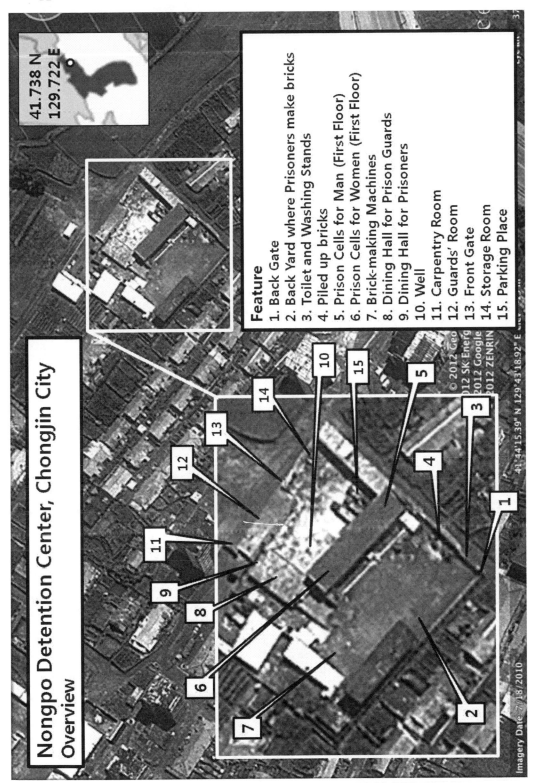

Nongpo Detention Center, Chongjin City
Overview

41.738 N
129.722 E

Feature
1. Back Gate
2. Back Yard where Prisoners make bricks
3. Toilet and Washing Stands
4. Piled up bricks
5. Prison Cells for Man (First Floor)
6. Prison Cells for Women (First Floor)
7. Brick-making Machines
8. Dining Hall for Prison Guards
9. Dining Hall for Prisoners
10. Well
11. Carpentry Room
12. Guards' Room
13. Front Gate
14. Storage Room
15. Parking Place